Contents

Acknowledgments

In a study that spans twenty-five years, it is difficult to acknowledge the magnitude of love, support, and ideas I have received from others. Foremost, I want to thank my mother, father, sisters, brother, brothers-in-law, nieces, and nephews, and my husband for their unfailing love and support. I dedicate this book to all of you. I also want to thank David's family for their love and support. My family has played a special role in this study. *Mil gracias, mami,* for being involved in the first phase and for helping me open so many doors. I love you, Francesca, Roy, Madelene, Jeanette, Cristian, Elliot, and Kim for always being there for me. A special hug to Jeanette and Elliot, whose love and encouragement sustained my spirits throughout this project. Elliot, thank you for your hard work and patience in creating the genealogical charts in this book. I would also like to thank Kristi Long and Adi Hovav for their editorial support.

I am also grateful for the love and friendship of many dear friends. Thank you Jóse Sanchez and Alice Colón for being there at every stage of this work and for the countless stimulating ideas we shared. I would also like to thank Rosalind Petchesky, Karen Sacks, Ruth Zambrana, and Mike Rose for reading an earlier version of my work. Lynn Chancer, thank you for your advice and sustaining friendship, especially during the final stage of this book. Other good friends that have always supported my work and believed this project would some day come to a happy completion are Julia Andino, Patricia Antoniello, Nilda and Paul Bloomberg, Arlene Dávila, Sean Krebs, Ana Maria Morales, Luchi Sanchez, Carol Smith, and Barbara Winslow. A special thanks to Barbara for the many weekends you provided your friends with a space to write at "Barbara's Bellagio Retreat." I would also like to acknowledge and thank Jody Carlson for her generous heart in helping me develop the methodology for this study. I also want to thank *las mujeres* from our Latina feminist group for their camaraderie and friendship. My students and colleagues have also been a source of support for me at City College. Leith Mullings, you are a beaming light in my life. Thank you for paving the path for me and other women of color to walk on. I also want to remember the late Elliot Skinner for his kindness and courage.

I am also fortunate to have been the recipient of a postdoctoral award from the Ford Fellowships Program. I want to thank the former director Tom Rozzell and his amazing staff; Christine O'Brien, the perpetual guardian angel of the Ford Fellows; Joan Rosenthal; Margaret Petrochenkov; and others who have been part of the Ford family for many years. I would also like to acknowledge the PSC/CUNY Faculty Research Program and the Intercambio Program at the Center for Puerto Rican Studies for the research support they have given me. My husband, David, has also played a major role in encouraging me to bring this book to its final stage. I thank you for sharing your love and ideas with me and for patiently reading and editing countless drafts of this manuscript. If that isn't love I don't know what is. Last but certainly not least, *gracias* to the women and their families in this ethnography and to the hundreds of women I have worked with in the past that have made this journey a true inspiration.

Introduction

"My first pregnancy was a surprise." Nancy, a thirty-one-year-old Puerto Rican woman in New York, leaned forward and spoke with a sense of urgency. "I was only seventeen years old at the time. I wasn't taking the pill on a regular basis. I didn't feel good taking the pill. I also tried the coil, but it got to the point where I could hardly walk from the pain and the doctor took it out. I tried the diaphragm but my husband didn't like it. I waited three years to have my second baby. I had my kids three years apart. The crazy thing was that for my third pregnancy I had twins. That was my last pregnancy."

Nancy only wanted to have three children. She had problems with the pill, IUD, and diaphragm and then had twins in her last pregnancy. She decided to have *la operación,* the colloquial term for sterilization, at the age of twenty-five once she exceeded her desired family size.[1]

Nancy was going through a divorce at the time (1981). Her eyes flashed as she discussed her husband, the ordeals of motherhood, and the lack of her husband's support.

> My husband helps a little but it's the kids who really help the most. That is why I think women should have the final decision about whether or not she gets sterilized. Because the woman, she's the one that's going to go through the changes. She's the one that is going to bring them up. Men go to work and bring in the bread but there are few men who help out altogether. They might help here and there but it's the woman who has to deal with the burden of the housework. We have a twenty-four-hour job. That's why the decision to get operated was my decision because men aren't always around to help. . . . If you have maybe one or two children, that's different, but after you have a

few, for him to say no, you'll just continue reproducing and not getting any place because it's hard to be a mother.

Nancy was also familiar with sterilization because her mother and sister and most of her friends had undergone la operación. As Nancy put it, "When my children were small I had a part time job and I received public assistance. My husband and I were having problems and I decided to get sterilized. After we broke up I was not in a steady relationship. I had a lot of mental anguish and financial problems, too. Most of the women in my family were sterilized. My girlfriend recommended it to me, and I decided it was the best thing for me at the time."

Like Nancy, the women in this ethnography reported that most of the women in their families were also sterilized. I took a genealogy of each family to map these patterns, and I found that in Nancy's family her mother, sisters, nieces, aunts, godmothers, and sister-in-laws were almost all sterilized. They either had a tubal ligation, a hysterectomy, or a combination of a tubal ligation and a hysterectomy. In the broadest sense, sterilization also includes vasectomies for men. In this book, I will focus on both tubal ligation and hysterectomies among Puerto Rican women. I include women with hysterectomies because in a survey I took during the first phase of this longitudinal study, based on a random sample, I found that eighteen out of the ninety-six sterilized women (almost one in five) had hysterectomies. I was struck by this high number. Moreover, it is an extreme form of sterilization that up until the 1970s was sometimes used as birth control.

Nancy's financial situation was similar to the other women in this study. Most were living below the poverty line. Like most of the women in this study she married young and did not graduate from high school. In 1981, her annual income of $6,228 supported her and her four children. In 2006, her household income per capita (calculated on the salaries of two working adults) was $23,102 for two adults working full time.[2] Fortunately for Nancy, when her children were younger her mother, doña Rosario, and niece, Sonia, provided her with a strong social support system. They lived just a few miles away and doña Rosario frequently babysat for Nancy's children. In brief, Nancy was sterilized because of a combination of reasons—financial pressures, marital difficulties, and problems with birth control.

Sonia, Nancy's niece, provides a poignant example of women's experience with sterilization in the younger generation. We met in 1981 when Sonia was twenty-two years old. Like her sister she was married at the age of seventeen. She was bright, energetic, and highly motivated to get out of her impoverished situation. Before she met her husband, Nelson, Sonia worked as a full-time secretary in an office. After she was five months pregnant with her second child, she decided to stay at home, although she planned to go back to work as soon as her baby was born. One of her life goals was to travel with her husband. At first, Sonia only wanted a one-child family. She decided to get sterilized at the age of twenty-two because she already had a one-year-old daughter and was pregnant with her second child. Her second child was an accident and she wanted to make sure she did not have more than two children. Although Sonia was happy in her relationship with Nelson, she was unhappy about their poverty and desperately wanted to improve their living conditions. The only way Sonia could see her way out of their poverty was to limit their family size through sterilization.

Carmen is Sonia's mother and Nancy's sister. She has a third-grade level of education and married Alex when she was eighteen years old. She has struggled with poverty and sexism all of her life. In 1981, when I started this longitudinal study, she was forty-seven and had several grandchildren. Like several Puerto Rican women in this ethnography, she had an unnecessary hysterectomy instead of the tubal ligation she desired. In her words, "I was shocked when I went in for a gynecological examination and found out that my uterus had been taken out. I could not believe that a doctor had done this to me. I felt violated, ashamed, and stupid. All I could think was what my husband would think of me now."

Nancy, Sonia, and Carmen's lives represent a range of the individual, social, cultural, and medical inequities that have led thousands of Puerto Rican women across several generations, some in the same families, to have tubal ligations and hysterectomies. Their lives typify the social conditions, gender subordination, family conflicts, cultural beliefs, and medical disparities and inequities that are reflected in the high rate of sterilization and hysterectomies (of which I found many were unnecessary) among Puerto Rican women in New York City.

This account of Puerto Rican women's history with sterilization is a compelling case study of reproductive rights, human rights, and reproductive freedom. It also resonates with the experiences of other women in national and international arenas. Indeed, the ethnographic material presented here provides a local perspective and a broader analysis of the confluence of individual, cultural, social, historical, and global conditions that influence women's fertility decisions and circumscribe their reproductive options. In essence, it reveals the variety of ways that poor women cope with, negotiate, challenge, and take control of their daily lives. In order to obtain a nuanced view of Puerto Rican women's sterilization experiences, it is important to focus on the diverse reasons that motivated their decisions and to explore the range of their social circumstances, their gender awareness, and the interplay between agency and constraint through a more comprehensive model.

Sterilization is a controversial topic because it is associated with abuse. Sterilization abuse takes place when an individual is sterilized without her knowledge or consent or when an individual is targeted for sterilization because of her race/ethnicity, gender, and/or class. While there is sterilization abuse, not all Puerto Rican women who get sterilized are victims of sterilization abuse. Although there have been many cases of sterilization abuse in the Puerto Rican community, the majority of women I interviewed did not think of themselves as victims of abuse. Neither did they perceive themselves as exercising complete volition when it came to choosing methods of birth control and larger issues of reproduction. Instead, they were women like Nancy and Sonia who claimed they wanted to get sterilized because of myriad individual reasons, and did so with respect to particular cultural, social, and historical conditions. This does not minimize the problem of sterilization abuse. It contributes a different dimension and analysis of Puerto Rican women's experiences with la operación.

Although sterilization abuse is an important subject that merits serious consideration, I have not made this the focus of my book for two reasons. First, feminists have written extensively about this subject (CARASA 1979; CESA 1976), and second, I believe it is a straightforward issue: sterilization abuse is a violation of human rights because the state interferes with the fundamental individual right to decide if, when, and how many children one will have (Colón-Warren 1991; Chavkin 2005; Hartmann 1995; Petchesky 1984; Roberts 1997). On the other hand, I have chosen to focus on the more complicated and more difficult to understand subject of how poor women exercise reproductive agency within a parameter of oppressive social, cultural, and individual circumstances and how they negotiate these multiple dimensions. For example, even though Nancy does not fully exercise reproductive freedom, she cannot be labeled a victim of sterilization abuse because she made a proactive decision to get sterilized. However, even though she is making a decision, neither can one say she is demonstrating full reproductive freedom.

Reproductive freedom consists of individuals having the right to decide if, when, and how many children they will have without violence or coercion. It also includes having the best social conditions that enable a family to have children—for example, having viable birth control options, quality prenatal and child care, and a support system that allows women and men to raise children in the most healthy environment. *Optimal* reproductive freedom is something more. It necessitates that individuals and society also have reached the level of individual, educational, and cultural awareness that promotes egalitarian gender relationships, responsible parenting, and emotional and social intelligence (Goleman 1995, 2007). Nancy's case study shows not only that Nancy does not exercise optimal reproductive freedom but also that she, like the other women in this study, does not even exercise the same degree of reproductive freedom as middle-class women. I will explore this issue further through their stories.

The Increasing Rate of Sterilization

In the twenty-first century, sterilization has become one of the most popular methods of fertility control worldwide (Chandra 1998; Hartmann 1995), second only to the pill. In the United States during the 1960s, it became a popular form of fertility control in response to international concerns about population explosions in developing countries (Ehrlich 1968). In countries like China, Brazil, India, Indonesia, Columbia, Mexico, Peru, and Puerto Rico, "birth control" became a euphemism for sterilization. Despite its widespread use, though, sterilization is the least acknowledged and studied method of fertility control, and its original purpose as population control has become minimized or even disguised through the terminology of birth control.

Exemplifying this invisibility, on March 10, 2002, the *New York Times* reported that birthrates in Third World nations like Brazil, Mexico, the Philippines, and Egypt had dropped since the late 1960s (Crossette 2002). Yet, the experts were at a loss to explain this dramatic demographic decline. Speculating about the reasons for this unexpected drop in fertility rates, they suggested cultural factors, changes in attitudes, the influence of the media on people's self-image, declining infant mortality, and urbanization. Oddly enough, what none of them recognized was the significant role that sterilization has played in reducing the rate of population growth in Third World nations. Few people publicly acknowledge the link between sterilization and population control, and even fewer question the relationship between poor women's socially oppressed conditions, gender subordination, the lack of access to viable birth control and comprehensive health care, and the increasing use of surgical methods of fertility control, namely tubal ligation as a primary form of fertility control (Crossette 2002; Hartmann 1995).

A distinction needs to be made between birth control and population control. Birth control developed to meet women's needs to space births and/or prevent pregnancy. On the other hand, when birth control is designed to meet the requirements of the state, then it is population control. Population control takes place when a government of a country implements a strategy to control the birth rate or growth of a given population either through reproductive measures or migration; it embraces the neo-Malthusian ideology that population growth causes poverty and underdevelopment. Any method of birth control, particularly sterilization, can be used as population control when policy makers and other officials target women and men by administering contraceptives that, once administered, women have no control over—for example, sterilization, Norplant, or Depo-Provera (Fathalla 1996; Hartmann 1995; Lindemann and Lindemann 1995; Moskowitz et al. 1995; Steinbeck 1995).[3] Although sterilization is a form of birth control, it is at the extreme end of the birth control continuum. In most cases it ends women's ability to have children.

Historically, sterilization has been used as the favored means of population control. In the first half of the twentieth century sterilization was used as population control in Puerto Rico. Yet today Puerto Rican women have come to think of it, and use it, as birth control. Hence, in discussing the experiences of Puerto Rican women with sterilization, we need to keep in mind the distinction between sterilization as population control and as birth control. Perhaps the most important distinction to be made is between population control as a state policy and birth control as a woman's human and reproductive right.

Since the 1960s, the high rate of sterilization among Puerto Rican women has been a controversial topic because of Puerto Rican women's history of population control and sterilization abuse in the United States. In 1982, the rate of female sterilization in Puerto Rico was 39 percent for women within the reproductive age group of fifteen to forty-five. In contrast, in New York City, where my research took place, in 1995 Hispanic women had a rate of sterilization of 50 percent in comparison to 27.6 percent for white women, 25.8 percent for black women, and 2.4 percent for Asian women (Laraque et al. 1995, 2). The rate of sterilization for Hispanic women may be higher than 50 percent because they were both counted in the black and white categories (2). Because Puerto Ricans still constitute a large number of Hispanics in New York City and have a long history of sterilization, it is reasonable to assume that a large percentage of these sterilized women are Puerto Rican. A survey of 128 Puerto Rican women that I conducted in one neighborhood in Brooklyn (Bushwick) corroborates this deduction. I found that 47 percent of the Puerto Rican women twenty-one years and older were surgically sterilized. But these numbers only tell a portion of the story. We need to look behind the numbers and explore women's experiences, their understanding of sterilization, and the life events that led them to make these fertility decisions. Ethnography and life history offer the means to do so.

This book tells the story of five households of fifteen Puerto Rican women who live in Bushwick, Brooklyn, a neighborhood that I have followed for twenty-five years (1981–2006). The research is unique because there is a dearth of empirical data on this subject; to my knowledge, this is the only ethnographic, longitudinal, and intergenerational study of Puerto Rican women of its kind. Each household consists of three generations of women, most of whom have been sterilized. Some of the women in the immigrant generation had hysterectomies in addition to tubal ligations. Their lives represent the stories of Puerto Rican women in particular and the views and experiences of Latinas in general.

I intend to provide a far-ranging analysis that extends beyond the narrow issue of sterilization among women, particularly tubal ligations and, to a lesser degree (because it was less prevalent among the participants of the study), hysterectomies. The book explores the ways in which women's migration experiences, their struggles within a changing urban economy, their social support systems or lack thereof, their relationship with men, women, and children, their gender awareness and their personal aspirations and desires all affected their fertility decisions. I also consider how these women's lack of access to quality housing, jobs, education, and decent health care services have shaped and limited their perceptions of their reproductive options. Because men play an important role in women's lives and influence their fertility decisions, I also include men's views and perspectives of sterilization.

This case study examines the myriad forces that maintain a high rate of sterilization among Puerto Rican women in the United States. It does so through an integral analysis that transcends the binary model of agency and constraint. An integral analysis takes into account the personal, cultural, social, and historical forces that comprise Puerto Rican women's reproductive decisions and experiences. By examining the women's decisions and experiences within an integral model, it is possible to see that they do not exercise complete reproductive freedom, nor are they victims. This analysis helps move the debate beyond the fragmented and simplistic binary framework and provides a more nuanced understanding of how Puerto Rican women negotiate their reproductive experiences within cultural, social, and historical contexts.

A Trajectory in Exploring the Question of La Operación

I first became interested in why Puerto Rican women have such a high rate of sterilization when I was a second-year graduate student in anthropology. That year I went to a small town on the north coast of Puerto Rico known as Barceloneta to study how women's lives had changed with respect to employment and education over a twenty-year period (1956 to 1976). In 1976, this small town had a population size of twenty thousand. When I asked women about their children and whether they wanted to have more, they often told me that they were sterilized. I found it remarkable that such a large number of women had been sterilized. What I did not know at the time was that Barceloneta was considered the mecca of sterilization in Puerto Rico. In other words, even though sterilization was promoted throughout the island, Barceloneta was known as a place where many clinics were located and where women from all over the island came for the procedure. In fact, sterilization became so popular that women colloquially referred to it as "la operación," a term still used today.

This popularity was largely the result of governmental policy. In 1970, the mayor of Barceloneta initiated a sterilization campaign for the town, with the goal of reducing its birth rate. This campaign was so successful that the mayor had to close down several grammar schools because there were not enough school-aged children.

When I returned to New York, I searched the literature for causes of the high rate of sterilization among Puerto Rican women and began to probe for answers to the following questions. What was the nature of Puerto Rican women's fertility experiences? Was sterilization voluntary, coerced, or something else? I found that explanations for the high rate of sterilization in Puerto Rico fell into two opposing schools of thought. In one school, Puerto Rican women were presented as free agents who make entirely voluntary decisions (Cofresi 1951; Presser 1973, 1978; Stycos, Hill, and Back 1959). In another, representing exactly the opposite interpretation, Puerto Rican women were presented as victims of population control (Mass 1976; Marreo 1977).

The first school of thought argues that a high rate of sterilization among Puerto Rican women evidences reproductive freedom because it derives from Puerto Rican women's "free will" and their individual cultural preference for la operación. Social scientists who adapt this approach gloss over the influence of social constraints and oppression as well as the historical role of population control in Puerto Rico. They relegate all responsibility to Puerto Rican women as individuals, abstracting their culture from its historical context and the social and material conditions that promoted sterilization, such as the health care industry, poverty, and institutional racism women encountered in social service and welfare agencies.

The opposing argument states that all sterilized Puerto Rican women are victims. Social scientists who promote this view tend to attribute high rates of sterilization among Puerto Rican almost exclusively to population control policies and colonialism. They assume that Puerto Rican women are powerless and therefore do not exercise any control over their fertility. Neither group of social scientists distinguishes the varying degrees of control among the fertility experiences of Puerto Rican women, nor have they offered a more nuanced and complex framework of understanding.

These conflicting explanations of agent and victim in the literature were striking. I continued to think and read about this issue. I wanted to understand the conditions under which women who had been socialized to be mothers and wives, and who love children so much, would put an end to their fertility. I was also intrigued by how the sterilization procedure that had been developed under a colonial framework on the island was maintained and perpetuated in New York City, and how it became a widespread social and cultural practice.

Instead of going back to Puerto Rico, I decided to undertake this investigation in my own backyard, in the adjoining neighborhood in Brooklyn where I was born and raised. As a Latina of working-class origin, I was also motivated by the fact that in the 1970s very little research about Puerto Ricans had been undertaken by Latinos or Latinas in our own communities. Equally troubling was that the scarce literature depicted Puerto Rican women as subordinate and passive. For example, I was disturbed to come across a book in 1976 by an Argentine male author entitled *The Puerto Rican Woman* that depicted Puerto Rican women as paragons of passivity. That image contradicted my own impressions growing up in Brooklyn. Most of the Latinas with whom I was familiar were strong-willed, independent women who had overcome many obstacles in their lives and who successfully struggled on a daily basis to keep their families safe and intact. After the initial phase of research (a survey) I continued working with five families over an extensive period of time. This extended project culminated in twenty-five years of research with these same families.

Prior to starting my fieldwork, I worked with predominately liberal, white, middle-class women who fought for the reproductive rights of poor women through social justice groups such as the Committee to End Sterilization Abuse (CESA) and the Committee for Abortion Rights and Against Sterilization Abuse (CARASA). In the 1970s, these women, along with health and community activists, focused their organizing efforts on eliminating sterilization abuse (though the main focus of the feminist agenda was abortion rights). At the time, sterilization abuse was already recognized as a common problem, particularly among poor women of color (CARASA 1979; CESA 1976; Davis 1981; Velez 1978). Women in CESA and CARASA, among them Helen Rodriguez, Karen Stamm, Rosalind Petchesky, and Esther Armstrong, played a vital role in documenting, advocating, and litigating for victims of sterilization abuse. I was excited to begin the fieldwork in my community. Having lived through the turbulent history of protesting sterilization abuse, I was baffled to find that many of the poor Puerto Rican women I met actively sought sterilization. Like most people during those years, I assumed that sterilized women were usually victims; looking back, I realize that I, too, employed the dominant binary framework that lumped everyone into categories of victim or agent. Eventually, though, I learned that although there have been many cases of abuse among the Puerto Rican women I worked with, not everyone had been victimized. On the contrary, even though poor women were targets of population control, they did not follow population policy blindly; they exercised a certain degree of agency, even though when we talked about sterilization in detail they said they did it because they felt they had no other choice and did not feel they enjoyed complete reproductive freedom.

My research reformulates this oppositional framework and critiques the paradigm of choice.[4] In brief, it rejects the notion that Puerto Rican women are either voluntary agents or powerless victims and demonstrates that neither of these polar extremes presents an integral picture of most poor women's reproductive experiences. An integral analysis takes into account the individual, cultural, social, and historical forces that influence and shape Puerto Rican women's reproductive decisions and experiences. Sterilization has been discussed within a binary framework that opposes "choice" or agency to victimization or constraint. As I talked to the women it became evident that this framework was too simple and did not reflect their understanding of their experiences. I will consider this issue in detail throughout the book, first by focusing on Puerto Rican women's stories about la operación and related issues. In the final chapter I will return to consider alternatives to the binary model of choice and victimization.

One benefit of the ethnographic method is that it enables us to see the nuances involved in the way terms such as "choice" and "constraint" actually operate. One social factor that constrains poor women's reproductive freedom on several levels is their lack of access to quality health care services. For example, as a matter of course, many health providers in public hospitals and clinics that women use recommend tubal ligation to poor women more frequently than to middle-class women (New York City Health and Hospital Corporation 1982) and spend less time educating them about temporary methods of birth control. This was apparent among the women in this study because even though three-quarters of them had used birth control, only 7.8 percent had used the diaphragm (Lopez 1985, 126). Finally, women who do not have access to quality health care services tend not to know how to utilize the birth control pill properly, and they also tend to be misinformed about the permanent nature of sterilization. I observed this frequently when I accompanied these women to public hospitals and clinics.

Despite the multiple forces that constrain, shape, and influence women's reproductive options and decisions, most of the women featured in this book had a strong sense of self-entitlement about their bodies. They believed, and adamantly argued, for their right to make decisions about their bodies: no one had the right to tell them what to do with them. Thus, many of the women's views of sterilization conflicted with the arguments put forth by women in CESA (1976), CARASA (1979), and other organizations, and with what I knew about Puerto Rican women's colonial history and oppression. This led me to question what reproductive rights meant to them. In doing preliminary research with the women, I learned about a range of practical factors and conditions that sometimes led them to either opt for or accept sterilization. Among these practical factors was achieving their desired family size; their desire to have more time and energy to properly care for the children they already had; their wish to do other things with their lives in addition to having children; and, in some cases, their desire to reduce further involvement in a troublesome domestic relationship.

These reasons made sense to me because I was aware that Puerto Rican women viewed sterilization as permanent (cut) and temporary (tied) birth control, and many women seemed happy with either. What, then, was the problem? I was perturbed and discussed my concerns with some of my progressive Puerto Rican friends who, along with other women's groups and other Puerto Rican scholars and activists, continued to emphasize these women's social and historical oppression and to gloss over the aspect of their obvious individual agency. For example, once when I was interviewed on a radio talk show by Piri Thomas, the author of *Down These Mean Streets*, three male community activists—also guests on the show—became upset with me when I stated that many working-class women actively sought sterilization and did not consider themselves victims of sterilization abuse. Even though I spoke about Puerto Rican women's colonial history and the role of Puerto Rico's oppressive population policy, explaining the complex and dialectical nature of Puerto Rican women's experiences, the men became agitated and had a hard time hearing what I was saying. They thought that, by acknowledging any degree of agency and/or cultural beliefs in Puerto Rican women's decision-making process, I was erasing their oppression and implying, therefore, that all was well.

On the one hand, I understood these young men were interpreting what I was saying from a binary perspective. On the other, I was at a loss to explain the two horns of the dilemma, essentially because I was still trapped in the predominantly binary way of thinking about this issue myself. If I emphasized the individual practical reasons why a large number of Puerto Rican women opted for sterilization and acknowledged that most women did not consider themselves victims of sterilization abuse, the "left" accused me of betraying Puerto Ricans because they thought I was denying the existence (and persistence) of a problem. But if I stressed Puerto Rican women's history of oppression and population control to the exclusion of women's agency, I knew I was presenting a simplistic notion of women's actual experiences. What I wish I had been able to articulate then, and what I understand more clearly now, is that there are different degrees of agency, resistance, and reproductive freedom and these are not mutually exclusive.

To reiterate then, a relatively small number of Puerto Rican women represent a classic case of sterilization abuse. However, the majority of the women I interviewed opted for tubal ligation due to a lack of options based on their poverty, cultural familiarity with la operación, problems with birth control, and gender subordination in their personal relationships. Consequently, although most Puerto Rican women make decisions and are not victims of sterilization abuse in the classic sense, this does not mean that they are not oppressed or that they are exercising optimal reproductive freedom.

I was grateful Piri Thomas understood that I was trying to develop a more complex argument, and for his asking the young men not to interrupt but to listen to what I was saying because "I knew what I was talking about." To conclude the radio dialogue, I asked these young men if they had ever talked to their sterilized mothers and sisters about why they had undergone la operación; this question stopped them dead in their tracks, forcing them to admit they had never broached the topic. Since then, I have continually found among many men this lack of gender awareness of and consideration for women's needs and concerns. In later chapters, I will discuss how sexism as manifested in women's relationships and in female subordination has also contributed to some women's decisions to seek sterilization.

In another situation, I had the opposite experience than the one I described above. I was on a television program with a small group of Latinas and one of the foundation officers of Planned Parenthood. This time when I spoke about Puerto Rican women's desire to get sterilized and the steps they took to have the operation, this officer insisted that if Puerto Rican women were seeking this operation, then as far as she was concerned "there was no problem because they were exercising free choice." Once again I was stumped about how to respond because I did not want to deny Puerto Rican women's agency; however, later, I realized that while there were "elements of agency" in most Puerto Rican women's decisions to seek sterilization, they were not exercising complete reproductive freedom. Yet, as quickly as the young Puerto Rican men dismissed Puerto Rican women's agency, the foundation officer dismissed the oppressive colonial population control policies and current poverty that constrained Puerto Ricans' reproductive options that failed to provide them with other social and birth control options. Because they were both thinking in binary absolute black and white terms, they could not see the total dimension of the issue. Since my graduate school years I have heard similar arguments as the one the Planned Parenthood foundation officer posed. The argument is that regardless of a woman's race or class, all women's reproductive options are constrained because all women confront sexism and have problems with the limitations of the contraceptives on the market. While I agree that no one yet exercises optimal reproductive freedom, I argue that middle-class women tend to exercise more degrees of freedom than poor and working-class women, especially women of color.

Even though years have passed since I and others (Chancer 1998; Colón 1999; Gordon 1990; Petchesky 2003; Petchesky and Judd 1998) have criticized binary thinking, it is my experience that many students continue to think about women's reproductive rights issues like sterilization in the same dualistic fashion. For example, in 2001 I gave a talk to an undergraduate class on "Latinas and Health." As I lectured to approximately thirty Latinas of different Spanish origin groups, I was disturbed to find that the young women, twenty to twenty-five years younger than I, were still adhering to the old binary framework of agency and victim developed in the 1970s. When I criticized the oppositional way of thinking as linear and simplistic, and tried to show them the multiple problems with it, I was surprised to find that a large number of these women—like their male counterparts twenty years earlier—became angry and insisted that all poor sterilized women were victims. After a lengthy discussion, though, a handful of these young women became convinced that this was a more complex issue when a few women in the class announced that they were sterilized. They went on to say that, for the first time, I was describing and analyzing their experiences in a way that helped them see the oppression while at the same time validating that, given their situation, they had done the best thing they could. I felt reassured by their statements because when I discuss this subject with my students, it is always very important for me that my sterilized students do not end up feeling as if they have been duped and had no agency. Once again, even in the twenty-first century, this classroom experience made me realize how difficult it is to grasp all of the contradictions involved in order to understand this issue on different levels.

Based on these experiences, I brought four basic questions to my subsequent fieldwork. First, what constituted choice and reproductive freedom in the context of poor women's lives? If women said they wanted to get sterilized, did this mean that they were making voluntary decisions and that, in fact, sterilization was a choice? Since the language of choice and reproductive rights is pivotal to a discussion of reproductive freedom, I consistently raised a second question: was a voluntary "choice" based on reproductive freedom even possible in the context of these poor women's lives, given their social conditions and colonial history? Were these women and I conceptualizing the term "voluntary" in different ways? Third, I inquired into Puerto Rican women's actual experiences with sterilization. This set of questions led me to my fourth and final query. Given that all women's birth control options are limited regardless of race/ethnicity and class, was there something that made Puerto Rican women's fertility experiences different from millions of women of other racial/ethnic backgrounds who are sterilized in the United States and abroad each year?

The best way I found to expand the knowledge about reproductive rights and freedom was to talk to poor and nonwhite women and men who underwent this reproductive surgery. In order to get the full picture of how women think about their fertility and make fertility decisions, I had to get a feel for what their daily lives were like. Although this was not easy and presented many challenges for me, it was not an altogether impossible task either: I was born and raised in the area where I did the research, and I am a Puerto Rican woman from the same working-class background as most of the women in this study.

Although my background differed from theirs in some ways, I am fluent in Spanish (and Spanglish) and familiar with nonverbal forms of communication, which was a great advantage to me in bridging our differences. Overall, the intergenerational and longitudinal perspectives of this study enabled me to glimpse the variety of ways Puerto Rican families have changed in Brooklyn since the 1960s as well as the nature of the communities wherein they reside.

An integral understanding of how Puerto Rican women negotiate their reproduction in this study also tells how other poor and marginalized women in the United States may perceive and act upon sterilization. This ethnography also offers insight into a better understanding of how women in Third World countries cope with similar issues of poverty, lack of access to quality health care, sexism, family size, etc. Even though Puerto Rican women's experiences are distinctive in some ways, they share many factors with other minority women in the United States and with women of color internationally. For example, from a personal perspective, along with Latin American and other poor women of color in the United States all women want to use birth control to control their fertility. In cultural terms, women recommend sterilization to one another through family and interpersonal relationships and share the meaning of sterilization as birth control. With regard to social structural constraints, women worldwide get sterilized due to economic hardship, but other factors are equally compelling; for example, troublesome patriarchal relationships, problems with contraceptives, and the fact that women are primarily responsible for birth control, child rearing, and domestic work while lacking access to government-sponsored child care.

METHODOLOGICAL CHALLENGES

Undertaking a longitudinal ethnographic study and collecting data in a metropolis like New York City presents many challenges. My main challenge in collecting data for this research was to document the richness of experiences captured by the ethnographic approach at the same time I made the findings more broadly quantifiable and, therefore, generalizable. To accomplish these goals, I combined traditional anthropological methods like participant observations and the collection of oral histories with traditional sociological methods like systematically listing the residents in the neighborhood (a census) and an in-depth survey. The survey provided me with comprehensive background information about the women who lived in the locale. I used this survey to provide background information on the women in the study and to compare the women in the longitudinal phase with the women in the neighborhood at large. In addition, I used survey data and stories from the ethnographic sample in chapter 7.

Because half of the women in this study were Spanish dominant and the other half were English dominant, I developed a questionnaire in Spanish and in English. I also translated all of the quotes and oral history material from Spanish to English. I cross-checked my translations by asking some of the bilingual women in this study to translate a question or phrase on a piece of paper. I translated the same question or phrase and then we compared translations. I selected the translation that was closest in meaning to the original.

In 1981, I hired and trained four women from this community and neighborhood to help me take a census of 880 households; we then went door to door to determine where the sterilized Puerto Rican women were located. One of the women I trained was my mother because she lived in the neighborhood; she helped me to establish and build rapport with the first-generation women. From this list, I randomly selected and then personally interviewed a survey sample size of 128 women from different parts of the neighborhood (96 sterilized and 32 nonsterilized). I included 128 women in the neighborhood because I wanted to ensure a more representative picture of women from the entire neighborhood before completing the survey. This was important because there is significant variation in the physical and economic conditions within the neighborhood. Also, even though all the women were poor, I found considerable variation among them with respect to their life conditions, gender awareness, and life perspectives.

For this book, I focused on a subsample of five families I selected from the survey. I refer to these three generations of women as first, second, and third generation. The first generation is the immigrant women who were born in Puerto Rico. The majority of the second-generation women were born in New York. I chose these families because they represented, according to results from the survey I took earlier in the initial phase of research, a range of experiences that Puerto Rican women have had with sterilization. The survey was not intergenerational. However, because I found that a significant number of the daughters of first-generation women in the survey lived in the neighborhood, I was also able to include them in this study. Although I did participant observation throughout 1981–2006, I collected and updated oral histories from the first- and second-generation women in 1986, 1996, and 2006. The women in the second generation also had children. However, in the 1980s and 1990s most of their children were too young to interview. Therefore, I decided to undertake a longitudinal study to enable me to speak with the next generation of young women and young men when they were in their late teens through their mid-twenties and then again when they were in their thirties. I kept in touch with these women by phone and visited a few times a year, especially during the holidays and on special celebrations.

The survey provides a broader picture of women's lives, enabling me to see trends and make generalizations. For example, the survey I took allowed me to discover and document that 47 percent of the Puerto Rican women living in this neighborhood over the age of twenty-one were surgically sterilized. This was a significant finding. However, what quantitative data cannot tell us is why something is occurring. This is where the ethnographic method comes in. The ethnographic method provides a nuanced view of women's daily lives, helping us understand the myriad forces that affect their fertility decisions everyday

Although I initially worried that my Ph.D. could create a social gap between me and the women in this ethnography, I found they were impressed that I was the only daughter in my working-class family who had earned a doctorate. Regardless of my educational status, I ultimately had to prove myself, and what really made a difference was the time I spent with them. I genuinely wanted to learn from the women I met and came to know. For example, I spent many hours cooking with the women whose stories are recounted here, taking care of their children, and running errands with them. An important factor that helped me to undertake this research and understand the complexity of this issue was staying in touch with the women in this community for the past twenty-five years and witnessing the changes that have taken place in their lives and in this neighborhood. Of course I could not, and do not, presume to speak for all of these women: I have instead tried to let them tell their own stories.

THE STRUCTURE OF THE BOOK

Chapter 1 provides a historical overview of Puerto Rico's birth control movement. In this chapter, I show that Puerto Rican women's experiences of individual "choice" regarding sterilization and migration were facilitated by Puerto Rico's colonial status, the widespread acceptance of sterilization among the medical profession, the government's ambivalence toward temporary methods of birth control, and by sexist population policies.

Chapter 2 consists of a comparison of women's experiences across generations. Here, I explore what Puerto Rican women in each generation share in common. In this chapter, too, I provide an overview of Puerto Rico's history so as to contextualize the lives of the women in each generation. Because most of the women in the second and third generations were born and/or raised in New York, this chapter also describes New York City's changing economy and the effects of these changes on the second and third generations.

Chapters 3, 4, 5, and 6 consist of Puerto Rican women's narratives. These chapters provide a broad trajectory of the lives of fifteen women from the five households that I have been following for the past twenty-five years. The stories illustrate, through the voices of the women themselves, how they have asserted agency while resisting and negotiating patriarchy, poverty, and the health care system in their everyday lives.[5]

Chapter 7 examines how many women's lack of access to quality health care services, combined with stereotypes of the poor held by medical personnel including doctors, compromise their health treatment and reproductive freedom. The goal of this chapter is to examine how women struggle with and negotiate the health care system. It also explores how their reproductive health decisions are sometimes limited by their lack of knowledge about their bodies (e.g., fibroid tumors), lack of knowledge about how to find the best hospital to meet their needs, and how to evaluate a doctor's medical expertise. It also explores the high rate of misinformation about sterilization among Puerto Rican women and its varied meanings to the women in this study.

Chapter 8 summarizes and analyzes the women's stories within the broader framework of an integral model of reproductive freedom, which includes the personal, cultural, social, and historical realms of women's lives. This means looking at women's reproductive experiences from their subjective perspective, cultural meaning and relationships, social structural constraints, and historical framework. I extend the current thinking about reproductive rights by suggesting ways that the dominant models could be expanded and improved.

PART I

The Globalization of Sterilization

CHAPTER 1

The Birth Control Movement in Puerto Rico

After the Spanish American War in 1898, Puerto Rico, Cuba, and the Philippines became colonies of the United States. The U.S. rulers were enthralled by the ideology of Manifest Destiny, which promoted American expansion into the lands occupied by nonwhite peoples in the name of a "civilizing" mission. In 1899, one year after the United States took possession of Puerto Rico, neo-Malthusian ideology, based on the revival of the ideas of Thomas Malthus (1766–1834), came into vogue.

In the eighteenth century, Malthus argued that poverty stemmed from the proliferation of the poor. The neo-Malthusian revival at the turn of the twentieth century built upon these ideas and on the implications of Darwin's theory of evolution in considering the problems of population and economic development. Driven by neo-Malthusian ideology, U.S. officials blamed Puerto Rico's poverty and underdevelopment on what they defined as an overpopulation problem. The application of neo-Malthusian and eugenic approaches to population and development within the colonial relationship between Puerto Rico and the United States played a critical role in the development of the island's birth control movement and continues to have an adverse effect on Puerto Ricans living in the mainland United States today. In order to understand the role that la operación continues to play in the reproductive choices of Puerto Rican women, we must first consider how the colonial context facilitated a particular approach to population and to birth control in Puerto Rico.

MALTHUSIAN MISERY AND EUGENIC SUPREMACY

Puerto Rico's birth control movement has its roots in the Malthusian and eugenic philosophies that originated in Europe in the eighteenth and nineteenth

3

centuries. Thomas Malthus, considered the father of population policy control, was a British aristocrat and clergyman who lived in England during the second half of the industrial revolution. He argued that poverty was caused by over-population. According to Malthus's mathematical formula, resources multiplied only arithmetically (1, 2, 3, 4) while the population multiplied geometrically (2, 4, 8, 16, 32). In other words, Malthus maintained that world population would rapidly outpace the earth's capacity for food production unless preventive checks were put in place. As a staunch believer in the "great biological law"—that is, that the rich were genetically superior to the poor—he went so far as to argue that one of the checks that God sent were the plagues to eradicate the "burdensome and unworthy poor." Malthus viciously fought against the poor laws in England that offered hungry workers a bit of relief after they had been disenfranchised from their land and forced to work under inhumane conditions for meager wages, because he thought the effect of the poor laws would be to encourage the poor to have more children rather than fewer.

In the early part of the twentieth century, the Malthusian explanation for poverty was applied to the Third World and strengthened by the eugenic ide-ology. Malthus's ideas about population were also revived at the turn of the twentieth century. Neo-Malthusianism further built on the original theory by incorporating elements of social Darwinism. Social Darwinism was an attempt to apply the principles of Darwin's theory of evolution to social life, with unfor-tunate consequences. The theory was closely associated with capitalist expansion and colonialism and developed in a social context of increased immigration to the United States and rising social unrest in response to inequality. Social Dar-winism provided an ideology to justify inequality by arguing that societies were shaped by a principle of survival of the fittest. Social Darwinism was further bolstered by eugenics. Francis Galton, the father of modern eugenics, coined the term, meaning "to improve the race." Like Malthus, his thesis was based on the premise that the rich were superior to the poor and therefore were justified in considering themselves to be biologically and socially more fit to reproduce. In practice, those considered unfit to reproduce were the poor and nonwhite.

Proponents of eugenics were concerned with a program of improving the population of the United States, a project that was inexorably tied to racism. Eugenicists classified people on the basis of race and assumed the superiority of certain races over others. Furthermore, intelligence and social problems such as crime were considered hereditary. The belief was that if an individual was a crim-inal, their children would be criminals, and they would pass those genes down the family line. The theory also assumed a differential distribution of character-istics like intelligence or criminality on the basis of race. By blaming the genetic makeup of the poor for society's ills, the rich and powerful created a convenient justification for their racist and classist beliefs. In this xenophobic environment,

Moving from neglect to more active sterilization

Malthus's neglect of the poor was not sufficient; something had to be done about it. And this was to be done by the control and management of reproduction. The primary goal of the eugenic movement in the United States was to sterilize any individual that was considered genetically or intellectually inferior.

The Eugenic ideology was so pervasive at the time that it became an integral part of the U.S. birth control movement in the early part of the twentieth century. Its influence promoted class inequality and led to a double standard in the ways which women of different classes, races, and/or ethnic groups were treated, especially with respect to birth control. This is aptly exemplified during the first wave of feminism. For example, in the early part of the twentieth century, feminists like Margaret Sanger fought for the reproductive rights of all women to be voluntary mothers. Once eugenics came into vogue, however, she jumped on the bandwagon. Sanger used eugenics as a rationale to convince the powers-that-be that even though all women needed birth control, the state would greatly benefit if poor (and nonwhite) women, in particular, had access to it. As a result, while birth control was considered a privilege for upper-class white women, it was deemed mandatory for poor black and some white women, especially those considered "mentally challenged" (Davis 1981; Gordon 1990; Petchesky 1984; Roberts 1997).

By the turn of the twentieth century, many Americans embraced the belief that selected breeding through eugenics could improve society. Eugenics was so popular that it led to compulsory sterilization laws for the "feeble-minded" and "physically defective," passed in twenty-seven U.S. states by 1932.[1] As Petchesky (1984, 87) points out, "Between 1907 and 1945, 45,000 mentally challenged persons in the United States were surgically sterilized without their consent. The systemic character of sterilization procedures reached the point where many mentally challenged or unstable persons were being admitted to the institutions merely to be sterilized and then released."

COMPULSORY STERILIZATION of undesired bodies

By 1945, a campaign ensued against the sterilization of the mentally challenged in Virginia and compulsory sterilization was outlawed throughout the United States. However, sterilization abuse continued to take place, especially among poor women of color; for example, a disturbing case in 1969 in South Carolina that galvanized the women's reproductive rights movement. The Relf sisters, twelve- and fourteen-year-old African American girls, were sterilized without their mother's consent because a few racist doctors and nurses feared they would otherwise become unwed mothers (CARASA 1979).

oh fuck this is so violent

POLICY SOLUTIONS TO OVERPOPULATION

Since the United States occupied Puerto Rico in 1898, the island has been characterized by policy makers and journalists as suffering from a prevailing problem of overpopulation, and the policies of emigration and population control that developed in response to this problem were influenced by neo-Malthusian and eugenic approaches. In 1901, when the population of the island was approximately one million, the first civilian governor of Puerto Rico, Charles Allen, declared, "Porto Rico has plenty of laborers and poor people generally. What the Island needs are men with capital, energy and enterprise" (History Task Force 1982, 15). Allen vigorously promoted the emigration of what he considered to be "excess people." Governor Arthur Yager followed in his footsteps in 1915, when he stated that the only effective remedy to the "crowd of surplus population" was the "transfer of larger numbers of Porto Ricans to some other region" (History Task Force 1979, 110). Inspired by eugenic and neo-Malthusian theories of population growth, Governor Yager further justified his policy by invoking the powers of a "great biological law" that "we can neither alter nor repeal" (History Task Force 1979, 110).

Overpopulation does not exist in a vacuum. It occurs in relationship to economic production and to the kind and number of jobs available, among other factors. In the case of Puerto Rico, two factors contributed to overpopulation: the economic policies that arose from Puerto Rico's dependent relationship to the United States and the government's restructuring of the economy and the population through emigration and sterilization. Neo-Malthusian and eugenic ideologies shaped this process, which has important implications for the development of strategies for birth control in Puerto Rico (History Task Force 1979).

The first phase of the reshaping of Puerto Rico's economy focused on emigration as the solution to the overpopulation problem. In 1917 the U.S.-appointed governor of Puerto Rico approved several expeditions to Hawaii, other islands in the Caribbean, and the U.S. mainland. Although prior to this period Puerto Ricans had migrated in smaller numbers, this era marked the beginning of the first wave of migration officially organized by the government (History Task Force 1979, 110–111; 1982, 15).

At the beginning of the twentieth century, Puerto Rico was still an agricultural society. Its economy consisted of the production of tobacco, sugar, coffee, and citrus fruit. In just twenty years of U.S. rule, Puerto Rico's economy became absorbed into that of the United States. An important development that drastically altered Puerto Rico's economic structure, and contributed to the so-called overpopulation problem, began with the arrival of North American corporations soon after colonization. These corporations took land from peasants and replaced subsistence crops with profitable sugar commodity agriculture. This changed Puerto Rican agriculture from subsistence farming to a one-crop economy. The cultivation of a single crop disrupted land settlement patterns and uprooted thousands of peasants from their land (History Task Force 1979; Mass 1976; Sanabria 2000).

The shift from a subsistence to a mono-crop economy led to seasonal internal migration, because the peasants could no longer live off the land they had no choice but to move to follow the jobs. This created many redundant workers who could not find work in the emerging commercial and industrial businesses. The internal migration of an uprooted rural population to urban areas led to high unemployment and the rise of urban poverty.

One solution to having too many workers was emigration. The granting of U.S. citizenship to Puerto Ricans in 1917 helped bring this about. During the 1940s and 1950s almost one million Puerto Ricans left the island and came to the continental United States. One of the most significant themes in the history of Puerto Rico during the twentieth century has been the constant emigration of its people, promoted by government agencies as a remedy to the alleged chronic overpopulation problem of the island (History Task Force 1986; Sanabria 2000).

But emigration is only half of the story. The reshaping of the Puerto Rican population and economy was not accomplished by emigration alone. A complementary government policy of sterilization arose simultaneously, and the Puerto Rican and U.S. governments developed Puerto Rico's economy through both emigration and sterilization, especially during the industrialization phase known as Operation Bootstrap. In essence, migration was used as the temporary response to Puerto Rico's overpopulation problem, while sterilization became the permanent solution (Ayala and Bernabe 2000; Bonilla and Campos 1986; Colón-Warren et al. 1999; History Task Force 1979).

It is difficult to collect reliable statistics about the number of women who underwent sterilization under their program because the Puerto Rican government has always denied that Puerto Rico ever had an official sterilization policy.[2] Statistics are difficult to find because, by not keeping records, it is as if this policy never existed. However, as a wise Spanish saying goes, you cannot cover the sky with your hands. There are other sources of information, including life history interviews such as those that I have conducted, which suggest the presence of a widespread government-backed sterilization policy in Puerto Rico during this period. I would argue that whether the policy was official or unofficial, the ultimate result—a population with one of the highest rates or sterilization in the world, often as a result of lack of alternatives—is the same. I would argue that sterilization became so widespread because it was part of a government-orchestrated program of population control and also because it filled a gap in the birth control market. For example, I found that Puerto Rican women accepted sterilization on the island in large numbers because they wanted to control their fertility and there were no other reliable methods of birth control available there in the early part of the twentieth century. As one of the older woman in this study explained, "There were no contraceptives back then. The only way to avoid having children was getting sterilized—free. I just got my husband's signature, went in and got operated on."

The Growing Rate of Sterilization in Puerto Rico

Operation Bootstrap, the industrialization program that began in the 1940s, offered U.S. corporations operating in Puerto Rico tax-free status, cheap labor, and attractive profits. The economic restructuring under Operation Bootstrap reinforced the neo-Malthusian ideology and unofficial sterilization policy that dominated Puerto Rico's approach to population control. Already in 1946, 6.5 percent of all Puerto Rican women had been sterilized in government hospitals and private clinics. By 1953 17 percent—almost one-fifth of all Puerto Rican women—had been sterilized. In the 1960s, as economic and social conditions worsened, it became obvious that Operation Bootstrap's industrialization program had not succeeded in producing enough jobs to accommodate all of the displaced agricultural workers. The government again invoked the argument of overpopulation: too many poor who were to blame for their plight.

To further aggravate these difficult economic circumstances, adverse economic conditions in the United States caused a reverse migration trend—of Puerto Ricans leaving and returning to Puerto Rico (Hernandez-Alvarez 1976). At the same time, large numbers of Dominicans and Cubans migrated to Puerto Rico (Duany 2002; History Task Force 1979). Government administrators became concerned about the burden this influx of people put on the saturated labor market and the increased demands for social services. Consequently, it is no surprise that sterilization was seen as the solution for controlling the growth of the island population and that fertility termination programs were intensified (History Task Force 1979; Mass 1976). In 1974, according to government statistics, 200,000, or 35 percent, of women in Puerto Rico had been sterilized. The average age was twenty-six. As Bonilla and Campos (1986, 26) note, "The demographic effects of this and other methods of population control have exceeded the expectations of Puerto Rican planners and their preceptors in the United States. The island's rate of natural increase has taken a decisive drop, from 2.7 percent during the decade of the 1950s to 1.7 percent in the decade ending in 1980. Equally impressive is the nearly 40 percent reduction in fertility between 1960 and 1980."[3]

Even if sterilization was not part of Puerto Rico's official population control program, it was the only effective method of fertility control consistently made available to Puerto Rican women for long periods of time. Because the government unofficially sanctioned sterilization, doctors approved of it as a way to control Puerto Rico's overpopulation problem. Women wanted to control their

fertility, and by 1982 39 percent of the female population on the island was surgically sterilized (Vazquez-Calzada and Carnivali 1982).[4]

In Puerto Rico, then, what appeared as individual choice with respect to
migration and sterilization was facilitated by the development of capitalism
on the island (History Task Force 1979). The policies of the United States and
colonial governments were such that migration and sterilization were used as
alternate and reinforcing mechanisms. Migration was seen as the temporary
method—the escape valve—while sterilization, or la operación—was considered the permanent solution (Bonilla and Campos 1986). Yet after four decades
of industrialization, massive migration, and large-scale sterilization, Puerto
Rico continues to experience widespread poverty and dependency, and these
problems are still blamed on an overpopulation problem. In January 2007 the
official unemployment rate for Puerto Rico was 12 percent (U.S. Bureau of
Labor Statistics 2007), almost half (45.4 percent) of the population lived below
the poverty line (U.S. Census Bureau 2006) as defined by federal standards, and
60 percent depended on food stamps and other government subsidies for their
daily sustenance (Rivera-Batiz and Santiago 1996). Obviously, overpopulation
cannot be the only reason for Puerto Rico's poverty and underdevelopment.

The Origins of Puerto Rico's
Birth Control Movement: 1925–1948

Puerto Rico's birth control movement and the Puerto Rican community's predisposition toward la operación developed intrinsically within this framework
of political, economic, ideological, and social constraints. From the onset of the
twentieth century, the development of Puerto Rico's birth control movement
was based on the premise that Puerto Rico's poverty and underdevelopment
were caused by overpopulation and that the eugenic and neo-Malthusian ideologies provided the solution. Numerous North American and Puerto Rican
groups—both for and against birth control—participated in the development
of Puerto Rico's birth control movement (Briggs 2002; Colón et. al. 1999; Earnhardt 1982; Henderson 1976; Lopez 1985; Presser 1973; Ramirez de Arellano and
Seipp 1983; Ramos-Bellido 1977; Schoen 2005; Vazquez-Calzada 1988). Although
they all basically agreed that the Puerto Rican problem stemmed from its
overpopulation crisis, they disagreed about the nature of its origins as well as
the solution. The conservative eugenicists, mostly North American officials in
powerful government and administrative positions, attributed Puerto Rican
"backwardness to the tropical climate and their inferior stock" (Briggs 2002,
100). Like their European counterparts, they considered poor Puerto Ricans
unfit for reproduction. Their solution to Puerto Rico's overpopulation problem
was sterilization and emigration. In contrast, the moderate eugenicists were

mostly Puerto Rican social workers, health professionals, and nurses. They worked in Puerto Rico's birth control leagues, maternal and child health centers, and hospitals and clinics that made up Puerto Rico's natal and prenatal services. Although they, too, believed the view that Puerto Rico's problems originated from overpopulation, as progressive eugenicists they did not blame the social problems of Puerto Ricans to their genetic inferiority. Their plan for reform was to lower the birth rate through birth control and sterilization and improve the living conditions of the poor (Briggs 2002).

The Catholic Church and the Puerto Rican Nationalist Party, known as the Independentistas, had opposed birth control and sterilization on national, religious, and cultural grounds since the early part of the twentieth century. They considered birth control and sterilization part of a North American plan of genocide (Schoen 2005, 204–205). As Ramos-Bellido (1977) notes, the Independentistas feared that through birth control, the colonial power could eliminate Puerto Rican cultural values by wiping out Puerto Ricans. They argued that birth control could destroy the chance for radical political change that might arise from poverty caused by overpopulation and economic disparity (Ramos-Bellido 1977). Despite their differences, as Briggs (2002) points out, the Independentistas and the Catholic Church both adopted patriarchal attitudes toward motherhood and gender. They both saw women as weak and defenseless, as well as easily fooled and manipulated (Briggs 2002; Colón et. al 1999; Crespo-Kebler 2001a).

Throughout history women have wanted to control their fertility, and Puerto Rican women were no exception to this rule (Briggs 2002; Colón et al 1999; Crespo-Kebler 2001a; Gordon 1990; Hartmann 1995; Lopez 1993). For example, Puerto Rican upper- and middle-class feminists and reformers were fighting for birth control on the island in the early part of the twentieth century, long before North American women joined their struggle (Azize-Vargas 2000, Briggs 2002, 90, Colón et. al 1999, 54; Crespo-Kebler 2001a, 57; Schoen 2005, 213). Some of the Puerto Rican women who worked in the birth control organizations were both feminists and nationalists, and as a consequence they endorsed and embraced voluntary motherhood and independence for Puerto Rico (Briggs 2002; Colón et al. 1999, 54; Schoen 2005).

THE TRAJECTORY OF PUERTO RICO'S BIRTH CONTROL POLICY

The moderate (progressive) eugenicist family planning specialists arose in Puerto Rico in the early part of the twentieth century. In 1925 Dr. José Lanauze Rolon, a black physician, and other prominent citizens organized "The League for the Control of Natality." They did so not just because of an overpopulation problem, but also in order to reduce population growth and to improve the conditions of the working class. They launched this league in Puerto Rico to challenge and repeal the Comstock Law, a federal law that made birth control illegal (Colón et al. 1999, 52; Gordon 1990, 257, 274–290, 302–317, 321–340; Ramos-Bellido 1977, 69). As Briggs notes, members of Rolon's league were involved in a broadly progressive movement, and they also fought to "combat ignorance, poverty, and crime" and to implement the minimum wage in Puerto Rico (Briggs 2002, 91–92; Colón-Warren 1999; Ramirez de Arellano and Seipp 1983). Even though their clinic did not provide any birth control services, the league was pressured to close in 1928 by the Catholic Church because it lacked funds (Alvarado and Tietze 1947, 15–18; Earnhardt 1982, 12; Ramos-Bellido 1977, 70).

The first birth control clinic that opened in Puerto Rico, known as the Birth Control League of Puerto Rico, was established in San Juan in 1925. Unlike the League for the Control of Natality, this clinic may have provided clinical services as well as family planning advice to poor and working-class people (Colón et. al. 1999; Ramirez de Arellano and Seipp 1983, 29; Vazquez-Calzada 1988). The clinic was closed after two years, once again due to religious opposition, lack of public support, and a scarcity of funds (Alvarado and Tietze 1947, 15–18).

In summary, between 1925 and 1932, Puerto Rican public health officials organized two leagues to promote temporary methods of birth control in Puerto Rico. As far as the records show, neither of these leagues offered contraceptive services, given the limitations set by the Comstock Law. This means that most of poor Puerto Rican women had no legal access to contraceptives until the Comstock law was repealed in 1937.

The lack of access to contraception, among other reasons, set the stage for the widespread acceptance of sterilization among Puerto Ricans in the 1930s. Other factors included widespread poverty, the Great Depression, the eugenic ideology, and Puerto Rican feminists' and public health officials' support for birth control.

The Great Depression and hurricane San Felipe, which destroyed the island in 1928 and left thousands of Puerto Ricans in desperate straits, contributed to widespread and dire poverty on the island. Also, the significant increase of unemployed workers throughout the United States during the 1930s rekindled the eugenic movement in the continental United States. This campaign called for the sterilization of individuals who were regarded socially and genetically undesirable. Based on the eugenic laws of the United States, the Puerto Rican legislature passed two additional laws that established an insular eugenics board to sterilize any incarcerated persons suffering from a mental disease, mental retardation, epilepsy, and sexual perversion, and permitted physicians to provide birth control information and prescribe contraceptives to patients because of their physical, mental, or socioeconomic conditions (Ramos-Bellido 1977, 72). According to Earnhardt:

> After the Comstock law was repealed in 1937 two acts were passed in Puerto Rico. Law 33, which legalized contraception and Law 136, which "authorized the Commissioner of Health to (a) license physicians (and midwife nurses under their supervision) to 'teach and practice eugenic principles' and (b) to promote the 'teaching and divulgation of eugenic principles' in public health facilities. (Thus, private and public physicians might advise on or practice or provide contraceptive measures to legally or consensually married persons whenever justified on the basis of personal health, eugenic principles, or 'financial poverty or poor social living conditions'); and (3) the third law created a Eugenic Board which might under certain conditions order the sterilization of the mentally diseased or retarded, epileptics and sexual perverts" (Earnhardt 1982, 28).[5]

In sum, one (legal) act encouraged the sterilization of the poor and the other permitted tubal ligation for health and other reasons. Puerto Ricans rejected the clause that promoted sterilization based on poverty, since the majority of Puerto Ricans were poor and they felt they were being targeted for population control. Consequently, most sterilization operations were performed for health reasons, which were considered more socially acceptable. This act condoned sterilization for the majority of the Puerto Rican population because most were poor, malnourished, and in poor health (Earnhardt 1982, 33; Gordon 1990; Lopez 1985; Ramos-Bellido 1977, 73). The potential impact of such legislation on Puerto Rican society was enormous. Between 1947 and 1982 the rate of sterilization rose from 6.6 percent to 39.0 percent (Vazquez-Calzada 1988).

Because of Puerto Rico's colonial relationship with the United States, Puerto Rico's birth control history was strongly intertwined with the politics of birth control in the United States. For example, with the inauguration of Franklin D. Roosevelt in 1933, the population control policy of birth control in Puerto Rico received stronger government support than ever before. One of the agencies created under the New Deal was the Federal Emergency Relief Administration (FERA), which provided funds to state and local governments (Briggs 2002; Colón et al. 1999; Earnhardt 1982, 25; Ramirez de Arellano and Seipp 1983, 31). In 1933, the FERA selected James Bourne to direct the Puerto Rican Emergency Relief Administration (PRERA). With the mind-set of a (progressive) moderate eugenicist, James Bourne used the PRERA money to fund birth control on the island and to provide direct relief.

From the beginning of his tenure, Bourne attributed Puerto Rico's social problems to overpopulation. For example, in a report he submitted to President Roosevelt known as "A Constructive Plan for Puerto Rico," he argued that overpopulation was the island's most serious problem and recommended birth control and emigration as the solutions (Ramirez de Arellano and Seipp 1983, 32). However, as a progressive eugenicist, he believed the social situation of Puerto Ricans could improve through changes in the environment. Therefore, in his report Bourne also addressed Puerto Rico's immediate health problems such as malaria and tuberculosis and suggested the establishment of a latrine system (Ramirez de Arellano and Seipp 1983, 32).

In 1934, Rexford Tugwell, later appointed as governor of Puerto Rico, was sent to the island by Roosevelt to make recommendations on the reconstruction of Puerto Rico's economy, which was severely devastated by the Depression. On the same airplane was Mrs. Eleanor Roosevelt, who also expressed interest in solving Puerto Rico's problems. Both Tugwell and Mrs. Roosevelt played an influential role in advising the president of the federal role in Puerto Rico's reconstruction (Earnhardt 1982, 18–20; Ramirez de Arellano and Seipp 1983, 33). When Tugwell returned to Washington he presented President Roosevelt with a reconstruction plan for Puerto Rico. Despite his reservations about the dysgenic effects of birth control, he recommended it as a major solution to Puerto Rico's overpopulation problem primarily because the president and Mrs. Roosevelt both approved of birth control (Earnhardt 1982, 19).

Tugwell also recommended that a small committee of Puerto Rican officials come to Washington and identify the services they felt Puerto Rico needed. Among the group of Puerto Rican officials who convened in Washington was Luis Muñoz Marín, who would become Puerto Rico's first elected governor. The recommendation that this committee made for Puerto Rico's reconstruction came to be known as the "Chardon Plan." Their report defined Puerto Rico's problems as landlessness, unemployment, and overpopulation, for which they recommended land reform and industrialization (Earnhardt 1982, 20). These recommendations, however, were not popular with landowners and therefore were not implemented. In contrast to Tugwell's position, the report recommended emigration rather than birth control as the solution to Puerto Rican overpopulation (Ramirez de Arellano and Seipp 1983, 36).

Despite the recommendations made by the Puerto Rican officials, the Catholic Church's opposition to birth control, and Tugwell's own personal reservations about birth control, Tugwell recommended birth control only because he knew that Roosevelt favored it over emigration (Earnhardt 1982, 19; Vazquez-Calzada 1988). Consequently, in 1934 funds from the Puerto Rican Emergency Relief Administration (PRERA) were directed toward the creation of the maternal health clinic, an experimental birth control clinic that was a division of the School of Tropical Medicine. Dr. José Belaval was appointed director of this clinic. Although President Roosevelt officially denied that the U.S. government was sponsoring birth control in Puerto Rico, there is little doubt that he was aware of the establishment of this clinic. According to Earnhardt (1982, 19), "it is quite apparent that President Roosevelt himself approved personally if not officially of the opening of the PRERA" maternal health clinic (with an emphasis on birth control). At the very least, the president should have known of the impending PRERA maternal health program when he visited Puerto Rico in July—where at a dinner in the government house he told an audience including the Reverend Edwin Byrne, Catholic bishop of San Juan, that "his administration would not favor birth control being enforced in Puerto Rico by the Government." James Bourne was present at the same dinner, and he reports that at this approximate time he promised Roosevelt that he would "take the heat of birth control" (Earnhardt 1982, 22).

The controversy over the use of U.S. funds to sponsor birth control clinics in Puerto Rico escalated when the island's church hierarchy joined the protest (Ramirez de Arellano and Seipp 1983, 38). After a great deal of commotion, PRERA was dissolved through bureaucratic restructuring on September 30, 1935. Despite the dissolution of PRERA, the federal birth control program on the island was expanded. On the day following PRERA's dissolution, birth control efforts were taken over by a new federal agency: The Federal Emergency Relief Administration for Puerto Rico (FERA-PR), with James Bourne as its director. From October 1935 to June 1936 the FERA-PR expanded the federal birth control effort. Under its auspices, fifty-three to sixty-seven maternal clinics were opened around the island, and by June 1936 over 10,000 women had been provided with birth control services (Earnhardt 1982, 25; Schoen 2005; Vazquez-Calzada 1988). Although there are no records indicating the kinds of birth control methods these clinics distributed, from the data that is available it can be surmised that they were natural methods of birth control such as rhythm or withdrawal and/or mechanical methods, such as a condom or diaphragm. Although condoms were available at this early date, they might not have been readily accessible since birth control was still against the law in Puerto Rico.

The FERA-PR birth control campaign came to an abrupt end on June 30, 1936, when the Roosevelt administration switched from a "relief" plan for Puerto Rico to a "reconstruction" strategy with the creation of the Puerto Rico Reconstruction Administration (PRRA). However, before all of Puerto Rico's contraceptive clinics were closed, one more effort was made to revive Puerto Rico's birth control program. In 1936, PRRA allocated $225,000 to a national health program, which endorsed fertility control. The Catholic Church in the United States put an end to this last-minute effort, however, by exerting pressure in Washington, particularly during Roosevelt's second electoral campaign. As Earnhardt notes, Dr. Gruening, the director of the PRRA, described the order from Washington to terminate the program immediately in the following way: "In August 1936, Jim Farley (President Roosevelt's chief political advisor) called and said 'what the hell is going on in Puerto Rico . . . Whatever it is, stop it. It's hurting the (national Democratic) campaign. We've had three bishops in here this morning.' And I knew what he meant. So I did tell all of the workers in the organization that they could no longer do this" (Earnhardt 1982, 26).

Monopolizing Puerto Rico's Birth Control Market

As Briggs notes, the era of the progressive nurse and social work control over birth control was short-lived (Briggs 2002, 101–102). By 1936, Puerto Rico's birth control movement shifted from moderate to conservative eugenicists, personified by Clarence Gamble, an individual who played a major role in the development of Puerto Rico's birth control movement (Briggs 2002, 102; Earnhardt 1982; Ramirez de Arellano and Seipp 1983). As I noted previously, in the election year Roosevelt put an end to the federal aid, leaving a gap in the Puerto Rican birth control market. Clarence Gamble, a North American philanthropist, physician, and researcher, and heir to the Proctor and Gamble soap fortune, saw the gap and quickly seized the opportunity by founding (and funding) a private birth control organization called the Maternal and Child Health Association. According to Briggs, "This Association was so similar to the federally funded Maternal Health clinic that Gamble hired most of the same individuals who worked for the previous clinic" (Briggs 2002, 102). Ultimately Gamble's goal was to corner the birth control market.

Gamble's motives were self-serving. Briggs found that with this association he promoted his own private stock of spermicidal jellies that he wanted to test instead of funding the more reliable diaphragms that were already on the market. As a conservative eugenicist he believed that these methods were better suited for the "limited intelligence" of the poor (Briggs 2002, 102). In 1937, he opened up twenty-three birth control clinics in Puerto Rico and tested contraceptives on fifteen hundred women that the FDA had not approved in the U.S. market at the time (Ramirez de Arellano and Seipp 1983, 45; Schoen 2005, 205). The methods tested in these clinics for future use in the United States were the diaphragm, foam powder and sponge, and spermicidal powder and jelly (Ramirez de Arellano and Seipp 1983, 47). In two years, these clinics serviced free of charge approximately five thousand lower-income couples (Earnhardt 1982, 27; Ramirez de Arellano and Seipp 1983, 56). In keeping with the pattern of the past, the clinics were forced to close in 1939 because of religious and political opposition.

Despite its short-lived existence, the Maternal and Child Health Association played a vital role in the development of Puerto Rico's birth control history. It

was the first organization to collect data systematically and to conduct program evaluation demonstrating the need for contraception among the Puerto
Rican population (Alvarado and Tietze 1947, 16). The association helped to
galvanize a variety of private groups interested in the legalization of birth control in Puerto Rico (Earnhardt 1982, 25, 26). And, most important, in 1937 the
Maternal Association was a catalyst for the introduction of birth control and
sterilization legislation. This legislation established licensing procedures for
doctors to practice and disseminate information about sterilization and birth
control for both sexes. This legislation represented a major gain for those who
had fought for birth control in Puerto Rico (Vazquez-Calzada 1988).

Between the 1930s and the 1950s Gamble turned Puerto Rico into his own
personal birth control laboratory (Briggs 2002, 107). By the end of the 1930s,
Gamble monopolized the birth control market with his ineffective contraceptive foam and jellies (Briggs 2002, 102, 108; Schoen 2005, 207). It is not
surprising that by the time sterilization became legal in 1937, la operación
was the only effective method of fertility control on the island, and women
readily accepted it primarily because it worked. The colonial discourse that
overpopulation was the cause of poverty echoed throughout Puerto Rico in
the 1940s. In Briggs words:

> Huge numbers of social scientists were funded to do research on the Puerto
> Rican family with the goal of developing a model that could be used in the
> rest of the overpopulated Third World. The Puerto Rican woman was rep-
> resented as a victim of machismo. For liberals, she was victimized by her
> endless children, and they longed to rescue her from her own ignorance and
> "macho" Puerto Rican men who proved their virility through her suffering
> maternity; for conservatives, she was a "demon mother" whose dangerous
> fecundity could not be halted by strong measures—sterilization, high doses
> of hormones, perhaps a contraceptive agent in the water. (Briggs 2002, 110)

In the 1940s, free of the Comstock law, Puerto Rican professionals took up
the birth control cause again, despite the protests of the church. Their work and
the general encouragement from Gamble and indirect acceptance from Marín
led to Puerto Rican women's involvement with birth control. For example, the
rate of birth control utilization shot up from 34 percent in 1939 to 74 percent in
1968 (Briggs 2002, 122).

GAMBLE AND SANGER'S BIRTH CONTROL EXPERIMENTATION

The use of Puerto Rico as a laboratory for testing new methods of birth control
continued beyond the demise of the Maternal and Child Heath Association.
Clarence Gamble, and even the well-known feminist Margaret Sanger, played

a key role in the testing of the birth control pill on Puerto Rican women in
1956. Gamble collaborated with Searle, the pharmaceutical company that tested
the pill in Puerto Rico.[6] Between the 1940s and 1950s the pharmaceuticals
sponsored contraceptive research on the island (Briggs 2002; Henderson 1976).
The largest trial started in 1956 (Colón-Warren 1999, 56; Briggs 2002, 135–136;
Schoen 2005, 208–215). It involved poor women in a housing project in Rio Pie-
dras and included patients of Ryder hospital. More than a breach of ethics, this
trial also took unnecessary risks with women's health (Briggs 2002, 100). Many
women became quite sick from taking the pill; some were even hospitalized.
However, Schoen's study reveals that women volunteered to be part of these
birth control trials because they were desperate for birth control (Schoen 2005,
208). According to Schoen, hundreds of Puerto Rican women volunteered to
participate in the birth control trails because they sought sterilization but had
been rejected because they did not have three children. According to Rule 120,
if a woman's age multiplied by the number of children she has does not add up
to the number 120, the doctor will not sterilize her. In this context, Schoen's
point supports my argument that Puerto Rican women accepted sterilization
in such large numbers because they desperately wanted to control their fertility
and they were not offered viable options.

Sanger, a Conservative Feminist Eugenicist

Margaret Sanger participated in the testing of the birth control pill on Puerto
Rican women. She supported this experimentation by recruiting a wealthy
female patron, Katherine Dexter McCormick, to fund research on the pill
(Chesler 1992). It is ironic that two American female physicians conducted the
birth control trials (Briggs 2002; Schoen 2005). This action speaks volumes
about the limits of female solidarity and reveals Sanger's classist and racist
biases. As Briggs underscores, "The trials—and the pill generally—have been
criticized as an example of male and masculinist science being callous about
women's bodies. But it bears underlining that the people most directly involved
in these trials were women and feminists. Sanger and McCormick supported
and shepherded the work of Pincus and his lab, even when Planned Parenthood
of America Association dropped it" (Briggs 2002, 137).

Furthermore, as Briggs notes, if Sanger had had her way she would have
begun testing the pill on Puerto Rican women as early as 1941. This trial failed
because the patients recruited from Presbyterian hospital (San Juan) were educated and refused to participate in this trial study to the end (Briggs 2002, 140;
Schoen 2005, 210–211).

It should be noted that access to legal abortion in Puerto Rico was not initially
brought about by an internal feminist movement; rather, it was a consequence of

its legalization in the continental United States. This is another example of how U.S. policy was automatically made law in Puerto Rico (Azize-Vargas and Aviles 1997, Colón, et. al. 1999, 2). However, it is important to note that even though abortions were not legalized in Puerto Rico until 1973, they were still performed. In fact, in the 1950s Puerto Rico was known as an abortion haven, and through the 1970s thousands of women, particularly women from the mainland United States, had abortions in Puerto Rico (Colón, et. al. 1999; Ramirez de Arellano and Seipp 1983). For local women, however, the lack of legal abortion services and stigma associated with abortion limited their reproductive choices and induced many women to accept sterilization, which was legal and more socially accepted.

CONCLUSION

As Briggs's and other scholars' work highlights, the outcome of Puerto Rico's birth control movement, an approach to birth control that encouraged wide-spread use of sterilization, was a combination of the struggle between the island's own internal pressure groups and those of the United States. Myriad forces played an important role in shaping Puerto Rico's birth control move-ment and in constraining Puerto Rican women's reproductive rights: the Com-stock Law that made birth control illegal; the struggle between progressive and moderate eugenicists, each group promoting what they thought was best for Puerto Ricans and for their own agendas; the adamant opposition of the Catholic Church and Nationalist Party toward birth control and sterilization; the feminist consciousness of Puerto Rican women's groups; and the privatiza-tion of Puerto Rico's birth control market in different periods of the island's history. The latter had particularly challenging consequences, as by the early 1940s, by eliminating the more effective diaphragm from the market, Clarence Gamble literally provided Puerto Rican women with no other choice but to accept tubal ligation or continue to have children. The high rate of steriliza-tion among Puerto Rican women was also influenced by the ambivalence of the U.S. and Puerto Rican governments toward temporary methods of birth control and the sexist orientation of policy makers.

Puerto Rico's colonial social framework also played a crucial role in con-straining women's fertility options. Federal funding was not consistently avail-able for temporary methods of birth control in Puerto Rico until 1968. Private funding often came with commercial agendas that were not necessarily in the best interests of Puerto Rican women. Abortion was not legalized in Puerto Rico until 1973 (through *Roe v. Wade*) and even then it was highly stigmatized.[7] As in most Latin American countries, birth control was used in Puerto Rico to solve the overpopulation problem instead of to empower women to control their fertility.

The Catholic Church adamantly opposed sterilization, contraceptives, and abortion, yet they considered la operación the lesser of the two evils because it took place prior to conception. In the long run the church preached that in time this "sin" could be absolved through confession and prayer. Consequently, Puerto Rican women accepted and opted for sterilization primarily because of the lack of viable individual birth control alternatives and social/personal hardships. In essence, Puerto Rican women were denied full reproductive freedom.

All of these factors must be examined within the larger colonial context of the United States' and Puerto Rico's endorsement of neo-Malthusian and eugenic ideologies. These presumed that overpopulation was the cause of Puerto Rico's underdevelopment and poverty, and the eugenicists' view that the poor were unfit to reproduce because they were poor and nonwhite was explicitly incorporated into government policy at various points in the twentieth century. Policy development also took place within a social context that was geared toward U.S. markets and profits, which contributed to an increasing number of surplus workers. Women's fertility alternatives were also influenced by the widespread acceptance of sterilization among the medical profession based on their beliefs that lower population growth would lead to more prosperity for the individual as well as for the island.

Even though sterilization was initially imposed on women through Puerto Rico's population policy (through a colonial regime), many women used it after having several children because it provided them with the only practical way to control their fertility. This is especially true after Puerto Rico shifted — *why* from an agrarian to an industrial society. After several generations, sterilization became a large number of Puerto Rican women's preferred method of fertility control, and they began to seek it out for themselves. *a combination of things all resulting in greater sensibility due to these outside factors*

CHAPTER 2

Gender Awareness
across Generations

The colonial history of Puerto Rico and the history of birth control on the island have influenced the lives of three generations of women in my study. Despite individual variations, each generation shares certain common orientations that stem from the intersection of their gender, race, age, and class, and are influenced by the era in which they grew up, as well as the sociopolitical environment. Thus, before I move on to the stories of individual families, I would like to consider the common experiences faced by the women of each generation.

My study focuses on Puerto Rican women living in New York City, whom I will term, for heuristic purposes, the first, second, and third generations. These are the mothers, daughters, and granddaughters in the households I followed for twenty-five years. The mothers (first generation) were born 1914–1922. The daughters (second generation) were born 1934–1952. The granddaughters (third generation) were born 1959–1981. The first generation of women share experiences of emigrating from agrarian communities in Puerto Rico to industrial New York City in search of work. Women in the second generation were mostly born in New York. They lived through an era of rapid social change as the city shifted from an industrial to a service economy, and the civil rights movement and the second wave of feminism challenged Americans to think about race and gender in new ways. The third generation women grew up in a postindustrial and post–civil rights city, facing gentrification and the challenges of a new economic and social structure.

My main concern in this chapter is to consider the impact of these significant social, economic, and political changes on women's gender awareness. The choices women make (or do not make) about reproduction, fertility control, and parenting are linked with their understanding of themselves as women, and with their larger understanding of gender roles and values, as well as their social circumstances.

The women I have termed "first generation" grew up in preindustrial, agricultural Puerto Rico, where they were raised in wooden shacks with no running water or electricity. Their stories of life on the island were generally stories of poverty. When they were children, they were so poor that they only had one pair of shoes. To preserve them they only wore them during school and in church. Doña Rosario explained, "We went to school barefooted and put our shoes on only when we were in school. We had one pair of shoes, which we wore on Sundays to go to church. When the service was over, we would take off our shoes at the church door. Everyone took his or her shoes off, even the elders." At the time the first generation women were growing up, in the 1920s and 1930s, Puerto Rico was undergoing economic changes under a colonial regime. The island underwent a transition from subsistence to a monocrop economy that resulted in widespread displacement and impoverishment of the rural population. Additionally, because these working-class women grew up with such few amenities and work was so labor intensive, physically they worked harder than any subsequent generation of Puerto Rican women. The combination of hard work, poor living conditions, and tropical island diseases adversely affected their health and the health of their children. Doña Rosario explained, "I was born in Puerto Rico in 1917. There was no electric light, and to cook we had to fetch water from the river. We had to cook with firewood. We went to the hills to find the wood and cut it down. The wash had to be done in the river. We would get up at five in the morning and sometimes we would not go to bed till twelve at night."

In Puerto Rican agricultural society, children had economic value. Children played an important role in domestic labor and agricultural production. Because domestic work was so labor intensive, women needed help around the house and young girls often filled the role of surrogate mother. Depending on their age, girls were required to help with the household chores and care for the younger children. Doña Rosario continued,

> When I was growing up children worked plenty. After going to school kids came home to work: to plant bananas, yams, and cut firewood. We pressed clothes with huge irons heated by coal; we cooked with firewood and washed clothes in the river. When I was growing up we had two small houses. We lived in one and rented the other to sugar cane cutters who worked in a nearby sugar plantation. My parents always had ten to fifteen men living in

that house. For a small fee we washed their clothing and cooked for them. They lived with us during the week and went home on weekends.

We washed in the river from Monday through Wednesday. Sometimes we got up at four in the morning and washed from 7 to 11. Then we went home to cook and then returned to the river. By three we went back to cook again. I started to do chores like this when I was twelve years old. Before I was twelve, I helped but my sisters were in charge. Since I am the youngest I was the one with the fewest chores. While my sister cooked, I would look for firewood and help with the wash and ironing. When I was growing up children earned their keep. Everyone was more responsible then.

Because their parents needed their labor, children only went to school until the first or second grade. Doña Rosario explained,

> I have three years of schooling. In those days parents did not send their children to school because they had to work. At that time we lived on a farm and there were all kinds of animals, and we had to plant everything, even the rice.
>
> When I was five years old my father said everyone in this house is going to work. I cried and pleaded with my father to let me stay in school, and I would do all of my chores because I wanted to go to school, but he said no, and when he said no, the answer was no.

Young girls not only performed adult household chores but also, between 1900 and 1920, at the height of the needlework industry in Puerto Rico, worked for wages at home, sewing alongside their mothers and mothers. For example, by the age of nine or ten, young girls had already started working in the needlework industry, embroidering handkerchiefs and sewing gloves at home piecemeal. In doña Rosario's words, "We sewed handkerchiefs and gloves at home. They paid a penny for each handkerchief. I began to sew when I was seven years old. We used a gas lamp for light. Often there was so much smoke we had to swallow it. Sometimes we stayed up all night sewing. At times I sewed five-dozen handkerchiefs in one night."

Large families are common in agricultural societies, and women of this generation tended to have large families. For example, by the age of fifteen or sixteen, most of the women were mothers. By the time they were twenty-five or twenty-six years old, these poor and often malnourished women sometimes had as many as nine or ten consecutive pregnancies. Puerto Ricans also had many children because they knew that they would not all survive. In the 1940s, the infant mortality rate in Puerto Rico was 72.4 infant deaths per thousand (Vazquez-Calzada 1988, 235) as compared to 47.0 per thousand in the United States (Linder and Grove 1943).

Doña Caridad's mother was a midwife in the early part of the twentieth century, and she vividly recalls the wretched conditions poor women lived and gave birth in:

My mother was a midwife. She took out the rotted kids from poor women's bellies. She also frequently positioned the babies in women's bellies before they gave birth. If she could not position them correctly she sent the woman to see a doctor, if there was one available. My mother helped these women, and these *barrio* (small town) women paid more attention to what my mother said than to the doctors.

I'll never forget the sight of those poor women with their newborn babies on the floor. In that era the beds were hard like a rock, for those lucky enough to have a bed. We put rags on these hard mattresses, and that is where these poor souls, who had just given birth, rested. That is why a law should be passed that women should not have more children. Because the fathers would make these babies and then abandon the women, and the children had nothing to eat, and look at the situation they would come to. Children had nothing to eat. Nothing. Everything was a disaster.

I was a young girl when my mother assisted other women in giving birth. She would say to me: "bring me whatever old clothing we have to lay so and so on the floor because she is such a poor soul she has no bed. I brought her whatever clothing I could find and some chicken broth as well. We raised chickens at home and part of my job was to make and bring my mother soup.

One other reason women in this generation had large families was because they did not have access to temporary methods of birth control. Because most women in this generation were born in the early part of the twentieth century, several were in their early twenties in 1937, the year when sterilization became legal. Until that year, birth control was illegal under the Comstock law in Puerto Rico and the United States. Even after the Comstock law was repealed in 1937, access to contraceptives for many poor women was minimal, either because poor women could not afford them, they lived too far away from the health clinics and public transportation was not available, or the Catholic Church frequently forced these clinics to close.[2]

Not only did women give birth under difficult conditions and take full responsibility for the domestic work and the children, but poor women often did men's work as well. For example, doña Rosario took over her first husband's job when he fell sick and died so that her family could survive.

My first husband worked in the cane fields. I married him when I was fifteen and had five children with him. (I had my children every two years. They

were born in 1934, 1936, 1938, 1940, and 1944.) He died of tuberculosis when
I was 24. I was both the woman and the man of the house. Many women
worked like men to earn a few dollars. Many of them picked coffee, cut
sugar cane, and spread fertilizer. I even plowed with oxen and sowed rice and
pigeon peas. I also packed sugar cane and the cane flower. I had to carry the
cane on my shoulders to the place where the oxen cart picked it up.

Some women from the first generation expressed resignation about having as many children as "God" gave them. Other women, like doña Rosario,
opted for, accepted, and actively sought la operación after going through one
pregnancy after another and finding that she could not feed the children she
already had. She confessed to me that when she was eight months pregnant, she
tried to abort by picking up a huge basin of water.

In addition to the hardships of motherhood, poor health, and poverty
these women confronted daily, they also had to deal with the inequities of
the patriarchal family. For example, many of the women also had to accept
their husbands' infidelity and sometimes violent behavior. In that era, sexual
double standards were accepted as the norm. A significant number of men had
extramarital affairs and children with other women. Even though women did
not like it, and resisted it, they had to accommodate and tolerate such behavior because they could not afford to raise their children by themselves. For
example, although doña Rosario worked hard, she found she could not survive
with her children on the meager income she earned. Before she migrated she
tried to leave her second husband, but she went back to him because her family
would not support her.

I met my second husband Victor two years after my first husband died. We
had a problematic relationship because he drank, was a womanizer, and a
gambler. At that time I was twenty-six years old. I had five children with
him. The children were almost born one right after the other [*the children
were born in 1945, 1946, 1948, 1949, and 1950*]. During my last pregnancy I had
twins. They died one week apart from cholera.

I left him twice. The first time I moved in with his mother and the second
time with my sister. When I moved in with his mother she gave us a small
corner of a room because that's all the space she had. We slept on the floor.
When I moved in with my sister, I had to take care of my kids, and her six
stepchildren. I washed, cooked, and cleaned around the clock. I couldn't
keep up with the workload. I had to do everything because my sister had
to take care of other things. It was easier to live with my husband than take
care of twelve kids every day. The workload finally forced me to go back to
my husband.

Although doña Rosario and don Victor had a problematic relationship, she claims he also worked hard and supported her and their children, at least while they were in Puerto Rico. In order to do so he migrated to the U.S. mainland to work in migrant camps, or "farms" as they referred to them. According to doña Rosario,

> Victor supported the children and me; to provide for us he had to go work in camps in the United States. In Puerto Rico he worked in the sugar cane fields. He ground the sugar cane and separated the juice from the fiber. He took the sugar cane pulp to the laboratory. When he left for the United States for several months he had to cook his own meals. He did not like that.
>
> He left every two or three months. When the cane work disappeared the government started to give him social security. He built this house. It used to be made of wood, now it is made of cement. Afterwards the government brought food stamps to Puerto Rico. When the kids were young I used to receive a supplement for them; they gave us flour and milk.

Like women, men were also subjected to the gendered nature of work on the sugar plantations. According to don Victor, men's lives were hard in that era, too. Prior to the industrialization of Puerto Rico, the only jobs available to poor men were the backbreaking cutting and packing of sugar cane in the fields or the arduous task of picking coffee and tobacco leaves in the center of the island for pennies a day. That is, if they were lucky enough to find a job. Because the sugar cane crop took six months to plant and another six months to mature, the men who worked in the fields were unemployed for six months out of the year. In order to survive the so-called "dead season," they migrated to the interior of the island to pick coffee beans or tobacco. If they were not able to find work there, they had no choice but to migrate to other parts of the Caribbean, or temporarily move to the U.S. mainland as migrant workers. Don Victor explains,

> I studied till the second grade and started to work in the sugar cane when I was fourteen years old. I also spread fertilizer for six months of the year, and cut weeds with my machete and did various other things. I rose at five in the morning and was out in the field at seven A.M. We worked till four in the evening. We worked nine hours a day every day, Monday to Saturday. On Saturday we only worked half a day. We ate lunch and rested from twelve to one. The most I earned was from seven to ten dollars a week.
>
> From the ages of fourteen to nineteen I worked as a *pinche*, who is the guy who goes to town, picks up lunch and puts it in a canteen for the men working in the field. When I was nineteen I started to chop cane. We'd work in the hot sun till we dropped.

I came to Lyons, New York, to work in 1951 because I could not find work in Puerto Rico. When a man has a family he has to do something. Even though I emigrated there to work, I had to pay my own airfare. They took it right out of my salary. I lived in a camp with about four hundred other men. I would get up at dawn and work all day picking string beans, peaches, and apples. They gave us a bed and food. We went back to the barracks in the evening; they served us a hot meal. We took a shower and went to sleep so that we could start the same routine all over the next day. I got paid next to nothing and the work conditions were difficult. Most of the men were totally frustrated.

I also migrated to a place near Philadelphia in 1952 to pick string beans, apples, peaches, and gladiolas. They paid us one dollar an hour and provided us with food and a bed. I spent five months on the farm and I didn't wait around for winter.

When I returned to Puerto Rico I worked as a carpenter's assistant. I would bring him water. I was his apprentice until I learned the trade. I never wanted to return to work in the farms in the United States. I was an apprentice for six months until I learned enough to find work on my own. Afterwards I helped build houses, doing whatever they needed me to do. In Puerto Rico it was easier to earn a living than in New York. There I was in my own home. In my home I ate the food I liked. My health suffered in the United States. I developed ulcers and a hernia.

In the 1940s, thousands of Puerto Ricans migrated to the east coast of the United States in search of work. Entire families migrated to the United States. Doña Rosario said, "I left Puerto Rico because the situation was so bad that when it rained we would all get wet because our roof was full of holes. Sometimes we might find a *pana* (breadfruit) but other times there wasn't even that." Like other women in her situation, doña Rosario was resolved not to live in dire poverty any longer. So, when she saw other men migrating to the United States she took action. First, she convinced her husband to go to Florida ahead of her, and while he was gone she clandestinely arranged to get sterilized without his permission. She wanted to get sterilized before she joined him because she feared getting pregnant again and not being able to work. During that era corrupt politicians running for mayor in small towns unofficially provided free sterilization in exchange for a vote. This reveals that by the late 1950s la operación had become so widespread that resourceful women like doña Rosario learned to navigate the system to get their needs met.[3]

As the counterpart story to this, in New York City I spoke to a few Puerto Rican women living in Brooklyn who told me that in the 1950s they returned to Puerto Rico to get sterilized there because la operación was not yet legal in the United States. According to these women, they did this because they needed to work, they could not afford to have more children, and they could not get sterilized in New York. In Puerto Rico they understood the politics of how to obtain a cheap or free operation. Doña Rosario's story highlights the active role some women played in getting sterilized.

Like doña Rosario and don Victor, between the 1940s and 1950s thousands of other Puerto Ricans eagerly migrated to New York City in search of work. A large number of Puerto Rican women were motivated to get sterilized before they migrated so that they could work in New York. This is partially exemplified by the fact that 50 percent of the ninety-six sterilized women interviewed for the survey of this study were sterilized in Puerto Rico before they migrated. The other half was sterilized in New York. In fact, Puerto Ricans were predisposed to having smaller families even before they migrated to New York in the 1950s. With the onset of industrialization in Puerto Rico in the 1940s—the building of hospitals, roads, schools, and the implementation of in-door plumbing and electricity—the birth rate on the island dropped as infant mortality declined and the rate of tubal ligation increased.

Essentially, Puerto Rican women subscribed to the middle-class ideology that small families were a symbol of upward mobility. This image is corroborated by one of the women in the classic documentary *La Operación* (1977). In her words, "We would tell each other the belief that the only way to succeed was to have a smaller family" ("Nosotros nos hacíamos la propaganda unos a los otros que para truinfar se tenía que tener menos familia"). Puerto Rican women figured out other strategies to enable them to work when they migrated to the United States. For example, a few women in this study came up with the innovative idea of bringing a younger woman with them when they migrated so that she could babysit for their children while they worked. Another widespread plan was to temporarily leave their small children in Puerto Rico with their parents and other family members until they found an apartment, a job, and someone to babysit for the children. As one of the women in this study stated,

> When you are going to migrate, you either have to find somebody to take care of your children or take them with you. In that regard its harder here [New York] than in Puerto Rico. And mothers usually want and need to work. How can a woman work when she has more than two or three kids? I know women who work with four kids and I don't know how they do it. There must be someone from the family who takes care of the kids because a stranger isn't going to do it. In order to work with four kids the child care must cost very little; otherwise, you spend all of your money on the babysitter. Sometimes there is a day care center but the majority of times there is not.

LIFE IN NUEVA YORK

Most of the women in the second generation were either born or raised in New York City and have lived there at least since they were two or three years old. In contrast to the first generation, they grew up in a diverse metropolis where they had basic amenities such as housing with running water, electricity, and indoor plumbing. They also had access to public education and health services. However, the women of the second generation and their children continued to experience racism, urban poverty, and rapid changes in New York City's economy.

In the 1940s and 1950s, almost one million Puerto Ricans migrated to New York City and a booming postwar economy. During this time the manufacturing industry in New York was thriving. Blue-collar workers were in demand, and Puerto Rican women found a niche in manufacturing, particularly in the garment industry (Ortiz 1996; Sanchez-Korral 1994; Silvestrini-Pachecho 1986). Puerto Rican women were skilled seamstresses who had either learned to sew from their mothers and grandmothers, who had worked in the needlework industry in Puerto Rico during the early part of the twentieth century, or from the manufacturing industry that developed in Puerto Rico in the 1940s. In the 1950s Puerto Rican women had the highest rate of labor force participation of any other group (Ortiz 1996).

In the 1950s, New York City was going through radical structural changes (Rodriguez 1989; Sanchez-Korral 1994). The restructuring of the city's economy was linked to major economic and global shifts that became apparent in the United States after World War II. Across the nation, the automation of industry began a process of transformation that developed into a new information and technological era. In New York City a series of bridges and highways were built to connect the different boroughs and facilitate industrial production. The mechanization of agriculture in the south and west also displaced African Americans from their jobs and created the impetus for migration to the industrial north. Furthermore, while Puerto Ricans and African Americans were moving into New York, a white flight was taking place from Manhattan to the suburbs (Rodriguez 1991).

FROM AN INDUSTRIAL TO A SERVICE ECONOMY

By the early 1960s, New York City's economy underwent a transition from an industrial to a service economy, and the manufacturing industry left New York in search of cheaper labor and bigger profits. From 1960 to 1980 in New York City there was a total loss in all jobs from 946.8 thousand to 498.7 thousand (Sassen 1988; Waldinger 1996). Although it was difficult for Puerto Ricans in New York to make ends meet in the manufacturing industry when jobs were plentiful, their situation became more precarious as jobs became scarce. Puerto Ricans lost thousands of jobs, and as the last immigrants hired, they were the first fired. Puerto Rican women were disproportionately concentrated in the manufacturing sector, even throughout this period of economic change. In 1978, 31 percent of Puerto Rican women were employed as blue-collar workers in contrast to 14 percent of all U.S. women (Morgan 1981; Ortiz 1996; Rosemary and Colón-Warren 1996).[4]

In sum, the exodus of the manufacturing industry from New York led to the decline of blue-collar jobs, massive unemployment, the rise of female-headed households, the feminization of poverty for poor women of all ethnic/racial groups, and an increase in enrollment in entitlement programs such as Aid for Dependent Children (AFDC). As the economy in New York shifted, the civil rights movement swept the country. The black and feminist movements were challenging the status quo and traditional gender roles as politicians were scrambling for explanations and solutions for poverty. In the 1960s and 1970s, the dominant explanation for poverty and social inequality shifted from genetic determinism to cultural reductionism. For example, in the 1960s policy makers and social scientists in the United States developed deficiency models that accentuated the weaknesses of the poor, ignored their strengths, and blamed their poverty on individual failure, their families, and their culture. Daniel Moynihan published the first explanation for poverty in his article "The Negro Family: The Case for National Action," which appeared in The Moynihan Report (1965). Despite the fact that Patrick Moynihan looked at the structural forces that led to inequality and argued that the family organization of African Americans was an adaptation to environmental conditions, Moynihan still concluded that the causes of poverty for black Americans were the matriarchal family that emasculated black men, sexual promiscuity that led to illegitimate children, and welfare dependency (Briggs 2002; Piven and Cloward 1979, 338; Roberts 1997, 16).

Oscar Lewis (1966), the anthropologist who coined the phrase "the culture of poverty," contended only a short time later in his bestseller La Vida that the cause of Puerto Rican poverty was the female-headed household; the inability to save, plan, or defer gratification; and sexual promiscuity. He based his ethnography on a dysfunctional family with a history of prostitution and mental illness who lived in Puerto Rico's most notorious slum, known as La Perla. According to Lewis, by the time children turned six or seven, they were so warped by the culture of poverty that even if offered social opportunities they would not be able to take advantage of them. A la Moynihan, the culture of poverty thesis ignores the strengths of the poor and the social causes of poverty. Rather, it assumes pathology. Moynihan and Lewis blamed poverty on the female-headed matriarchal household, and even though they did not ignore how this family organization was an adaptation to persistent poverty and social marginalization, this distinction was lost on the lay public. Despite Lewis's disclaimer that the culture of poverty only applied to a subculture of socially marginalized individuals such as prostitutes, alcoholics, and drug addicts, a number of academics, policy makers, government officials, and the lay public assumed all poor racialized minorities were part of the culture of poverty (Briggs 2002, Sanchez-Korral 2005; Rodriguez 2005).

The culture of poverty thesis was popularized in the 1960s and 1970s and took on a life of its own. This occurred because the culture of poverty thesis provided a conservative solution that placed the burden of change on the family rather than on society (Leacock 1971; Valentine 1968; Chase 1980). Consequently, despite the fact that Moynihan and Lewis considered social structural inequities and took into account historical forces, the outcome of their analysis was not as they had intended. The culture of poverty thesis pathologized the poor and blamed their culture and family organization for their poverty. As Leith Mullings so aptly stated, this is "old wine in new bottles" (Mullings 1978).

With the deindustrialization of the United States between the 1960s and 1970s, Solinger observed that the lay public's hostility toward racial minority women increased as the welfare rolls grew (Solinger 2001). By the 1980s the pendulum had swung full circle and the United States soon entered a political period of neoconservative social and economic structures under Ronald Reagan. This social climate inspired the popular—and very politicized—stereotype of the welfare queen. The origin of the term arose under the presidency of Ronald Reagan, when he perpetuated the myth that a large number of African Americans on welfare tricked taxpayers out of their hard-earned money to buy beer for themselves instead of milk for their hungry children (Briggs 2002). The insidious image of the welfare queen, whom Reagan portrayed as bad mothers because of their alleged neglect of their children, dehumanized poor minority women and created outright public hostility toward them. The stigmatized image of African Americans taking advantage of the welfare system was generalized to all racialized minorities, especially Puerto Rican women. In other words, it was easier for populist politicians to blame poverty on women and individual family failure than to talk about the deindustrialization of urban America—corporate greed, social inequities, and institutional racism—because that would have shifted societal responsibility to the government.

The identities and gender awareness of the second generation of women in this study were shaped by this period of economic and social change. I recall many conversations with the women in this study when they expressed indignation about the stereotype that all Puerto Ricans had children to get on welfare. By the late 1980s William Julius Wilson revitalized the culture of poverty thesis in his underclass model, which, once again, blamed the poor's poverty on their family structure and culture (Wilson 1987).

In the 1970s New York City underwent a profound fiscal crisis. Services suffered throughout the city, unemployment soared, the economy stagnated, and the more affluent abandoned the city for the suburbs. The neighborhood where the women in this study lived became more marginalized. For example, by the 1970s Bushwick was characterized by abandonment and eviction, and much of it was in a state of neglect. Landlords invested little money on repairs (Cohen 1982, 1983); therefore, many of these tenements were in a poor state of disrepair and without heat and hot water in the winter. Fire, whether accidental or deliberate, was a major cause of the housing crisis. As one fireman put it, "Once these tenements fall into neglect, the final blow comes in the form of a fire frequently set by landlords eager to collect on the fire insurance."[5] According to a housing report prepared by the City of New York, between June 1977 and 1983 close to half of the tenements in this area were destroyed by fire (New York City, Department of City Planning 1981, 211).

By the time the third generation came of age in the twenty-first century, the neighborhood where they had grown up had changed in some significant ways. By the mid-1980s the economy of New York City was recovering as the financial services industry and other postindustrial economic sectors grew, and once again Manhattan became a fashionable and desirable place to live. Space was quickly becoming a premium and real estate prices were rising precipitously as prosperous white professionals began to move into the city. At this time landlords started to convert apartments into condominiums and co-ops. In order to make space for the upcoming generations of young urban professionals who could afford to pay the higher rents, the poor were slowly evicted from the neighborhoods they had lived in for generations. This process, known as gentrification, started in Manhattan and later spread to the outer boroughs. It did not happen overnight nor did it take place evenly across entire neighborhoods. In fact it has taken twenty-five years for the neighborhood I did fieldwork in to start showing visible signs of change.

Like Manhattan, the rents in the outer boroughs such as Brooklyn have continued to escalate at an alarming rate for its poor residents. New York City in general has become one of the most expensive cities in the United States. In the neighborhood in which I worked (and grew up), old abandoned factories were converted into condominiums. As the remaining vestiges of New York City's industrial infrastructure are being swept away, this neighborhood is shaped by the local refraction of complex social and economic processes that are taking place nationally and globally.

By 2005 the value of real estate had changed significantly in this neighborhood. Not only had the price of real estate risen, but the demographic makeup of the neighborhood had changed as well. This neighborhood changed from a predominantly Puerto Rican one to a Mexican and Ecuadorian locale. But higher rents have not necessarily meant better housing. As the super of one tenement told me, even though the neighborhood has improved and landlords charge higher rents, who has that benefited?

Although the third generation women in my study have seen their neighborhoods transformed as New York City has developed a vigorous postindustrial economy, they, along with the city's working-class and minority populations, have seldom been the beneficiaries of that economy. The cost of living in New York has soared while higher levels of education are now required to compete in the market. And, Puerto Ricans continue to have one of the highest high school attrition and unemployment rates in the city (Rivera-Batiz and Santiago 1996). This is especially problematic in an information-based economy where an education is the only vehicle of upward mobility for most working-class communities.

SHIFTING GENDER ROLES

The lives of the pioneer Puerto Rican men and women who migrated to New York City were difficult, and the environment in which they raised their children was frequently harsh. With the demise of the manufacturing industry in New York City, Puerto Rican men and women struggled to stay employed. They also struggled with changing gender awareness.

One of the most significant changes Puerto Rican women have experienced in New York is the change in the traditional patriarchal family. The women in the first generation struggled with marital conflict and survival as access to jobs and resources diminished in New York. These struggles led to separation and divorce and changes within the family organization for many Puerto Rican families. For example, between 1970 and 1990, the rate of female-headed households with children eighteen years or younger increased for all women. According to the 1970 census, the rate of female-headed households for families of all ethnicities and races was 17.2 percent. In 1980, it climbed to 27.8 percent, and in 1990 it reached 30.1 percent. Comparing these percentages by ethnic/racial groups, in 1970 the rate of female-headed households for white households was 11.9 percent; for black households it was 34.5 percent; and for Hispanic households it was 18.0 percent. By 1980, these rates had risen considerably. For white households it was 40.8 percent; for black households it was 67.6 percent; and for Hispanic households it was 48.7 percent. In 1990, the rate of female-headed households for white households increased to 40.4 percent. It was 73.0 percent for black households and 45.7 percent for Hispanic households (Kasarda 1993, 271). The primary role women play in the family is reflected in the popular saying developed among Puerto Ricans. Changes in family organization are reflected in the saying that developed from the collective wisdom of the first generation Puerto Rican women: madre una, padre cien (any man can father a child, but there is only one mother). Therefore, given the rate of Hispanic female-headed households, this saying reflects the important role that many mothers play in their children's lives as their primary support system. For this reason, after most of the women in the second generation married they chose to continue to live in close proximity to their mothers.

The restructuring of New York City's economy and changes within family organization slowly led to some changes within traditional gender roles. Myriad forces shaped the changing gender awareness of Puerto Rican women in New York, particularly the civil rights and women's liberation movements, and most of the women of the younger generations were exposed to new and radical ideas about feminism and racial equality to some degree.

Puerto Rican men and women have been portrayed in the literature through dualistic concepts of machismo and marianismo. In the same way the binary model fails to capture the nuances of Puerto Rican women's reproductive experiences, this dualism fails to do justice to the complexity of women's lives. According to marianismo, women are defined as dependent, passive, asexual, martyrs, and morally superior to men (Gil and Vasquez 1996; Stevens 1973). In contrast, Puerto Rican men have been depicted as authoritarian, self-centered, sexually aggressive, and mired in rigid gender roles. Puerto Rican men and women are more complex than these prototypes. Like Western women, Puerto Rican women have traditionally been socialized to be good mothers, wives, and daughters, to be nurturers, to conform to traditional gender roles, to repress their discontent, and to sacrifice themselves for others. Puerto Rican men have been socialized to be good providers and enjoy male privilege. However, with few exceptions, I did not find any individual in this study that embodied the absolute prototype of machismo and marianismo (Bidegain 1989; Ehlers 1992). I found that changes in gender roles did not occur in linear fashion. For example, women's behaviors varied both within and across generations. This defied the expectation that the older generation was always more traditional than the younger generation or that the younger generation was more liberated. What I did find was that men and women share a range of conventional and unconventional behaviors. For example, some of the women in the first generation like doña Rosario were traditional but fiercely proactive and independent. For many women, their independence was born in Puerto Rico out of economic need and cultivated in New York as they adapted to the other harsh realities of a city in transition. Some scholars argue that marianismo cannot be analyzed in a vacuum, that women's gender roles must be grounded in the choices they make according to their economic conditions (Ehlers Bachrach 1991). I believe a combination of factors such as traditional expectations, self-esteem and self-awareness, and economic conditions shape and influence gender roles.

Changing gender roles not only stemmed from society at large but were also based on the radical changes that were taking place in the second generation women's own homes as their parents struggled to adapt to their new lives. Many of the second generation developed a higher level of gender awareness from watching their mothers suffer in troubled marriages they could not afford to leave or change. As Sonia noted, "While I was growing up, I watched my mother suffer in silence—I swore to myself I would never be like my mother." However, even though some first generation women were conventional and served as the transmitters of cultural traditions (Toro-Morn 2005, 141), many were unconventional in other ways. For example, some were single parents because they had divorced their husbands and raised their children alone. Nancy (second generation) expressed, "I had a kick-ass mother. Yeah, she was traditional when it came to things like cooking and cleaning and making Daddy feel good, but when he crossed her he was out of the house in a minute. It got to the point where she only let him come back to visit when she felt like it."

Even though the majority of the women in the second generation remarried, a large number of them were divorced themselves because they were less inclined than their mothers to stay in an unhappy marriage. Lourdes and her husband broke up because she felt she could not pull her life together when she was with him. Despite the hardships she went through, she had a strong support system in a woman who lived in her building that was a surrogate mother to her. Lourdes explains, "Sometimes women are better off alone than with a man ("Mejor sola que mal accompanada"). After we were separated two of my neighbors babysat for the children while I worked and went to school at night. I couldn't have gone to school without their help."

INTERGENERATIONAL CONFLICT

Most parents in the first generation were protective of their children, male and female. Some parents were so strict they literally did not allow their children to go anywhere other than to school and church unless accompanied by a parent or sibling. Parents were in part overprotective because they feared for the safety of their children in this new environment, especially for the chastity of their daughters. These young women and men struggled with their parents over issues such as dating, curfews, privacy, and normative gender role expectations. Even though parents were protective of their sons, they were more protective of their daughters. Like their mothers, second generation daughters were socialized into traditional gender roles and were expected to be virgins and to live at home until they married. Relatively speaking, most of these second generation women had a little more individual freedom than their mothers, who in some cases were not allowed to leave their house without their husband's permission in Puerto Rico. This was especially true if their parents led traditional lives in small towns on the island.

In the early twentieth century Puerto Rican adolescent girls and boys were not allowed to be alone. Therefore, normative practices in North American culture such as dating and socializing with male friends were not acceptable to most second generation immigrant parents. Consequently, if young women wanted to go to a party, their parents might compromise by having her take a younger sibling with them as a chaperone. Young men and women had strict curfews. Lourdes's account reflects the cultural differences between the immigrant parents and their children that created intergenerational clashes: "When I was 18 years old I was absolutely mortified when my mother told me that if I did not take my younger brother to the party with me I could not go. No one else took a younger brother or sister to a party. I felt like a prisoner when I was growing up. Even though I knew they meant well, I felt suffocated by my parents' overprotectiveness and felt miserable most of my life. That is why I married my husband, to get out of my mother's house the first opportunity I had."

Puerto Rican Women's Ways of Knowing

But even in the midst of this intergenerational conflict, women of the first generation began to see different possibilities for their daughters. One of the colloquial phrases women developed out of their collective wisdom and experiences and repeated to their children, especially to their daughters, was [potential] "mírate en este espejo." When women say this to their daughters, they mean, look into the mirror of my life and do not make the same mistakes that I did. They want their daughters to go to school so that they will be more independent and have more options than they did. As Sonia reflects, "I learned a lot ["don't make the same mistakes I made"] about how not to live my life from my mother. Whenever she thought I was making the wrong life choices when I was growing up, she would look at me with that sad and wise expression and say, 'Mírate en este espejo [look in this mirror] and don't make the foolish mistakes I made.' That saying has always stayed with me because my mother suffered a lot in life because she hung in there blindly with my father when she should have left that marriage a long time ago."

Other sayings that first generation and a few second generation women shared with me when they began their stories were, "my life has been a veil of tears" (mi vida es un paño de lágrimas) and "I have shed tears of blood" (lágrimas de sangre). Both of these phrases express the level of sorrow some of the women in this study experienced.

The women in the third generation were also familiar with the traditional folk saying, "estudia por si tu marido te sale sin verguenza" (study in case your husband turns out to have no shame) (Crespo 2000). Although each generation has added their own twist to the saying, the meaning is essentially the same. Both warn that a woman should take care of herself in whatever way is necessary so that she can be independent and/or not live with regrets in the future.

The women in the first and second generations wanted their daughters to marry and have a family, but they also wanted them to study so they could have more opportunities than they had. They wanted their sons to do well, too. Although women did not develop a particular saying for boys, according to Frankie, his mother always told him, "Study so you don't end up like me."

The Men—Tradition and Transition

According to some of the women in the second generation, many of the men of their age cohort were as sexist as their fathers. Some of the men of this generation did not want their wives to work outside of the home. In some cases these women were trapped in the double shift syndrome, fully responsible for the children and domestic work while also earning income outside the home. In other cases, even some of the men who did not work and therefore could not fulfill their traditional male role as the provider of the family still refused to help with childcare and domestic work.

This was the case with Jorge. I interviewed him when he was forty-one years old and divorced. Jorge was born and raised in New York with his mother and four sisters. He dropped out of high school in the tenth grade and started working at an early age to help his mother support the household. He acquired some work experience by doing construction work with his uncle, but work was not consistently available. In his words:

My dad left before I was born and I am the only son of five children, so basically my mother spoiled me rotten. When I was growing my aunts and uncles said to me only sissies cry. I was told I was the man of the house, so I had to be strong and protect the family. It was hard growing up male because my girlfriends and family had so many expectations of me.

My mother, she cooked, cleaned, and basically did everything for my sisters and me. She's still cooking, cleaning, ironing, and taking care of me. Since she never taught me to do anything around the house, I thought it was a woman's job to cook, clean, and take care of the kids. When I got married,

I expected my wife to do the same thing. I worked whenever I could find a gig, but these jobs were scarce. Sometimes I spent a lot of time at home. After I got married my wife complained I didn't do enough around the house. She was tired and irritable when she came home and complained she was too tired to come home and start cooking dinner and picking up around the apartment. After two years we split up, because even though I helped her it was too much for me that she expected me to cook and clean as well.

While sexism still prevails among a large sector of Puerto Rican men, some of the younger men are different. For example, as Lizzie, a third generation granddaughter, recalls, "I'm really proud of my brothers. All guys are not bums. Look at my brothers, how responsible and sweet they are with their wives and child. I hope one day I can meet someone nice like them, but if I don't I'll be okay, 'cause I'll have my career and like my mom, I'll always be able to take care of myself and help my family."

Although a few of the sons and daughters in the youngest generation completed high school and went to college, like Jorge, a large number of them dropped out of high school to help support their families. The high school dropout rate for Puerto Rican men was higher than it was for Puerto Rican women (Rivera-Batiz and Santiago 1996). As a consequence, the men of this generation suffered higher rates of unemployment than their female counterparts. For example, in the 1990s the labor force participation rates among Puerto Rican women rose, while it declined for men. In 1990 Puerto Rican women had a labor force participation rate of 43.3 percent, which rose to 47.6 percent by 1999. Among Puerto Rican men, however, the labor force participation rate dropped from 67.4 percent to 63.7 percent during the same period (Rivera-Batiz and Santiago 1996, 120–121).

CHANGES IN EDUCATION AND FERTILITY

In contrast to the first generation, their daughters' generation had higher levels of education (although lower levels than their peers) and more access to health care and birth control. For example, while the majority of women in the first generation only had a second or third grade educational level, most of their daughters graduated from high school, and a few continued on to higher education. Evelyn recalls, "The day I received my high school diploma was the proudest day of my life. I was the first one in my family who graduated from high school. My parents were so proud of me too, especially my mom, who always stressed the importance of an education."

The women in the second generation also had access to health care—which meant they had their babies in hospitals instead of at home with midwives—

and they also had access to birth control. Perhaps the greatest difference I found between the women in the first and second generations was that most of the older women did not have access to temporary methods of birth control when they were in their youth. This meant that the only method they had for controlling their fertility was sterilization. Now, it is also important to note that even though the women in the second generation had access to contraceptives, they also had problems with them. First, like other women, they experienced nausea, bloating, or other physical side effects with the pill, or their bodies rejected the intrauterine device (IUD). Second, they had limited knowledge of how to use these contraceptives effectively. Third, many of their husbands and boyfriends thought that birth control was a woman's responsibility. This situation became a major source of gender conflict because at least some of the women, who were born or raised in New York, had different ideas about sexuality, marriage, and domestic life than the men. As Nancy expressed, "My old man thinks that birth control is my responsibility because if I get pregnant I'm the one that's going to have it and primarily take care of the baby. That pisses me off 'cause he has a good time making the baby too. Why can't he wear a rubber?! I'm sick to death of always being in charge of everything—that is why some women like me got sterilized!"

The women in the second generation desired smaller families, and as a rule they had fewer children and did not have the children consecutively. For example, the women in the second generation had a median of three to four children as compared to the ten or eleven children common in the previous generation. Like their mothers, many second generation women still adhered to the patriarchal value of wanting a son before they were sterilized. A popular saying Puerto Rican women developed to indicate they are sterilized is "Cerramos la factoría" (We closed down the factory). They usually say this with a wink and a chuckle. Doña Rosario observed, "When women say they closed down the factory, we mean we are not going to have any more babies, or we have had all of the children that we want."

Interestingly, the women of the second generation frequently opted for sterilization as their primary method of birth control, even though they had greater access to temporary methods than their mothers did. There are a number of factors that contributed to the continued popularity of la operación: it was culturally familiar; the daughters desired fewer children than their mothers; it was difficult to support a large family in the economy; they suffered negative side effects from temporary methods of birth control; they became pregnant while using birth control; a large number of their female relatives and friends had been operated on and they recommended la operación to one another; and they took a pragmatic stance about the church telling them what to do with respect to birth control and la operación.

Latinas and Sexuality

Because Latinas were raised to repress their sexuality, many of the women in the first generation and even in the second generation were uncomfortable talking about sex. This was reflected in the fact that women frequently asked me to educate their children about birth control. Even though they came of age in the era of the women's liberation movement, they also grew up in the 1950s when "good girls" were virgins. In fact, the family's honor was tied up in its daughters' chaste status. This was Gladys's experience as she was growing up in Brooklyn.

> My generation never talked about sex when we were growing up, especially to our mothers. No one ever taught us anything about birth control either. As a young girl, I was naive about my body. Like many girls of my generation, I did not know what to expect even when I started to menstruate. I was traumatized when I got my period. I thought I had cut myself and I was bleeding to death. I told my mother. She said, "Tu eres señorita" [You're a woman now]. I didn't know what that meant; for me everything was new. Later on when I started to have sex, I had to hide my birth control pills from my mother's roving eyes. The day she found them and accused me of being a ho (whore) my world fell apart because I was a good and decent woman and wanted to live up to my mother's image.

Not all women were so reticent with their daughters. Because Gladys was raised so naively, she made sure that she taught her daughter and granddaughter about their bodies when they were old enough to understand. When her granddaughter Samantha was nine years old, she talked to her about her menstruation. "I got her a little book. I told her, 'You read it. If there is anything you don't understand, let me know.' 'I understand everything, Grandma.' By the time my daughter got her period she knew she was prepared for this event. She said to me, 'Mami que fun, I got my period. It happened on my birthday too.' I was on my way out to work. I told her you know what you have to do. You have everything in your room."

Sexual mores have changed radically from the second to the third generation. In fact, Gladys, who took care to instruct her daughter and granddaughter about sex and menstruation, is appalled at what is going on with children in the grammar school where she works. The two biggest health problems Gladys sees are incest and AIDS. According to Gladys, children are having sex even in elementary schools. In her words, "This is a problem because young children don't know what they are doing, and they do not use protection, so they risk pregnancy and AIDS."

Unfortunately, the up-and-coming generations of women also continue to face problems similar to those that confronted previous generations, such

as abusive relationships, a lack of emotional training and limited knowledge
about contraceptives, problems with temporary methods of birth control, sexist ideas that relegate the responsibility of birth control exclusively to women,
and the ongoing AIDS crisis.

Cultural beliefs about gender roles and sexuality have changed significantly
for this generation. They date, socialize with male and female friends, and are
able to stay out later than their mothers. Women's experiences with their parents vary according to how recently their parents migrated, as well as by family.
In most cases the women in the granddaughters' generation had a lot more personal freedom than their mothers and grandmothers. However, in other cases,
as with Jessica, their personal freedom was much more restricted.

> During high school I studied hard. I began to date even though it was against
> my mother's will. What I mean by dating is that I saw my boyfriend at school
> and spoke to him on the phone, but I was not allowed to go out with him.
> I felt restrained and left out of the whole teenage process. All the other kids
> in high school hung out and went out dancing, or went to the movies while
> I was home watching TV. There were many times in my life when I felt like
> running away. I hated my mother because she never let me breathe. I knew
> that her being strict was for my own good, but it was very difficult to accept
> at the age of fourteen when I should have been treated as a young adult.
> Because I was never allowed to hang out with my friends, it was very difficult
> for me to maintain friendships and relationships.

Some parents were strict with their sons, too, because they feared they could
get involved with the wrong friends and end up on drugs or dropping out of
school. According to one of the men in the grandson's generation:

> I know my sister thinks she is the only one who suffered while we were grow-
> ing up, but she's not the only one. It's no picnic growing up in the heart of
> Brooklyn. Outside school and home walls all around was crime and a lot
> of drug use. It was really difficult not to fall prey to either of the two. Many
> of my friends were smoking by the age of thirteen, some even got into vari-
> ous gangs on the block, such as Bloods and Crips. Many of them did all these
> things because of peer pressure. My parents kept tabs on where I was and
> who I was with. I had a curfew, and I needed to constantly ask for permission
> to do things. Some of the kids called me a fag when I went home early. I felt
> bad back then and still don't like to be reigned in, but at least now I realize
> what my parents were trying to protect me from.

A significant intergenerational gap about sex also persisted between the
three generations. These young women and men grew up during the AIDS
epidemic with contradictory and confusing messages. On the one hand, the

young women were exposed to explicit sex in the media and on the Internet; on the other hand, conservative fundamentalists, whose solution to the teenage pregnancy problem was "just say no," denied them sex education courses in school that would teach them about birth control, STDs, and AIDS. As Millie expresses, "Almost everyone I know knows someone who has HIV or has died of AIDS. My mother and father died of AIDS. This is the hardest experience I've ever gone through. I loved my mom and my dad. What would I tell young women out there today? You need to protect yourself 'cause one slip can kill you. It's really scary out there."

Women's attitudes have also changed with respect to marriage. In the first and second generations, having a child out of wedlock was considered a disgrace and tragedy to the family. Daughters were ostracized from their families and/or sent away to have their child elsewhere. This attitude differed significantly by the twenty-first century because of changes in family organization and changing gender roles within this working-class community. Nowadays the acceptance of women having children out of matrimony is reflected in television programs like *Friends* and *Sex in the City,* but perhaps even more important, young women have seen their mothers and grandmothers struggle with changing social, economic, and cultural circumstances that led many of them to raise families on their own.

Despite changing gender roles, most of the young women in this study idealized marriage and maintained some traditional beliefs, such as that domestic work and child rearing are still women's primary responsibility. The majority of the young women in this study would like to meet the right man for them. However, if he does not come along many of them feel they will raise their children without a man like some of their mothers did.

Younger women also want fewer children than their mothers and grandmothers. Although the women in the third generation are familiar with contraceptives, like their mothers they are not always well educated about them, especially the barrier methods. Therefore, some of them became pregnant accidentally, and like their forebears they decided to have their babies. Their views about abortion vary. Some feel that abortion is morally wrong; others feel it is their right to decide if they want to have an abortion. As Lizzie said, "I'm not telling anybody what to do, because it should be the woman who decides what she wants to do depending on her situation."

In summary, the younger generation has retained a strong Puerto Rican identity. Many have remained in the neighborhood near their families. Family networks are strong and remain essential for the survival and well-being of the family. While many changes have taken place over the three generations, one of the factors that remains the same is women's acceptance and misinformation about la operación. Like their female relatives, the majority of younger women plan to be sterilized after they achieve their desired family size. Like their mothers and grandmothers they are not fully aware that sterilization is, for the most part, permanent. In addition, because the majority of these young women are not religious, they are not aware and do not care about the church's view of tubal ligation. Like their mothers, they are culturally predisposed to sterilization and continue to consider la operación an important way to control their reproduction.

PART II

Cultural Continuities and Urban Change

CHAPTER 3

The Velez Family

POVERTY, THE CANCER SCARE, AND HYSTERECTOMIES

On a warm summer night in 1981 I walked four long blocks to where Evelyn lives. I was able to walk right into the tenement because of a broken front door. I found the family eating spaghetti and meatballs. Doña Hilda who was then 59 years old, was feeding her two granddaughters. When I inquired about Evelyn, doña Hilda looked at me sideways with a cross look on her face. In a loud, menacing voice, she demanded to know what I wanted with her daughter. I nervously explained my project. After looking me over carefully, she said in a somewhat tired voice that Evelyn probably forgot and had gone bowling. She invited me to come inside, and as she fed her granddaughters she allowed me to tape record our interview. We talked in between the girls' crying and screaming. They were not happy that I was taking up their grandmother's time, and in an attempt to regain her full attention they jumped, cried, and even sat on my tape recorder. At one point the two-year-old bit her grandmother's hand as she was feeding her. After doña Hilda quieted the girls down she was able to talk to me about her life.

DOÑA HILDA: FIRST GENERATION

I came to this country when I was eighteen years old because my aunt and my cousin lived here. Well, they said that dollars hit you in the face here and that the streets were paved with gold [*laughter*]. Well, the only thing that hit me in the face here was snow and mud. I came here because I wanted to work. I also came so if I hadn't I might have ended up in a delinquent home for criminals.

What happened was that in Puerto Rico a young man by the name of Raymond was courting me that my father, who was a Spaniard, did not consider white. One day my father said to me, rather than see you with Raymond, I would rather marry you off to one of my friends. Raymond had [a] gun and when he found out about this he came to my house and told me, "If I can't have you, no one else will." He wanted me to go away with him, but I did not want to run off with him, I wanted him to marry me. He threatened me and said, "I am going to bring my gun and if you don't come with me, I am going to kill your old man." My father was a captain in the military and he had a rifle. We lived in the country, so Raymond was on horseback when he came to see me. I fetched my father's rifle and I shot at him; I missed him but I shot the poor horse in the leg.

When my father heard the gunshot he ran out, but Raymond had already left. I told him what happened and he started to practice his (rifle) aim by shooting down almonds from the almond tree. I was so upset that in order to avoid a tragedy [Raymond returning to the house], I ran away from home that very evening. I walked for three hours from where we lived to Dorado, where I ran into a police officer that knew my family. He took me to his house, told my parents I was there, and my parents came to get me immediately. They tried to convince me to go home, but I refused because I was rebellious and scared of my boyfriend. My mother suggested that I go live with my aunt in New York for a while, and that is how I ended up in Brooklyn. I lived with my aunt and cousin for six months before I met Noel, the father of my first daughter, who now lives in Connecticut. He even went to Puerto Rico to ask my father for my hand in marriage. We were married right away and I had my first little girl within the year. We were happy for a while. Once I was living with Noel, I started to work in the fish store where he worked. After several years of marriage we split up because we were always arguing. He was a flirt, and I was not going to put up with that crap. A few years later I met Eddie, the father of my second child. I loved Eddie, but I didn't marry him because he drank too much and he was physically abusive. I had my second daughter Evelyn with Eddie.[1]

A Woman Should Have Her Children While She Is Young

Doña Hilda had two daughters. When she married Noel she was almost nineteen and she had her first daughter one year later. The majority of women in this study married before the age of twenty. That is one of the reasons two-thirds of these women were sterilized between the ages of twenty-five and twenty-nine.

Women should have their children when they are young and have the energy to take care of them. A child is the nicest thing that can happen in marriage. Children bring happiness to a home. I was married at the age of eighteen and a half. My first child was born at the age of nineteen. I became pregnant for the second time when my first child was a year and six months. Its better not to wait too long to have your children because when you really want a baby you might not be able to have one, or you might not have the energy to take care of them.

If a woman has a good marriage and a husband who is a good provider, and she lives well, I don't think she should use birth control. Why should she? In this case she has a good future and the respect that comes from a good marriage. She should have her children immediately and then get operated on. Do you understand? Now, it's different in a marriage where the husband is an alcoholic and the woman has bad habits too. A family like this should not have children.

Reasons for Getting Sterilized

Doña Hilda herself was not sterilized because she had a hysterectomy in 1956, when she was thirty-four years old, but she was familiar with and approved of la operación. In her opinion, good reasons for sterilization were economic hardship, difficult relationships, or achieving desired family size. Doña Hilda claims she would have been happy if she had a boy and a girl. She said that many of her friends were sterilized, among other reasons, because of financial hardship.

I think a woman should get sterilized after having three or four kids. It is easier to survive with fewer than four children. It is very hard for a woman to take care of five children by herself. In these days marriages do not last. The man falls in love with someone else, the woman is jealous, the husband leaves, and like that. Besides, with the way things are today, it is hard to raise, the way one should raise, more than four kids. I know. . . . I've been a church missionary and worked in schools. I've visited people's homes and I know how they live and the situation is hard. A mother by herself with three, four, or five kids has a hard time. All the money goes into paying the rent and bills. They are always complaining that they don't have enough money to buy their children the food and clothing they need.

If I had four kids, two boys and two girls, I would have gotten sterilized because in today's situation no mother should have more than four children. There is too much depression, drugs, and crime on the streets. The cost of food, everything is so expensive. The best solution is for a woman to have her tubes tied if she wants to stop having children, if she is having a hard time making ends meet. My daughter did that.

Doña Hilda told me she would have liked to have had four children, two boys and two girls, but she only had two daughters because of marital problems and severe economic difficulties.

Doña Hilda's second marriage was more problematic than her first relationship. Despite her view that a woman in a bad relationship should use birth control, she did not use birth control herself.

> I didn't use the birth control pill because I have a heart condition. I did not use the IUD because my uterus was too low and my doctor could not fit me. I did not use the IUD because I was afraid it would irritate my husband.

> We never talked about birth control. Even though he was an alcoholic, he always provided money for food and rent. You can see how I've ended up because if I did not leave him, I would be dead or he would be dead. I don't know. I'd be insane. He liked to gamble and drink, but he is a good person. If he didn't have the money for the rent, he'd get a loan. But he'd go crazy and he would beat me . . . yes, he beat me.

Moral Reasons for Having an Abortion

By the time doña Hilda became pregnant with Eddie's baby, their relationship was not going well. When she discovered she was pregnant, she unsuccessfully tried to abort her second daughter, Evelyn.

> I don't believe in abortions but I tried to have one. When I was pregnant with Evelyn I tried to poison myself. I don't believe in abortion, but my situation was very bad. My husband was drinking . . . I tried to abort her, but afterwards I regretted it. I suffered as a consequence of what I drank. I used *recación* and *tin de marrato,* two abortive herbs. Afterward I got scared. It's a blue pill that burns like acid. I wanted to die. When Evelyn was born she was so beautiful. I loved her very much. The only thing was she was born with problem skin. I drank too much Alka-Seltzer for that pregnancy.

The fact that doña Hilda tried to have an abortion even though she felt it was morally wrong reflects her desire to take care of herself and the family she already has. Other women recounted similar stories.

Doña Hilda, like many of the women in my survey (87 percent), was raised Catholic. Officially, the Catholic Church does not favor sterilization, yet only 32 percent of the women I surveyed felt that sterilization was against their religious beliefs. Yet, even when the women realized that sterilization was against their religious beliefs, they were still operated on because of economic and other pressing reasons. Doña Hilda, like the majority of these women, does not find sterilization and Catholicism to be incompatible. Her views, like those of many women, are profoundly pragmatic and are a good example of the way that women resist or rework Catholic dogma in everyday life. As she put it, "I practice religion my own way." According to doña Hilda, even if the Catholic

Church did not like it, if she had not had a hysterectomy, she nevertheless would have gotten sterilized because "God was not going to support her children."

mm

Hysterectomy, Fibroid Tumors, and the Cancer Scare

Doña Hilda was told she had a fibroid tumor at the age of thirty-four. Her doctor warned her that if she did not have a hysterectomy, it might turn into cancer. Doña Hilda became so frightened that she accepted the hysterectomy without eliciting a second opinion.

> Whenever I had sex it hurt. I told the doctor and he said it was nothing; this went on for years. Finally, one day I examined myself. I felt I had a little ball behind the neck of my uterus. The doctor told me that this cyst had not grown larger because I had stunted it with the vinegar douches I used weekly.
>
> After I found the cyst, I went to the hospital. Seven doctors examined me, but they couldn't find the problem. Then they called a cancer specialist. I told the doctor to look in the same way I had. Whenever I ran my fingers along the neck of my uterus, I got a pain. He did as I said and found the cyst. He asked me if I wanted to be operated and I said yes. He also asked me if I wanted to have more children. I told him that I did. He said that was going to be a problem because if they only operated me to remove the cyst, there was a chance some of the roots might remain and my ovaries could become infected. This, he said, would eventually lead to cancer.
>
> Because of this, I told him to operate me. After the hysterectomy, I developed other complications, like I couldn't hold my urine. I went to the hospital, and a different doctor scolded me for having had a hysterectomy because of a fibroid tumor. He said that the other doctor could have taken out the cyst without removing my uterus. I was devastated. I only agreed to have a hysterectomy because he told me I might develop cancer. I didn't get a second opinion because seven doctors had checked me at the first clinic and they all agreed I should have a hysterectomy. They also said that if I got pregnant again, I could lose the baby. According to them it was better to get operated on and avoid all of those problems. They even told me that I could liberate myself from my period. The reason I let seven doctors check me is because I was hoping that one of them would say I didn't need the operation. I was so scared.

Seeing multiple doctors, costs $$$

Ironically, doña Hilda experienced more pain and discomfort after the hysterectomy.

> I deeply regret having had a hysterectomy. First, I was too young to have that operation. After the hysterectomy I was going to get married, and I wanted to have more children but I couldn't. This led to a lot of problems in my marriage. Second, I have more pain now than I had before the hysterectomy.

For example, in the past before I got my period, I [would] get a headache and I would be in pain for a few hours. Now everything hurts for three or four days.

Like other women of color, doña Hilda's experiences with her hysterectomy are not exceptional. In a study of more than 53,000 women with hysterectomies, Kjerulff found that black women were more than twice as likely to have a hysterectomy because of a fibroid tumor (Kjerulff et al. 1993). There are also regional and class differences in the rates of hysterectomy. For example, rates were consistently higher for women in the South, where the standard of living is poorer and lowest among women in the Northeast (Kjerulff et al. 1993). Other studies found that there was a correlation between a higher rate of hysterectomies by race and region. For example, the Committee to End Sterilization Abuse found that poor black women in the South had a higher rate of hysterectomy than white women in the Northeast (CESA 1976). In fact, at that point (in the 1970s) they were so common that doctors referred to them as "Mississippi appendectomies."

The Second Cancer Scare

Doña Hilda went through the cancer scare experience twice. Eight years after she had the hysterectomy, a different doctor from the same hospital she went to during her first cancer scare found a liquid cyst in her right breast and told her that if he did not remove her breast she was liable to get breast cancer. Although doña Hilda was extremely upset about this news, her previous experience taught her something, and this time she sought a second opinion. To her relief she found that her condition, a benign liquid cyst, did not require a mastectomy. In her words:

Eight years after my hysterectomy a doctor found a liquid cyst in my right breast. If I squeezed it, blood would come out. It hurt. I went to the butcher shop [hospital] and a Chinese doctor told me I had cancer. He said they had to cut off my breast; otherwise, the cancer would spread to other parts of my body. I almost had a nervous breakdown. On that day alone I lost five pounds.

The doctor wanted me to sign the consent form immediately so that they could operate. I told him I was not going to sign anything until I spoke to the head doctor. He was the same doctor who told me that I should not have had a hysterectomy because of my fibroid tumor.

Doña Hilda claims that she was in a high state of anxiety when the head doctor saw her:

I asked him to examine me again. He took x-rays and did the test again. He took a cotton ball and took out a little bit of the liquid from my breast. The blood test was negative, but he said that in order to be sure they would have to take meat [a biopsy] out of my breast. Because the doctor saw how hysterical I was, he said he would do it himself. I was hospitalized for two days. He did the test, and thank God I didn't have cancer. I had liquid cyst in that breast. When I woke up from the tests in the hospital I kissed my doctor's hand. He told me: Don't believe everything everyone says. Don't get upset before you know for sure. You should always be sure first.

I almost sued that Chinese doctor for the brutal way he told me that I had cancer without doing the necessary test first. I could have lost my mind. I even said good-bye to my children. I didn't sue because I didn't want to harm anybody.

legal recourse

given wrong medical advice, unnecessary procedures

Doña Hilda's experience demonstrates the challenges that poor women often face in getting good medical advice, particularly when they lack adequate medical insurance to support further tests. This story was repeated many times during my study, but what is remarkable about doña Hilda's case is the way that she became much more proactive after learning that her first operation was unnecessary.

EVELYN: SECOND GENERATION

Evelyn was born and raised in Brooklyn. As a child, she spent a few months in Puerto Rico but did not live there for an extended period of time. My first introduction to Evelyn was at the clothing store where she worked as a salesperson. Loud music blared from the crackling speakers hanging on the walls, and racks of inexpensive clothing covered every inch of space.

When I met Evelyn she was twenty-five and divorced. She had married at twenty-two. In her words: "Married once, shacking up once and common-law second." Evelyn earned a GED and spent one year in a private technical school studying to be a nurse's aid. After she received her diploma, she worked at the hospital that she, her mother, and other women in the neighborhood referred to as the "butcher shop" (el matadero). Evelyn quit after her second daughter because it was too hard to work with small children, especially when she was constantly on call.

Sterilized at the age of 23, Evelyn lives in a violent, crime- and drug-ridden neighborhood. Evelyn feels the neighborhood she lives in strongly influenced her decision to get sterilized. She feared bad friends might corrupt her children, which made her unwilling to let them play outdoors. Fifty percent of the women in the survey voiced this concern. However, keeping the children indoors was stressful and not always an option because they lived in small apartments that were poorly ventilated. The children were often frustrated and wanted to play outside, especially during the warm weather.

Evelyn also lived with the gripping fear of getting robbed. Like most buildings in the area, the locks on the front door of her tenement were broken and anyone could walk in unannounced. Evelyn's doorbell did not work either. The residents tried to prevent robberies by owning guard dogs, installing alarms and police locks on their door, and/or by trying to spend as much time at home as possible. In the more dilapidated parts of the neighborhood, tenants put padlocks on their mailboxes to keep the burglars out. I was once astounded to see ten padlocks on one mailbox. This image reflected the seriousness of crime in the neighborhood.

It is difficult to describe the emotional wear and tear that the stress and worry about being robbed takes on a person's life. The women I worked with were constantly worried about walking into their apartment and not knowing if they and their families were safe. As Evelyn explained,

> Like I was robbed a few months ago. Ever since the burglary I stay home more. I came home one evening after work and they were here. I had a fight with him and I got cut. He got away. I'll fight anybody, especially for something I worked so hard for. They cleaned me out of a freshly paid-for Sony Trinitron [television]. They cleaned me out of jewelry, mine and the kids', money—my rent ... *Eran pinceros,* they were lock pickers, that's what got me, man. My mother was downstairs, too. I was at my mom's apartment, and I heard something, footsteps coming from my apartment that is above hers. This was very strange. I was sitting at the table. I was just about to have dinner. My mother watches her *novelas,* soap operas, real loud so I screamed to her, "Mami baja eso" [Lower that]. Quién esta arriba? Who's upstairs? I said *mami* nobody's upstairs, I just walked in. I came to eat. So we went out into the hallway, and I was gonna go for something but I saw my mother leave the door first. God ... so I ran out after her. I came up with nothing. Then this guy is coming down the stairs. They had just finished, you know, and he's got my record player. I got that piece back because in the other burglary they cleaned me out completely. I wasn't going to let them clean me out again. He's coming down the stairs and mami says, "A quien vd. esta buscando?" Who are you looking for? The guy says, "Yo estoy vendiendo una stereo, señora" [I'm selling a stereo player, madam]. I said ooohhhh ... let me see. So the guy opens the bag and shows me my stereo. He says, "I bought this off this guy, but I need some money and I wanna sell it." I says, "You ain't selling shit, cause that's mine!" He said, "Nahhhh, nahhh, I just brought this off this black dude. I wanna sell it, you know." I said, "Well, if it's yours, let's go up to my apartment and check my living room." He says, "Nooo, nooo, es mia" [No, no, it's mine]. So I said well let's go upstairs ... so I grabbed him and he dropped it there and mami picked it up. She backed off and I shoved him

to the wall. Big guy, too. Mami let out a yell and he pulled out the knife. He got my hand. If mami hadn't yelled, he might have gotten me in the chest. In this neighborhood, you live with this tension. You live with this shit.

In addition to living in a neighborhood with a high crime rate, Evelyn also had problems with birth control and complications with her pregnancies. Evelyn had two unintended pregnancies, even though she had been trained as a nurse's aid. Like her mother, her knowledge of contraceptives was limited. She chose to be sterilized postpartum at the age of twenty-three after her second child was born because she did not plan either of her pregnancies.

I tried the diaphragm, I tried the IUD, I tried the rhythm, I tried the foam, I tried the condom . . . I got pregnant for my first one, not the one I have now, but the one I lost, using cream and condom. After that I got pregnant for the second one. I was still using the foam and condom. After that I said, "Hmmmmmm." So I went back and they stuck me with a diaphragm, and I used all of them at once—the diaphragm, the foam, the condom, and the IUD—and I still became pregnant. I used the loop for two years. It got lost inside of me. That is how I lost that baby.

The most effective contraceptive Evelyn used was the IUD. The least effective was the rhythm method. She became pregnant twice while using a combination of the condom and foam, which could mean that she did not use them properly or simply that they are less reliable methods of birth control.

In the same way that living in a high crime rate neighborhood constrains poor women's reproductive options because they are afraid for their children's safety, their income will determine the types of health care facilities to which they have access, which in turn influences the types of birth control methods most frequently recommended to them.

Evelyn's decision to get sterilized was also influenced by her boyfriend's refusal to use a condom. In her experience only a few Latino men, like her first husband, were willing to use them. Others, like her present boyfriend, had the macho attitude that birth control was a woman's responsibility. Hector, Evelyn's boyfriend, explained, "I'm not gonna use the rubber. Eso no esta en na [there's no groove in that]. I can't feel anything with it on. It's better if she is sterilized. This way we don't have to worry about using nothing."

Evelyn commented:

I never learned anything about birth control from no man. Men are pretty dumb about those things. With my first husband we discussed condoms— and the foam—and he was very open about it. He wasn't bad about wearing condoms. Even though he didn't like them, he'd use it. My second old man was, "Ohhhh, I'm not going to wear that!" His attitude was that the woman has to take care of herself. It was a thing where both of you should be into it together since both of you are doing it. It's an attitude that many have.

Evelyn elaborated a bit more on machismo:

They get this attitude because of the macho atmosphere that they grow up in. Like I see women saying to their sons, you have to do this and you have to do that . . . and I hear people saying to them, you're gonna make that kid grow up like a faggot. I say to myself, that's ridiculous, that's a bad attitude. If a woman says something like that to her son, they're good, because at least it's coming from their mother, and the boys can feel, if my mother feels this way, then so can other women.

recognizing that women are coming from somewhere (example of mother)

Primary Sources of Information about Birth Control

Evelyn learned about birth control from her mother and from family planning counselors in the birth control clinics she visited. It is unusual for women in the first and second generations to talk about sex. However, doña Hilda taught her daughter that it was okay to use contraceptives, even though she never used them herself. Evelyn explained:

My mother was my main source of information about birth control. That's one good thing about my mother. She was always very open about sex, and everything else, since I was young. She started telling me everything when I was about eight years old, first with my period, telling me what to expect to happen. After I got my period she got into sex. It got to the point where she showed me pictures of female and male organs. She used to sit down with me and explain how, when, where. I never expected my mother to tell me these things, because I used to think that she was very old-fashioned, and in many ways she is. But thank God, because she taught me this. I didn't have to go out there and experiment like so many of these young girls do. That's why when my daughters get bigger I want them to know everything, too. Because I feel that a lot of these young girls are devirginized simply because they want to experiment, because they don't know what it's all about. They hear things and they want to find out if it's true. I've asked young girls, thirteen, fourteen, why did you do this? They say, "My mother never explained anything to me, and I wanted to find out." Around here, you see a lot of very young girls getting pregnant. Once they start having babies, that's it. When I was older I learned about birth control from my studies, doctors, and counselors in family planning clinics. I didn't learn anything from female friends.

Evelyn does not consider word-of-mouth sources to be reliable, because she knows a lot of older women who are misinformed about contraceptives.

No ... word-of-mouth sources like that are no good. Even older women don't know what they're talking about when it comes to sex or birth control. Some myths about preventing pregnancy are, oh, quick, run to the bathroom and take a piss. Quick douche. Don't have sex more than once. I've heard so many, it isn't funny. Douching with vinegar with water—that's the most common one. All it does is make you tight as hell.

In addition to fearing more accidental pregnancies, Evelyn was also motivated to undergo sterilization because of the medical complications she had with her first pregnancy. She suffered from preeclampsia and both of her daughters were caesarean deliveries. Evelyn's predisposition towards la operación was also reinforced by a social worker in the clinic she used.

I was sterilized when I was twenty-three years old, right after I had my second daughter. I had a lot of complications during both pregnancies. They were both caesarean deliveries. Then I got toxemia [preeclampsia]. The doctor was telling me that I shouldn't have a second one, but I wasn't going to raise an only child. Then we have to think about the inflation and everything; money is hard, money is tight. Under other circumstances I might not have gotten [economic constraints] sterilized, but, like I said, I had to take into consideration the way things are going. Things are just going higher and higher and higher. You know, you start to consider the ways things are today raising children, the crime, and everything.

When I had the baby, at first, I wasn't sure I was ready to get operated on, so I waited a couple of months after I had the baby. Then I did it. I read and signed the consent form. The person I was referred to explained everything even before I read it.

I have always gone to family planning clinics, and like I said, I tried other contraceptives that for me were total failures. I even took the pill for two or three years. This was the most effective method, but there are so many risks involved. I just couldn't take the chance. At the clinic a social worker told me about an alternative way and that's final sterilization. I already knew about it. She said there is an operation to try and have children again, but it's not that routine. She didn't have to worry, because once I did it I wasn't going to go back again and try to have another one. So I stopped using the pill, because I decided to have a baby. As soon as I had the baby, I had the operation. With the risk of getting pregnant no matter what I used, sterilization was my only alternative.

Evelyn made the decision to get sterilized on her own. She told her mother after she made up her mind to do it, and she did not consult with her boyfriend.

Women talk to their mothers or somebody that they know. Many of them will ask their companions. Some men are totally against it because they prefer *blch* to see their woman pregnant every year so that nobody looks at her. My boy-friend never suggested any reason why I shouldn't have the operation. A lot of my friends told me what if I meet somebody and they want you to have a baby? I said they'd just have to be happy with the two I have.

My mother knows I'm a headstrong person, and once I make a decision there is no turning me back. So I went to her and said, "Mami, I'm going to have the operation." No matter what she said, I had decided I was going to do it. She agreed with me, because she knew I had set my mind on it. She told me all the things that are involved and sometime afterwards told me, "Remember, after it's done you can't have anymore." That's all she ever said. Never made a big issue of it. Now we'll talk about it and she'll say, "I'm glad you did it 'cause I can't see you with a whole bunch of kids, and I can't see you getting sick the way you have." I guess in the back of her mind she wanted me to do it, too.

"Cutting" and "Tying" Tubes

Evelyn and I talked about Puerto Rican women's misconceptions about the "cutting" and "tying" of the fallopian tubes. In contrast to her mother, and most other women in this study, and perhaps because of her medical training as a nurse's aid, Evelyn was one of the few women in this study who was aware that a distinction did not exist between tying and cutting tubes. She understood that sterilization was permanent, while most women do not.

I don't think there's a difference between the cutting and the tying of the tubes. Doctors have told me that there isn't. Way back then, many women weren't being explained this operation—they were told that they tied it but they didn't understand that they had to cut it before they tied it. The thing is that now there is also burning. So that the women think that it's tying and that with time there are sutures that dissolve within the body and they can get pregnant again. If you notice that most of the women who say this are Spanish women—not American, not Italian, you know. I feel it's because of the language barrier—a lot of things get lost in translation, so they go around with this misconception.

COOKIE: THIRD GENERATION

During the years of my research, I watched Evelyn's daughters Cookie and Gabriela grow up. They are both good students and great, fun-loving girls with a strong sense of family and individual responsibility. In 1998, Gabriela was already in a four-year college. Cookie planned to follow in her older sister's footsteps when she graduated from high school. Despite her knowledge about birth control, Cookie was dismayed to learn that she was pregnant in her last year of high school, at eighteen years old. She had been having sex for a year but thought she was safe because she was taking the birth control pill. The father of the baby, Frankie, was also in his last year of high school. They talked about whether they should have an abortion but decided they wanted to have the baby. In Cookie's words,

> I felt bad that I got pregnant while I was on the pill 'cause my mami and *abuela* [grandma] taught me about birth control and encouraged me to use it when I was ready. I was on the pill for a year before I got pregnant. The pill started to make me feel sick, and one day I didn't take it. I didn't realize it was so easy to get pregnant if you skipped the pill for one day, but that's what happened. I was in my last year of high school, and I wanted to finish school and go to college. Frankie and I talked about having the baby, but I was afraid to tell mami and abuela because they want me to go to college like my sister. Frankie and I told them together, and after they calmed down my grandma asked us what we wanted to do. We told her we wanted the baby and we could get married and keep going to school. They were really upset with me because they had educated me about birth control.

After a tearful family discussion, doña Hilda and Evelyn accepted Cookie's pregnancy and agreed that she and Frankie should get married. In Cookie's words:

> I cried when I told mami and abuela that I was pregnant. We spent a lot of time talking it out. Mami said Frankie should stay in his family's apartment until we got married, and then he could move in with us. A month later we had a civil ceremony, nothing fancy, and then Frankie moved in with my family until we both graduated from high school. I asked to be transferred to a high school for pregnant girls, and I was lucky that they had space for me right away. It was a rough year being pregnant, going to school, and living with Frank, my mother, and my sister, Gabriela, but we were lucky to have such a loving and understanding family.
>
> After we graduated high school, Frankie got a full-time job as a doorman for a fancy building in Manhattan. I was only able to find a part-time job as a cashier in a supermarket nearby. I wanted to go to college part time, but the baby was too young, and I was exhausted from staying up with him at night and breastfeeding. A few months after the baby was born, we found an apartment near mami and moved out, but I had to start working full time 'cause Frankie couldn't make ends meet on his salary. Doña Hilda and Frankie's mother, doña Josefina, took turns babysitting for Carlito while we both worked. They were so wonderful and didn't charge us a penny. By the

time we picked him up in the evening, they had given him a bath, fed him, and even put on his pajamas, which made our lives so much easier. Mami even cooked for us everyday. Sure, we bought the groceries, but I was grateful that she cooked 'cause after standing on my feet all day, I didn't feel like coming home to cook.

Cookie admits that she would not have been able to finish high school and survive without her mother, grandmother, and mother-in-law's help. Financially they were not doing much better than Evelyn and doña Hilda. Neither of them earned more than minimum wage. When I asked Cookie and Frankie if they were planning to have more children, they responded they wanted one more child because they did not want their son to grow up by himself. However, after the second baby Frankie would have a vasectomy. In his words:

> We're being real careful not to get pregnant again 'cause we can't afford another baby right now. But I don't want Carlito to grow up as an only child so we're thinking of having another baby when he is two or three years old. I would like to have a little girl. I don't have no problem with having a vasectomy, it doesn't change anything like some guys think. Cookie told me she would have la operación, but I told her why should she have to go through all of the changes by herself. I think that's fair 'cause she's gonna have the baby.

Frankie's willingness to take an active role in managing family size—even to the point of undergoing sterilization himself—would have been largely unthinkable in previous generations in New York's Puerto Rican community. Even among contemporary young men, his stance is unusual. But younger men are beginning to become more involved in birth control and in parenting, and Frank's attitude is an example of the ways that gender roles are changing.

Summary: Proactive Approaches, Constrained Choices

The story of the Velez family demonstrates the proactive stance that many Puerto Rican women take toward controlling their bodies, and, more specifically, their fertility. The majority of times this means getting sterilized; sometimes it also means having an abortion. We can also see how their fertility decisions are influenced by the high rate of crime in the neighborhood, the high cost of having children, and by individual issues—in particular, problematic relationships and achieving desired family size. Doña Hilda's story illustrates a form of moral reasoning that insists that women need to take care of themselves so that they can continue to care for their families. Women are not always so clear on the need to care for themselves, as we will see in other stories (see also Acuña-Lillo 1988).

Doña Hilda's hysterectomy reveals a different set of issues. The key factors that affected her decision to have a hysterectomy were her lack of access to quality health care services, the cancer scare tactic used to pressure her into accepting a hysterectomy by the medical care system, and her inability to distinguish between a first and second medical opinion. For her first surgery, doña Hilda completely trusted her doctor and submitted herself to an unnecessary reproductive surgery. However, this experience taught her that she could not trust doctors blindly. Eight years later, when another doctor told her she needed to have a mastectomy, she sought a second opinion and, because the liquid cyst was benign, she saved herself from an unnecessary operation.

Finally, doña Hilda's story highlights poor women's lack of knowledge about the medical system. First, she did not understand what a second medical opinion is. In part this is because the poor are not educated to distinguish between an intern, resident, and a doctor in a hospital. By blurring this distinction, the medical establishment legitimates interns and bestows upon them the same authority as that of experienced specialists. Therefore, like other women in this study, doña Hilda believed that each intern that examined her constituted a separate opinion about her medical condition.

Her story also shows how patronizing some doctors can be, especially with poor women. For example, during her post-surgery examination for the hysterectomy, the doctor who examined her reprimanded doña Hilda for allowing a doctor to remove her uterus because of a fibroid tumor. Although he was right, this was an insensitive way to inform doña Hilda that her hysterectomy was unnecessary and that she had been duped by the medical system. He also blamed doña Hilda instead of holding accountable the unethical doctor who performed the unnecessary hysterectomy.

Evelyn, doña Hilda's daughter, does not share her mother's old-fashioned beliefs that women should have their children consecutively and then get sterilized. However, she does believe that women should have their children while they are young. Evelyn was the only woman in this study who was fully aware that sterilization was a permanent operation. She was motivated to get sterilized for a combination of financial, medical, and individual reasons. Evelyn was also familiar with la operación; also, though her mother was not sterilized, she had many friends that were. Moreover, her own mother believed that a woman in a good marriage should have her children consecutively, while she is still young, and then get sterilized. In addition, both of her pregnancies had been unintended, which means that she was not as knowledgeable about temporary methods of birth control as she thought, and her common-law husband refused to use condoms.

Evelyn is an example of a woman from the swing generation who came of age during the feminist and civil rights movements and began to question traditional structures of gender and authority. Evelyn took responsibility for her own fertility. However, as progressive as she was, it did not occur to her to ask her common-law husband to have a vasectomy, and she decided to get sterilized because it seemed to be the most reasonable and effective option open to her. But she decided that this was her decision to make. She did not consult with her mother or her partner before undergoing the procedure (although she appeared to know beforehand that at least her mother approved of her action). As we will see, husbands and male partners—either actual or hoped for—often play an important role in women's decisions about whether and when to undergo sterilization.

Cookie shares a number of cultural and moral values with her mother and grandmother. When she became pregnant she and her boyfriend Frankie decided to have the baby because she wanted to have it. (Her grandmother doña Hilda tried to abort Evelyn but regretted it later.) Cookie's family supported her desire to have the baby and provided a home for them until they graduated from high school and she had her son, Carlito. During this period, Cookie received a great deal of support from her family, which allowed her to continue her education while raising her young son.

Even though Cookie did not plan her first child, she is more knowledgeable about birth control and sterilization than women of her grandmother's—or even of her mother's—generation. She appeared to be well informed about the permanent nature of tubal ligation. Moreover, the idea of Frankie having a vasectomy instead of Cookie having la operación is a novel idea for this generation, which reflects a change in gender roles. Although Frankie's decision to have a vasectomy may not be typical, it is something more Puerto Rican couples are considering.

The story of the Velez family demonstrates the relationship between the cancer scare, fibroid tumors, and unnecessary hysterectomies for poor women of color such as doña Hilda. It also illustrates the multiple forces that influence and constrained Evelyn's reproductive options, such as the high crime rate in her neighborhood, her caesarean births, and her boyfriend's reluctance to use a condom. Cookie's accidental pregnancy led to a family crisis that her mother and grandmother resolved. Her story shows the important role that the family support system still plays in the continued survival of the upcoming generations.

CHAPTER 4

The Robles Family

SOCIAL CHANGE AND GENDER STRUGGLE

Early one morning I set out to find doña Rosario. It was a warm and humid August morning, one of those days when you perspire five minutes after you have stepped out of the shower if you do not have air-conditioning. Doña Rosario and her daughters lived in the more dilapidated quarters of the southern part of Bushwick. I walked south from where doña Hilda, Evelyn, Cookie, Frankie, Carlito, and Gabriela lived. Even though I grew up only ten blocks away, I was a stranger to the devastation and destruction that I witnessed here. In New York, one block can be radically different from another. A five-block radius can constitute a world of difference in the physical setting of a neighborhood. As I walked through these hot and noisy streets, I was not sure if I would be welcomed there.

Everyone appeared to be in the street that morning. The air vibrated with the mixed sounds of disco, hip-hop, reggaeton, and salsa music. Men and women talked and laughed as they sat on the front stoops of their tenements to escape the heat of their apartments. Early in the morning the rich aroma of Bustelo coffee wafted through the air, and as I passed by some apartment windows, I could smell the garlicky aroma of fried pork chops and sweet plantains. These women were taking advantage of the coolest part of the morning to cook lunch early. Mothers living on the ground floor called out of the windows to their children playing on the sidewalk. On some blocks the children screamed, laughed, and frolicked as they were sprayed with water from an open hydrant—their only relief from the sticky heat.

I finally arrived at doña Rosario's block. Across the street from where she lived was a large, dusty, rubble-filled lot where the ruins of a building still jutted out from the ground. The lot occupied half of the block. On the sidewalk in front of the lot and in front of the torn up pieces of concrete sat four or five Puerto Rican men around a small table. They were playing dominos and drinking beer. In order to avoid them, I automatically crossed the street, as all Latinas have been taught to do since we were young.

As I walked across the street, I tried to guess in which of the four- to five-story buildings doña Rosario lived. As I passed each one, I slowed down to locate the number of the building. It was a beautiful day, and this street had the feeling of an outdoor marketplace. A group of women were conversing on the front steps of doña Rosario's building. Feeling shy and a little awkward, I approached them and asked if doña Rosario lived there. Doña Rosario was among them. Before she identified herself, she demanded to know in a loud voice why I was looking for doña Rosario. When she raised her voice, all of the activity stopped and a silent hush fell over the block. Everyone stared at us, and I was momentarily stunned by her reaction and embarrassed by the attention.

As I nervously regained my composure, I explained that I was studying why such a large number of Puerto Rican women were sterilized. I told her I sought her out because I wanted to talk to women personally about their experiences. Timidly, I asked her if we could speak privately. After sizing me up for a few minutes, she seemed convinced and invited me to come up to her apartment.

She lived one flight up. Her granddaughter, who had just cleaned the apartment, was busy putting away groceries. The home was spotless and gleamed in the sunlight. It smelled clean and had the old familiar smell of King Pine, one of the favorite cleaning products of the Puerto Rican women I grew up with. Doña Rosario gave me motherly advice; she told me she went shopping every two or three weeks because it was more economical than buying groceries in the *bodega* at the corner. Bodegas are the only grocery shops in many poor neighborhoods in New York. They tend to have higher prices and more limited selection than the supermarkets that service prosperous locations. Buying food in poor neighborhoods is often more expensive than in middle-class areas. Before we started the interview, doña Rosario politely offered me a soda, which I accepted. (It is considered rude not to offer a visitor a beverage or something to eat when they visit, and equally impolite for the visitor to refuse it.)

Doña Rosario: First Generation

When I met doña Rosario she was sixty-four years old. She was born in Puerto Rico in 1917 and migrated to New York in 1953, at the age of thirty-six. Doña Rosario's husband came to the mainland first and worked in migrant camps in Florida. Several months later she followed him, although later she chose to settle in a different city. After a few minutes of small talk, doña Rosario started to tell me about her life.

When I saw that all the other men from Puerto Rico were leaving for the farms in Florida, I convinced my husband to migrate too. He didn't want to go, and I even made a promise (*promesa*) to God so that he would leave. He finally left because on the island there was no place where he could earn a dollar. He sent me twelve dollars every twelve days. By the time I paid for my bills, I'd begin to buy on credit again. There were no handkerchiefs to sew—there was nothing. I knew that we could not survive like this. The day my husband least expected it, I mortgaged our little shack, borrowed money to complete my airfare to Florida, which was only $45 and surprised him in Florida.

In Florida, the women worked alongside the men in the fields. Since there was no child care, poor women like doña Rosario worried about the logistics of migrating as well as how to take care of her children while she worked alongside her husband in a migrant camp. Like other women, she resolved this immediate problem by leaving most of her children with her relatives in Puerto Rico. In Florida, she resorted to desperate measures.

In Florida I worked like a man in a migrant camp planting and picking tomatoes, pimientos, squash, green beans, cabbage. I'd lock our four children in the shack so that I could work. The truck would pick us up at seven in the morning. We came home to eat at 11:30 and then didn't return till five. I hated to leave my eight-year-old daughter in charge of the seven, five, and two-and-a-half-year-old but what could I do? I brought them to Florida from Puerto Rico because my oldest daughter could no longer take care of them, and I needed them by my side. Otherwise, I would have gone back to Puerto Rico.

Before doña Rosario left for Florida, she arranged to get sterilized. She had wanted to get sterilized before, but her husband would not sign the consent form. Up until the 1950s women needed their husbands' permission for the operation. Therefore, she waited until he left for Florida to do it. By then she already had ten children and she did not want any more. Like other women who could not afford to pay for la operación, doña Rosario waited to get sterilized before the mayoral elections. Women not only exchanged a vote for a free tubal ligation in Puerto Rico but, after they migrated to New York in the 1950s, some of them returned to the island to get sterilized there because they knew how to negotiate the system and sterilization was still illegal in New York.

I love children and never thought of getting sterilized, but our economic situation was so hard that I couldn't go on like this anymore. While my husband was gone, I spoke to the mayor right before elections. At this time of year the mayor pays for the sterilization in exchange for a vote. A lot of woman got sterilized at this time.

Several years later, doña Rosario decided to move to New York because the next farm her husband was going to did not offer family housing. When doña Rosario first moved to New York she and five of her children stayed with her niece and her niece's husband in Manhattan.

> From Florida I moved to New York alone with my five children. I came in March and it was still very cold. We didn't have sweaters or anything. I left my other five children in Puerto Rico with my parents and eldest daughter while I got myself together. I came to live with my niece in New York.

In contrast to the norm of hospitality most Puerto Rican families are known for, doña Rosario's niece's husband found her a furnished room and asked her to leave a few days after she arrived. Doña Rosario was mortified but too proud to beg. She moved to a furnished room that same day.

> Because I had five children with me, in three days her husband put me out in the street. After my niece left for work one morning he told me that he had found a furnished room for us and there was a taxi outside waiting to take us there. He found me a furnished room and told me I had to leave while my niece was at work. When my niece came home they had a huge argument about this and broke up for a while. In the furnished room I lived on the third floor but had to cook in the basement.
>
> The owners would not allow the children to eat in the kitchen, so after I cooked, I had to walk up three flights of stairs with the children and the food. By the time we got upstairs the food was cold.
>
> After a few days I found a less expensive room. After paying the first week's rent in our second furnished room I was broke. I didn't even have enough money to buy food. The neighbors got together and brought food to us every day. They also brought me clothes to wash, and even lent me an iron and an ironing board so that I could earn a few dollars.
>
> I washed and ironed mostly for two men. I told my husband about this job in case he showed up unexpectedly he would know why I had other men's clothing in my room. My husband spent one week with us and the other in New Jersey in the migrant camp. He was jealous because he did not like me working for men, but since he threw away his money on other things, someone had to support the kids. Once he left and I did not hear from him in two years.

A few months later doña Rosario was able to find a five-room apartment where she lived with all her children.

> After the first month I sent for my other five children and there were ten of us in one room. We lived like sardines in a can. Some of them slept on the

floor and the others in the only bed we had. After a month I was able to find
a five-room apartment. I babysat for other children and took care of my own
kids. I've struggled a lot here. Even though it was tough in New York City, at
least I felt I had more control over my life here than I did in Puerto Rico.

In 1957 doña Rosario also bought a job in Astoria, Queens. In those days
people who could not find jobs paid a fee to an agency to get work.[1] Her older
daughter Carmen continued to take care of the children.

I began to work in New York in 1957. My first job was in Astoria, Long Island,
in a toy factory. I brought that job from an employment agency. After that I
worked in another factory in Brooklyn packing plastic curtains. I'd get up at
4:30 in the morning so that I could get to work by 7:30. Since I lived in the
Bronx, I had to make four changes on the train. Sometimes I would get out
of work at 5 P.M. If I worked overtime, I'd get out at 7 P.M. and I would not
get home till 10:00 that night, only to get up again at 4:30 in the morning
the next day.

After three years I had to stop working because one of my boys started
to play hooky from school. My eldest daughter, who took care of my kids,
moved and there was no one who could care for my children and home. I
suffered a lot and was forced to go back on welfare. I also had problems with
my health during that time.

Doña Rosario practically raised her children alone. In doña Rosario's
opinion, her husband became more irresponsible with her children after she
migrated to New York than when she was in Puerto Rico. She put up with his
bad behavior initially, but as soon as she became more independent by getting a
job and receiving welfare she changed the quality of her relationship with him.
Even though she still allowed him to visit her and the children, the minute he
did something she did not like she threw him out. In other words, the visits
took place on her terms. Doña Rosario became more aware of gender oppression when she moved to New York. This is her philosophy:

In the old days women were slaves. We had to put up with anything men
dished out—not anymore! After I began to receive welfare my husband
showed up. In the meantime he had wasted his money and barely helped
me out. So I told him I came here alone, and alone with my children I will
remain. If you want to visit your children fine, but don't go out of your way.
The abuse ends here. So every two or three months he would come to see us.
If he did something I did not like, I'd lock him out. He didn't want to put
up with anything, well, neither did I. This is the way we've continued to the
present [laughter]. And here I am today. I'd like to have the strength to work

like before. I don't like to stay home. I'm a happy person. When I danced, people used to make circles around me.

Doña Rosario adores her children. She refers to them as her treasure, she is especially proud of her daughters and grandchildren who are a daily part of her life. She beamed as she proudly describes Mother's Day at her home.

I don't regret that I had my children. I have thirty-five grandchildren. On Mother's Day they all come to visit me. There are so many of them that on Mother's Day no one else fits in this apartment. I love my grandchildren.

Nancy: Second Generation

I met Nancy when she was thirty-one years old. In 2006 she was fifty-six. Nancy is doña Rosario' youngest daughter. She was born in Puerto Rico but has lived in Brooklyn since she was three years old. Nancy dropped out of school at the age of seventeen because she was pregnant. In total she has had three pregnancies and four children. One set of her children was twins. When I interviewed her she was not in a steady relationship.

In 1981 Nancy was receiving Aid for Dependent Children. She was going to school to get her high school equivalency diploma. Nancy liked to work, but after she had her twins she became a stay-at-home mom because it was difficult to find someone to take care of two toddlers and a new set of twins. Before she had her twins, she worked as a bookkeeper for five years. However, in 1981 she and her four children lived on an annual income of $6,228. She was divorced and struggling, and her mother agreed that she should have her tubes cut. Nancy was sterilized at the age of twenty-seven. Her story is compelling because it shows how women's responsibility for birth control, child rearing, and domestic labor (patriarchy), along with financial constraints (poverty) and a woman's desire to do other things with her life (gender awareness) combine to limit a woman's perceptions of her fertility options. In her words:

Women get operated on because of a combination of reasons. It's not just money, it's everything combined. If you're alone that has a lot to do with it. If you're with somebody, the kind of relationship has a lot to do with it. You know—it's combined. It has to do with mental anguish. The mental thing can come if you're frustrated 'cause you don't have enough money to get what you want or to live comfortable anyway. Or you have problems with one kid, or you have problems with your old man—all these things combined. It puts your mind like wanting to do it. That's what happened to me. I can't afford to have another kid because money-wise it was tight. My situation with my old man wasn't good. The kids were giving me a hassle. I wanted to become somebody and I couldn't if I would have had more kids. I don't want to have one dangling on top of the other because that would be rough all around.

The double standards reflected in Nancy's everyday life wore her down and constrained her fertility options. After Nancy achieved her desired family size, she did not want more children. The more children women have, the more work there is because, as Nancy says, women have a twenty-four-hour job that does not end when the husband comes home.

According to Nancy, her husband did not want to use birth control. From her perspective, men do not want to share the responsibility.

My husband won't use birth control. I don't think men want to be respon-sible. I've asked some guys why they feel that way, and they have said to me, "well, why should we be! You girls have to take care of yourselves." I've argued to death with these guys, it blows my mind. To them it's like why should it be my business, they believe that it's yours to take care of.

Before Nancy was sterilized, she used the pill and the IUD. She had prob-lems with both methods of birth control. In her words:

I got pregnant using the pill. I don't think pills are effective at all. From my own experience they gave me a lot of side effects. I think I took the pill for about two years. After that I took them again because the doctor kept chang-ing them on me. I finally stopped. Then came the loop; the loop gave me a lot of cramps, and with my old man, it used to cut him. He couldn't penetrate because it cut him. I got rid of that one real quick.

To some extent Nancy also feels that the number of children a woman has depends on how much emotional support her husband gives her. Nancy's hus-band was not a very supportive man. At least 50 percent of the Puerto Rican women in my survey felt this way.

If you have maybe one or two children, that's different, but after you have a few kids, for him to say no, you'll just continue producing and not getting anyplace because it's hard. It depends on the situation too, what type of man you have. Does he deal with you when he comes home? Does he take over if he feels you're down and out? There are very few men that come home from work and, as tired as they are, take over or help the wife. My old man isn't one of them. So if he didn't approve of my decision, I would have done it anyway.

Like 50 percent of the women in the survey, Nancy regretted having been sterilized. Regret is a gray area contingent upon changes in a woman's life such as remarriage, the death of a child, or the improvement of a woman's socioeconomic situation. Like many other women in her age cohort, Nancy regretted having been sterilized because she feared she might meet the right man in the future who would want to have his own children.

> I sometimes regret getting sterilized for the same reasons some of my friends do. They've gone through one marriage, they've had it, and they figure it's time to cut it loose and, ahhh, they didn't realize that in the future, like this girl, she only had one kid and got sterilized. Now she's met this dynamite guy and she can't have more children. She was twenty-one when she got sterilized.

Nancy's fear did not materialize, and therefore her feelings of regret changed over time. Nancy stopped regretting her sterilization when she married a man who had grown children and who did not want any more kids. Although Nancy's desire to get sterilized was partially based on her desire to do other things with her life and not be responsible for all of the domestic work, her regret was conditional on her projection of what a man might want in the future.

CARMEN: SECOND GENERATION

Carmen is doña Rosario's eldest daughter and, like her mother, she also had a very difficult life. In contrast to her vivacious mother and younger sister Nancy, Carmen is a thin, pale, and long-suffering woman. In 1981 she was forty-seven years old. She has a third-grade level of education. Carmen married when she was nineteen years old and has six children. Carmen wanted to have a tubal ligation after her second child but did not because her husband refused to consent to the operation. According to Carmen, tying her tubes goes against her religious beliefs, but after having six children she felt there was nothing else she could do.

> I came to New York from Puerto Rico when I was twenty-three years old. Life was hard when I was growing up because I am the eldest of ten children. Ever since I can remember I helped my mother raise the other kids. I was always cooking, cleaning, and making them clothes. My husband Alex is also from the island. We met in church in New York and were married one year later. I had a child right away. My mother advised me to get sterilized after my second child. My sister and I were going to be sterilized on the same day. Three days before we had la operación, a woman died while they were operating on her, and my husband didn't let me do it. If I had gone against his will, he would have left me, and I didn't want him to go.

Alex did not give Carmen permission to have la operación until after she had her sixth child. He also refused to use birth control or to allow her to use it. Alex only agreed that Carmen could get sterilized after their sixth child because of the economic pressure of raising six children. After he consented to her tubal ligation, she went to a hospital in Manhattan to have la operación. Carmen does not speak English; therefore, she did not know how to tell the doctor that she wanted a tubal ligation. To the best of her ability, she described that she wanted an operation so that she would not have more children. Instead of performing a tubal ligation, the doctor performed an unnecessary hysterectomy.

> It was hard raising six children. Finally, Alex agreed to la operación because of the economic pressures and because men don't like it when we use contraceptives. So, when I was thirty-five, I went to the hospital and asked them to operate me so that I wouldn't have more children, and they took out my womb [uterus]. They told me my uterus was too low. I wasn't sick and they shouldn't have done this to me!
>
> I was shocked when I went for the gynecological examination and found out that my uterus had been taken out. I could not believe that a doctor had done this to me. I felt violated, ashamed and stupid. All I could think of was what would Alex think of me now.

Although Carmen signed a consent form, she claims she was not aware of what she was signing because she cannot read. According to the 1975 New York City sterilization guidelines, Carmen's reproductive rights were violated twice. The first time was when she signed a consent form without knowing what she was signing. The stipulation that a consent form must be in writing and be read orally was developed to protect illiterate women like Carmen. The second time was when the doctor performed the hysterectomy without her knowledge or consent.

To add insult to injury, the physician who Carmen consulted with after her surgery blamed her for allowing a doctor to perform an unnecessary hysterectomy on her. Doña Hilda, Evelyn's mother, had a similar experience. Once again, neither of these physicians held the doctors who violated Carmen's and doña Hilda's reproductive rights accountable for their unethical practice. In Carmen's words:

> A doctor at another hospital asked me why I didn't menstruate anymore. I told him and he scolded me and wanted to know why I had let those other doctors do this to me! I felt so bad. I didn't know they were going to do it. There are other operations for a woman not to have more babies that aren't this one. I never told my husband about this because he would think I am hueca [empty]. Since that doctor did this to me I am not the same person.

Carmen had a lot of problems after her hysterectomy. She became chronically depressed because she felt victimized, but she did not know how to redress her problem. She was afraid to tell Alex because he did not want her to get sterilized in the first place. As a result, she felt she had to suffer in silence. By *hueca* Carmen means she felt like a shell of a woman. In the Puerto Rican community there is a strong stigma associated with having a hysterectomy. The belief is that when a woman has a hysterectomy, she is hollow or empty inside; hence, she cannot receive or give sexual pleasure. Accordingly, women who have had hysterectomies feel embarrassed to talk about it because according to Puerto Rican beliefs they have lost their womanliness. For several years after her surgery, Carmen felt depressed and anxious. When she talked to me about it she still felt traumatized by this experience. Carmen's story reflects the inequities of the health care system and how sexism at home and in society at large affects women's lives.

Sonia: Third Generation

Sonia is doña Rosario's granddaughter and Carmen's daughter. Her story highlights the individual and psychological forces that lead younger women to get sterilized. We met when Sonia was twenty-two years old. In 2006 she was forty-seven. She and her husband, Nelson, live in the finished basement of her parents' small house in Brooklyn. They are poor, but they are working hard to build a better life for themselves. One of the ways Sonia plans to attain this goal is by getting sterilized. According to her, children are expensive and she does not intend to have any more. Sonia is sensitive about how society thinks of Puerto Ricans. She does not want to be stereotyped as a "baby maker" or a woman who has children to take advantage of welfare. In her words:

> I'm no baby maker. People think all Puerto Ricans are on welfare. They think we have no pride, that we have babies to take welfare. I'm sick to death of that attitude! We're poor but we are proud hard-working people. I don't want a handout from nobody.

Sonia's mother, Carmen, and father, Alex, lived upstairs in four small rooms. She and her family shared the small kitchen with her mother. Even though the house is crowded, Sonia claims that she is glad to share the household with her mother because, as she says, when her two-year-old makes her "crazy," she sends her upstairs while she gets much-needed rest.

Sonia has a high school diploma and is a bright, ambitious, and energetic person. Like her mother and grandmother, she married early, by the age of seventeen. Therefore, at the age of twenty-two (1981), she had a two-year-old daughter and was six months pregnant with her second child. At the time she was also completing the procedure for postpartum tubal ligation.

Men play an influential role in women's fertility decisions, particularly if they are married. Even though women feel that they should make the final decision about whether or not to get sterilized, most women agreed that if their husbands did not want them to do it, they would not because it would create marital conflict. According to Sonia:

> I discussed the idea of getting sterilized with my husband. His only objection was, what if one of our children dies? I told him, if God takes away one of our children, there's nothing I can do about it. I enjoyed them as much as I could. My child is a Christian. She will go with God. My husband agreed that I should get operated on because he told me he knew how fragile I was and how sick I got when I'm pregnant.

The first step in getting sterilized was signing a consent form. The sterilization consent process next consisted of two phases. In the first phase, Sonia attended a group counseling session. In the second phase, she met one-to-one with a social worker. These observations enabled me to see what the patient's procedure was like and assess the quality of the provider-patient dialogue. It also enabled me to explore what safeguards, if any, public hospitals provide against sterilization abuse.

I met Sonia and Carmen at the clinic, and the first person we came across was a clerk chatting on the phone. We waited ten minutes for her to acknowledge our presence. An hour later, we went into the group-counseling meeting. The person in charge of the meeting was Mrs. Gonzalez, a middle-aged, heavyset Puerto Rican woman. When we arrived there were already thirty women waiting. Some of the women had small children with them. The room was crowded and noisy. The women looked tired and hassled.

While we were waiting for the counseling session to begin, Sonia discovered that she had forgotten her birth certificate. She went promptly up to Mrs. Gonzalez to ask her if she needed it today because she was not sure if they would allow her to sign the consent form without showing her birth certificate. Her mother followed her. Mrs. Gonzalez had just started distributing the sterilization consent forms when Sonia intercepted her and asked if she could talk to her for a minute. Mrs. Gonzalez did not stop. Because Mrs. Gonzalez ignored her, Sonia ran after Mrs. Gonzalez trying to get her attention while Carmen ran after Sonia. Sonia was visibly upset. When she returned to her seat, I asked Sonia if she was okay, and in an exasperated voice she said to me that "she felt like a child" because Mrs. Gonzalez had asked her to sit down and had refused to listen to her. The counseling session was rushed, and Sonia, who had a high school diploma and was more articulate than most of the women there, was not able to entirely follow what Mrs. Gonzalez was saying.

Mrs. Gonzalez began the session by informing everyone that she was going to jump around so that she did not have to read everything on the consent form. She talked very fast in Spanish and set a harried and tense pace.

> They are going to cut your tubes. Read it fast because I know you pick up fast. Tubal ligation, counseling, fifth floor, room 514. Time 10 A.M. Dr. Ponce will cut your tubes. There are a number of different procedures used to perform this operation; some of them are laparacopia, colpotomia, etc. The anesthesia will be given through the spine.

After she said this in one breath, she paused and looked up for the first time and asked if anyone preferred if she spoke English. Sonia raised her hand. Once again, Mrs. Gonzalez dismissed her by stating that, since she was the only one, she would translate for her later.

During her presentation on tubal ligation, Mrs. Gonzalez used the colloquial language of "cutting" and "tying" because she was familiar with how women used to talk about la operación, and perhaps because she was trying to simplify the discussion for her patients. However, what Mrs. Gonzalez was not aware of or did not appear to be concerned about was the high rate of misinformation that Puerto Rican women have about the permanency of this surgical procedure. Her use of colloquial language did not help to dispel these misconceptions. The only hazard Mrs. Gonzalez warned her patients about was the possibility that another organ could be accidentally cut during the surgery.

At the end of her counseling session, Mrs. Gonzalez gave Sonia instructions in English on how to fill out the application. However, she refused to translate the session into English because she "knew" that Sonia had understood what she said in Spanish. Sonia did not respond.

Mrs. Gonzalez's counseling session demonstrates how the lack of access to quality health care services, and the large caseloads that hospital counselors are expected to handle, narrow poor women's fertility options. There were multiple problems with the way Mrs. Gonzalez conducted her counseling session. To begin with, she did not create a safe counseling environment that encouraged poor women to ask questions. On the contrary, when Sonia tried to talk to her, she ignored her. Second, she intimidated the women by setting a frenetic pace, speaking quickly and jumping around the consent form, which made it difficult for the women to follow her. No one asked Mrs. Gonzalez any questions, yet it was clear that some of the women were confused when they started to whisper to one another. Mrs. Gonzalez ignored this. Third, Mrs. Gonzalez added to Puerto Rican women's misinformation about the irreversibility of la operación by using colloquial language. She should have informed the women that, in general, tubal ligations are a permanent operation and that if they wanted to have more children, this would not be the fertility control method for them. Finally, at the end of the counseling session, it was unethical and inexcusable that Mrs. Gonzalez refused to translate to Sonia as she had said she would. It was even more presumptuous of her to assume that Sonia had understood everything that she said.

Although I am aware that health care providers in public hospitals are under considerable pressure to see large numbers of patients, and I am empathic about this, Mrs. Gonzalez's behavior was inexcusable. She could have asked the social worker that Sonia was going to see next to go over the materials with her again. I do not believe that Mrs. Gonzalez would have treated middle-class Latinas the way she treated Sonia and her other poor patients. Even though Sonia was one of the more educated women in this study, she admitted to me later that she felt intimidated by Mrs. Gonzalez.

After the group counseling session was over, Sonia met with a social worker on a one-to-one basis for a few minutes. I assumed that the goal of the individual session was to give women a chance to clarify any issue that they still did not understand after the group session. Carmen accompanied Sonia to this meeting because she was her legal witness. Although I was not officially allowed to attend this meeting, I was able to observe it because it took place in an open desk in the hallway of the hospital where anyone could stand around and hear the conversation. The meeting began with the social worker asking Sonia if she had any questions about the consent form. Sonia responded that her only concern was that she had forgotten her birth certificate, which provided proof that she was twenty-one years or older. Federal funds did not pay for a minor to be sterilized. The social worker replied that this was not a problem and she made another appointment for Sonia to bring it in. I was surprised Sonia did not tell this social worker about how Mrs. Gonzalez had ignored her and refused to translate the counseling session to her in English. The social worker did not volunteer any new information, and the entire meeting only lasted ten minutes. Later I asked Sonia why she did not tell the social worker about the problem she had with Mrs. Gonzalez. She responded that she did understand most of what Mrs. Gonzalez said, and she felt it was futile to tell the social worker because nothing ever changed. Sonia may appear passive when she expresses her belief that nothing will change even if she complains. Unfortunately, this is part of poor women's reality. Making changes in a hospital bureaucracy is exceedingly difficult.

After the individual session, a woman who was monitoring the sterilization guidelines came up to Sonia in the hospital corridor and asked her if the doctor was present during the sterilization counseling session. She expressed surprise when Sonia told her he was not there. This young woman was the only safety valve that the hospital had to monitor problems with the sterilization process in the hospital. Although the doctor's absence from the counseling session might have made a difference, that was not the only problem that occurred. This administrator needed to ask more open-ended questions to find out about the other problems women were having. Consequently, the sterilization monitoring system in this hospital was not working efficiently. I later found this woman and shared my observations with her.

After Sonia's son, Ricky Nelson, was born prematurely, she spent nine days in the hospital. The baby's lungs were underdeveloped and Sonia was afraid that he might not survive. She decided not to go through with the postpartum sterilization. In Sonia's words:

> The doctor who delivered my baby came to see me the day after he was born. He said he saw the baby and asked me if I was sure that I wanted to get sterilized. I told him I wasn't sure. He warned me that if any doctors came to see me and asked me to sign something, not to sign anything. After he left several doctors and nurses stopped by to ask me if I wanted to be sterilized.

This was not surprising since Sonia gave birth in a teaching hospital that has one of the highest rates of tubal ligation in New York City. Ricky Nelson survived. Three months later he was doing well, and Sonia told me she was caring for him and coping with the sibling rivalry. Sonia told me she planned to put the children in day care as soon as possible. Sonia went back to work after spending six months at home with her children. At the age of twenty-four, Sonia arranged to be sterilized with two children.

Summary and Conclusions

There are many parallels between the women in doña Rosario's family. All three generations of women are sterilized. With the exception of Carmen, they all decided to have their tubes "cut" because of the individual, cultural, and social conditions I have discussed. For varying reasons, they did not want more children. What the women in this extended family have in common is that they are all poor, have strong family values, and rely on each other for support. Moreover, all three generations worked and wanted a better life for themselves and their children.

Of all of doña Rosario's children Carmen had the most difficult life. Doña Rosario had ten children including Carmen. As her mother's eldest daughter, she inherited many of her mother's worries and became her siblings' surrogate mother. This means that there is a ten-year age difference between Nancy and Carmen. In addition to all of the responsibilities she had as a child, when her mother migrated to New York, Carmen was the primary caretaker. Like her mother, Carmen wanted to get sterilized after her second child, but her husband refused to consent until she had her sixth child. He also refused to use birth control. Carmen's husband's consent was important to her in contrast to her mother, doña Rosario, who took action into her own hands and was sterilized secretly after her husband left for Florida to work on a migrant camp. Other women's stories confirmed the significant role that men played in determining if, when, and how their wives underwent sterilization. Doña Rosario's action was not unusual, in that it demonstrates the need for women of that era to resort to informal (and, at times, secret) action in order to accomplish their goals. Like a few other mothers in the survey, doña Rosario had a combination of a tubal ligation and hysterectomy.

Like her mother, Carmen had an unnecessary hysterectomy. In contrast to doña Rosario, who had a hysterectomy for medical reasons, Carmen was a victim of hysterectomy abuse. With respect to her hysterectomy, Carmen simultaneously embodies elements of agency and abuse. The agency is reflected in her proactive behavior to get sterilized. Her abuse took place when the doctor performed the hysterectomy on her without her knowledge or consent. Carmen's story highlights class inequities, which takes the form of the medical abuse and the cultural role that machismo also plays in circumscribing women's reproductive options.

Nancy migrated to New York with her mother when she was three years old. Therefore, even though Nancy is female, she did not have the same responsibilities as Carmen. The difference in their experiences is reflected in their demeanor. In many ways, Nancy was more like her mother than Carmen. She had her mother's independent spirit. She owned and drove her own car. Like her mother she felt that women were treated like slaves and refused to live that way. Nancy left her first husband because she resented being treated like a maid.

Like her grandmother, Sonia was also vivacious and independent. In contrast to her female relatives, who ended up with more children than they wanted, she did not want more than two children. Like her aunt Nancy, and her mother Carmen, Sonia was not well informed about birth control. She had problems with the pill, IUD, and claimed that her second child was an accident, too, because of a defective condom. Sonia was not familiar with the diaphragm either. When I told her about it, she expressed interest but was afraid to experiment with something new because she was going through a difficult pregnancy and claimed she did not want to risk another one. Like her mother, grandmother, and aunt, she used sterilization to improve her life conditions. In Sonia's words:

> I don't intend to deprive myself anymore. What I had planned wasn't supposed to be like this. It's probably the way I was raised, the goals I had for myself. My mother told me that once I married, I would have a lot of children.

I told her no, I only wanted one. I want my own house. I am twenty-one years old. I also want to make sure that what happened to my mother didn't happen to me. She has six kids and she's still a slave. I want to study and go to school. My husband likes to travel. I want to live good. Will I want another child when I'm thirty? The answer is no. I won't be as young and I don't want to start this child-rearing thing all over again.

Sonia's mother, Carmen, actively supported her daughter's decision to get sterilized after her second child because this is what she herself had wanted to do when she was younger. Her grandmother also played an important role in encouraging her to undergo sterilization. Although doña Rosario did not advise Sonia to get sterilized directly, she did not discourage her either. Moreover, she served as a role model for her granddaughter. Doña Rosario felt that Sonia was young and that she was having children too quickly and that was going to ruin her life. In Spanish there is a phrase that women use to warn their daughters, sisters, and female friends when they believe they are having too many children too quickly. The saying is "se esta llenando de niños muy rápido" (careful, you are filling yourself up with children too quickly). Doña Rosario told me that if Sonia had not become more assertive her husband would control her life now. In this context, undergoing sterilization is often an act of asserting power (even constrained power) in a marriage, and it can expose the fault lines in gender and family relations. At times, encouraging or supporting the sterilization decision of one's friend or family member can be an important act of female solidarity.

What role do husbands play in influencing their wives' fertility decisions? How typical is Carmen's situation with her husband? All of the women in this extended family were married, but the extent that their husbands influenced their decisions to be sterilized varied. For example, doña Rosario's decision was clandestine. Although doña Rosario shares many characteristics with other women in her generation, her decision to undergo la operación is not representative. In addition, her marital relationship was unusual. She developed a long-distance relationship with her husband not only because he could not get a job in New York but also because she was tired of his double standards and preferred to see him intermittently.

Forty one percent of the women in this survey claimed that their husbands influenced their decision to be sterilized. This means men play a more significant role than perhaps some women claim they do. To follow up on this question, I asked the women if they had a problem with their husband as a result of their operation. Only 29 percent of the women in the study (n=96) claimed they had problems with their husbands. This is especially true if the men originally did not want their wives to get sterilized. I also came across a few cases of men who wanted their wives to get sterilized when the women did not want to.

As a woman raised in the United States, Nancy was very independent and resented her subordinate position vis-à-vis her first husband. Yet, even though she clearly rejected certain traditional female roles, she had internalized others, such as the belief that if she met the right man it was important to give him a child to solidify their relationship. In contrast, Carmen appeared to be the most passive of the women in this family. Even she wanted to get sterilized after her second child, but her husband did not give her his consent until she had her sixth child. Finally, Sonia was independent like her grandmother, doña Rosario. Even though she was happily married, she decided to get sterilized because she wanted a small family and desired to do other things in her life in addition to having children. Sonia had no problems convincing her husband that she wanted to get sterilized.

Sonia's story also illustrates how difficult it is for women to negotiate public hospitals, even when they have a high school diploma, speak English, and are proactive about their lives. Her story highlights an important issue. Even though the counselor for the sterilization counseling session was Puerto Rican and a woman, she was as patronizing as any male health provider could be. She was also clueless about the high rate of misinformation Puerto Rican women and other Latinas have about la operación. Her experiences reveal two myths. The first myth is that female health providers are inherently more sensitive than male health providers. The second one is that (on average) a Latina counselor is better than a non-Latina. Apparently what makes the difference is how mindful, well informed, and caring the individual is.

Overall, la operación appealed to these women for numerous reasons. On an individual level, they were familiar with the procedure because practically all of the women in their family had been sterilized. They were poor and, on a cultural level, their traditional gender roles relegated child rearing, domestic work, and birth control primarily to them. On a social level, they lacked access to quality health care services, they were not knowledgeable about temporary methods of birth control, and they did not have access to safe, convenient, affordable birth control. Without exception, all of the women in this extended family wanted to limit their family size; even doña Rosario was sterilized after she had ten children for fear of continuing to get pregnant. They accepted la operación because this was an effective option for them and they did not perceive other viable alternatives. La operación enabled them to limit their fertility so that they could do more with their own lives. Given their immediate circumstances all three generations perceived la operación as important for their basic well-being.

CHAPTER 5

The Gomez Family

UNDER THE KNIFE AGAIN— REVERSING LA OPERACIÓN

The Gomez family is headed by doña Margo and includes her daughters Lourdes and Gladys, and Lourdes's children, Lizzie, Luisito, and Roberto. This family differs from the Robles and Velez families in that Lourdes underwent a reversal sterilization. Her traumatic experiences with this surgery resonate with the lives of many poor women that have unsuccessfully attempted to have a child after having a tubal ligation. The Gomez family also highlights the complex relationships some women have with men and how men influence their fertility decisions. This case study also exemplifies how systems of reciprocity continue to operate among Puerto Ricans in New York as a cultural strategy of survival.

The Gomezes live a few blocks south of the Robles family in an equally poor but more desolate area. This part of the neighborhood has not changed much in the past twenty-five years. One of the few recent improvements is the allocation of federal funds to build two blocks of modest single-family houses, for which only a handful of the residents are eligible. Most of the residents in this community live in turn-of-the-century tenements that house six to eight families. In addition to this type of edifice, rows of gray, aluminum-sided, one-family homes comprise long stretches of drab, treeless blocks. Doña Margo owns one of these dwellings. Because she has always been enterprising, she bought the house twenty-five years ago; although it is old and needs repair, she is proud of it because she has almost paid off the mortgage.

The only amenities available in this part of the neighborhood are the intermittent bodegas that dot the locale. During the cold weather the streets are isolated and feel dangerous. As soon as the weather becomes milder, some blocks become hubs of activity, with people sitting on their stoops, children playing outdoors, and salsa and reggaeton music filling the air.

I met doña Margo in 1981, when she was sixty years old. In 2006 she was eighty-five. She was born in Puerto Rico and worked as a midwife. She had two daughters who lived in the neighborhood. Her story sheds light on the key role that some Puerto Rican women played in the survival of their families, and in the changing gender roles within the community.

Doña Margo: First Generation

Doña Margo was raised a Catholic but was also an avid believer in spiritualism. She was a clairvoyant and gifted healer from the age of fourteen. Like other women of her era, doña Margo assisted women at birth from a young age. At the age of ten, she helped her mother give birth to her sister. When she was fourteen, she started to work in a hospital. Doña Margo describes how she helped her mother deliver her sister:

> I learned through God's guidance who gave me the opportunity to do this. I predicted to my mother that when she was ready to give birth we would be alone and that I would help her, and that was exactly how that happened. When her labor pains began I massaged her to make sure the baby was in the right direction. A voice in my mind guided me. My mother was embarrassed, but I told her, open your legs because I know where the baby is coming from. Then I took the child out, she was half black. I took her by her feet and lightly hit her on her bottom. I wrapped her in a sheet. She was attached to the placenta, but I could not remove it until the midwife arrived. When my father came home, he could not believe that I had assisted my mother in giving birth. I worked as a midwife until 1952.

Doña Margo is a self-taught woman. She trained herself in many of the skills she has now. For example, by the age of ten she learned to sew on her own.

> I learned to sew by hand, making dresses for my little sister. My brother, who worked in a tailor's business, used to bring me pieces of cloth. I learned to cut cloth by watching my godmother, who was a skilled seamstress. She would give me a piece so that I could make something for my doll. I also learned to embroider in the same way. I embroidered the borders for handkerchiefs.

Doña Margo was more mature than other children her age. She prided herself on her ability to stay home and practice knitting and sewing while the other kids were playing.

> When I was growing up I never hung out in my neighbor's house; none of that for me when I was a girl. I learned to embroider and crochet as a young girl. I sewed dresses for the teachers. When I went to work for the Hilton

hotel I sewed men's shirts by hand for the tourists. I migrated to New York City when I was twenty-four. I arrived on July 11 and started working on July 12. In the mornings I worked in a factory in Manhattan sewing dresses and in the afternoon I worked in a different factory sewing men's sports jackets.

This skill served her well since it enabled her to find work when she migrated to New York.

Doña Margo had three years of high school, a higher level of education than most women of her generation and social class in Puerto Rico. She said she dropped out of high school in her fourth year because she could not afford to pay the tuition fee. Doña Margo wanted a better life—she was intelligent and street smart. For a few years she worked for a judge and, according to her, ran his office for him.

Doña Margo started to live with the judge in a common-law marriage at the age of fifteen. By the time she was seventeen years old, she had two daughters with him and was trained as a midwife. Because doña Margo grew up in a preindustrial society in Puerto Rico, she did not have access to birth control when she was growing up. As a midwife, she was eventually exposed to contraceptives, but, even in this capacity, she claimed they were not consistently available.

Doña Margo had an abortion after the birth of her second daughter because she became pregnant right away. Like other Puerto Rican women in this study, she was against abortions but felt it was a necessary evil. Although doña Margo was comfortable talking and joking about sex, she told me that this was a taboo subject with her mother and family when she was growing up. Moreover, this was also not a subject she ever discussed with either of her two husbands.

When I was a young girl I knew nothing about birth control in those days! After my first daughter, I went to clinics but it was far away and when I arrived they only had something for men. I didn't like that 'cause I wanted to be in control. Yeah, he'd say he would use it but sometimes he didn't and I would get pregnant. I would have used birth control if I had been able to get my hands on it, but sometimes there was none or the clinics were closed. My husband could have used a rubber but he wanted children. I had an abortion because what else could I do? I had just had two babies, one after the other, and here I was pregnant again! Abortion is a sin but sometimes a necessary sin.

In my time young women like me grew up innocent in the countryside where no one ever talked about sex. I met my first common-law husband when I was just a kid myself. I organized his office. I had my two girls with him. I suffered a lot with him. He was a womanizer. I caught him in bed with other women several times, and after putting up with his nonsense for more years than I care to mention I left for New York. When he saw that I was really leaving, he cried and begged me not to go, but it was too late. I left my two daughters with my parents and I went to New York by myself.

Doña Margo migrated to New York by herself in the 1950s, something not typical for women at that time. When she arrived, she temporarily moved in with one of her brothers; this, however, only lasted for a week. As doña Margo recounted, she was very independent and her brother wanted her to obey him. She then moved in with her sister, with whom she did not get along either, and shortly after she found a furnished room and moved out. Doña Margo felt her sister was selfish.

> Living with my family is like living with a bunch of animals, you never know when they are going to turn on you. I had my own mind and they were always telling me what to do. I first stayed with my brother, but I could not tolerate his moodiness. Afterwards I moved in with my sister but she started to bug me too. Just to give you an idea of what she was like, I froze my first winter in New York because I could not afford to buy a jacket. I wore several layers of sweaters to try and keep warm. My sister owned several jackets but never offered to lend me one. I figured I came to New York by myself and alone I will stay. I moved to a furnished room and kept sending my mother money.

Initially, doña Margo barely had enough money to survive by herself in New York, but she prided herself in sending her parents money to support them and her daughters. Without this money, her parents and daughters would not have been able to survive in Puerto Rico. Those who migrated, particularly those who left their children with their parents or other family members, had a strong sense of family obligation. These families practiced the age-old system of *hijos de crianza*, known as children by rearing. This is a cultural strategy that guarantees the well-being of children. It entails an informal understanding between adults that does not involve lawyers or any legal judicial intervention. In the Puerto Rican community (and other Latino communities as well), it is a common practice for children to spend a few months or years living with members of their extended families, especially grandparents. The poor have used this cultural strategy of survival to manage the distribution of scarce resources in the community and to provide their children with the best environment. Sometimes children may live in the same city as their parents, but, for financial or health reasons, their parents cannot take care of them. Then another family member will parent these children. In other cases children may move from household to household within the extended families as members migrate between Puerto Rico and the U.S. mainland.[1] As in doña Margo's case, when individuals migrate, remittances play an important role in supporting their children and other family members.

> Thanks to God as soon as I received my money for the week I had my envelope filled out for my parents and I'd fill out a money order that I would send them. I didn't want to mess around with their money, even if I didn't even have a nickel left to my name after I sent the check. Well at least the subway only cost a nickel at that time. A sandwich cost a quarter. I would buy myself a cup of coffee and a donut or whatever and that was my lunch.

Doña Margo was lonely in New York. A year after she was living in New York she met and moved in with her second common-law husband, Alfredo. A year later when she brought her parents and daughters to New York, she had already set up a household with him. Although this was a slightly unusual arrangement, doña Margo decided that her daughters would continue to live with her parents in a separate apartment she found for them, and she would continue to live with Alfredo. According to doña Margo, this was the best arrangement because the school that her daughters attended was closer to the apartment she found for her parents than to her own. Therefore, doña Margo's parents continued to raise her daughters Lourdes and Gladys.

Doña Margo was a good provider. After she brought her family to New York, she paid for their food and rent. Not only did doña Margo's parents raise Lourdes and Gladys; they also brought with them three other grandchildren they were raising in Puerto Rico, and doña Margo supported them as well. Doña Margo had a hard time supporting five kids and her parents by herself. In order to make ends meet, she worked in a factory all day sewing dresses, and in the evening she took on another job making sandwiches in a diner. Initially, doña Margo did not mind giving her mother money to support her brothers' and sister's kids. However, after a while she started to feel that her siblings were taking advantage of her. Doña Margo's mother was always very strict, and although doña Margo was now a grown woman supporting the entire family, she was afraid to tell her mother how she felt because it was considered disrespectful to question your parent's judgment.

> I sent for my parents to come to New York. They raised Lourdes and Gladys while I worked. I also supported three nieces because my mother was also raising some of her other grandchildren, too. I could not complain because in those days if a child lifted their eyes to look at their parent's face—there came the slap. I was afraid to tell my mother I couldn't do it anymore, so I found a third job working for a Sicilian family who owned their own factory. They hired me because they knew I was a talented pattern cutter and called on me whenever they needed me. The problem with that job was that they

wanted me to start working at 3:30 in the morning, so I was barely getting any sleep. I had three jobs, worked long hours, and earned very little money. Over the weekends I would even make *pasteles* to sell to neighbors, but I couldn't keep that up. One day I got really angry and told my mother that her other kids made children so that I would support them. It was too much for me to support all of these children. When my mother migrated there were seven of them including my two daughters.

A few years after doña Margo's mother came to New York she was diagnosed with cancer.

This was a horrible period of my life. Someone would call me from the hospital to tell me mother was in another crisis, and I drop everything and run to the hospital. I helped my mother till she died. Sometimes I even stayed with her overnight at the hospital and went straight to work from there the next day. It was hard for my father to manage on his own with the girls, although he did everything in the house from cooking to cleaning. After my mother died I started staying with my father and daughters at night. Alfredo moved in with us because he said he did not want either one of us to be alone. He treated my girls as if they were his own daughters. A few years later my father died of a heart attack. My daughters moved in with me.

At the age of thirty, doña Margo had a hysterectomy, which she claims was not medically indicated. Like doña Hilda, doña Margo's doctor told her that she had a fibroid tumor and that if he did not remove her uterus it could become cancerous. She was terrified of the idea of having cancer because she had just watched her mother die of it, so she accepted the hysterectomy without getting a second opinion, even though she had no symptoms, such as pain or abnormal bleeding, to indicate anything was wrong.

I was operated on in 1946. After the surgery the doctor told me that I did not have cancer. I was so relieved I thanked the Lord and did not ask any questions. It was only later that I realized that maybe there had never been anything wrong with me. Now I wish I could ask questions, but it's too late.

Doña Margo was also not sure about the kind of hysterectomy she had.

I guess it was a partial hysterectomy because I still feel like a woman down there, and if it had been a complete hysterectomy, I would not have any feelings. I know this because I went to a doctor's exam and the doctor touched me in my most painful spot [clitoris]. I was so embarrassed and mortified by the experience that I jumped off the table, got dressed and ran out of the doctor's office in a huff.

In addition to the hysterectomy, doña Margo had a mastectomy. She attributed her breast cancer to toxins she picked up when she was doing spiritual cleansings for other people:

> I have to do a mammogram soon because I still have one breast left. After they operated on it, it turned out that I didn't have cancer. Since I did spiritual cleansings, I may have caught something bad that one of my clients had. The doctors thought it was cancer, but it wasn't.

The experiences that doña Margo, doña Hilda, and other women in this study had with hysterectomies raises the question of why women who are so assertive in other parts of their lives appear to accept doctor's diagnoses and authority so passively. In doña Margo's case, the contrast is striking. There is no doubt that doña Margo is a resourceful and assertive woman. As a child, she was self-taught and self-disciplined. She migrated alone to New York and opted for her independence over living with a brother and sister when they tried to control her life. She found and juggled multiple jobs, brought her parents and daughters to New York, found a new relationship, and cared for her parents until they died. Yet, when faced with a medical dilemma like the possibility of cancer, she acquiesced to the doctor's recommendation.

This is a complex issue because on a certain level these women are assertive and on another level they appear to act helpless. How do we explain this? In understanding doña Margo's and doña Hilda's behavior, it is important to contextualize their reactions within the broader framework of most people's fear of cancer. The way people handle their fears is influenced by their personality, socialization, and class background. It might be that they reacted like most poor people would react when a doctor tells them they might get cancer if they do not have a certain medical procedure—they panic and acquiesce. This does not mean that doña Margo's and doña Hilda's acceptance of these procedures shows that poor and working-class Puerto Rican women do not resist and fight back when they perceive they are being misdiagnosed or treated unfairly in the health care system. After all, doña Hilda refused to have a mastectomy after her first experience with the cancer scare. The poor rely strongly on word-of-mouth information from other community members who have had experience with a particular doctor or medicine. I believe their reaction was based on the fact that they did not know how to evaluate doctors or how to research medical information, and therefore relied on the doctor as the ultimate authority. Moreover, like the majority of poor women in this study, doña Margo did not know what a fibroid was or how to evaluate her chances of getting cancer from a fibroid tumor. In contrast, a middle-class person would more likely obtain a second and third opinion, find the best medical help they could pay for, and undertake research to find out more about their condition and medical options.

LOURDES: SECOND GENERATION

Lourdes is doña Margo's first daughter. I first met her in 1981, when she was thirty-one years old and lived in the north end of the neighborhood. She is now fifty-six and lives in her mother's house, which is located on the south end. Lourdes had a total of four children, but the first one died of crib death. Her first was born in 1972; Roberto, in 1974; Luisito, in 1980; and Lizette, in 1981. Lourdes was sterilized after her fourth child. However, several years later, she had a reversal operation, technically known as a tuboplasty, because she wanted to have another child.

Lourdes and her sister, Gladys, had a tense relationship with their mother, doña Margo. According to Lourdes, her life changed drastically after her grandparents died and she moved in with her mother and stepfather. She lived with her grandparents for fourteen years before she moved back with her mother.

My mom raised her nieces, too. She helped raise a lot of children. We moved in with her after my grandparents died. It was hard. She was not used to us, and we were not used to her. She worked in a factory. Now we had a stepfather. We had to tippy-toe around—don't get him angry. She wanted to hold onto him. We wouldn't make him unhappy. My mother still kept in touch with our father who lived in Puerto Rico. My mother was fearsome. I'm still afraid of her. She would get into these fits and throw cups out of the window.

Lourdes said that by the time she and her sister Gladys moved in with their mother and stepfather, her parents were involved with the illegal numbers game *la bolita*, a very popular form of entertainment and gambling among the Puerto Rican community, especially from the 1950s through the 1990s. La bolita is played by selecting a number and playing it "straight" or in "combination." To play a number "straight" means to bet on it exactly as it is. To play it in "combination" means to combine the digits for every possible probability. Most people play their numbers in combination in order to increase their chances of winning. The bets an individual places on la bolita are small, from twenty-five cents to a dollar. Women and men collect bets by phone twice a day. The winning numbers are printed in Spanish newspapers such as *El Diario/La Prensa*.

Numbers for bets are selected in myriad ways. Puerto Ricans "dream of the numbers." For example, they might literally dream of a number or associate a particular dream with a number. In *botánicas* they sell a numbers book where an individual can look up their dream and see what number it is associated with. Puerto Ricans also choose numbers based on a person's birthday, an anniversary date, a street address, a person's license, and so forth.

When a person wins la bolita, he or she is expected to share the money with their friends, relatives, and even with the person who placed the bet for them. If the individual refuses to share, they are stigmatized as being *tacaño* (stingy). One of the worst stigmas in a poor community is to be labeled as stingy. The family and neighbors pressure that person to share by gossiping about him or her and embarrassing them by making the person the butt of their jokes in front of them. Usually the individual who is not willing to share succumbs to this kind of pressure.

Lourdes's description of doña Margo's fascination with la bolita illustrates these points. "It was hard for my mother to make ends meet. Sometimes she even held three jobs. Maybe she found this was an easier way to make money. She also liked the excitement of the gamble." On occasion her mother shared what she won with her and her sister. This went on for many years.

> My mother and stepfather earned a lot of money. They played the illegal numbers game, la bolita. Sometimes she used to give me a $100 bill. Even my grandmother played la bolita. My mother was always trying to earn a living. I remember that they sometimes sold liquor shots and the numbers. That was just part of our culture. My mother worked for the Italian guy. I think my mother was doing this till last year when my stepfather died. I don't hear people talking about it like they used to.

Doña Margo had a difficult relationship with her mother, and she reproduced this with her own daughters. According to Lourdes, both she and her sister married early to escape the family home. Immediately after she graduated from high school, Gladys married because she no longer wanted to live under the same roof with her mother. She graduated from high school in June and was married in July. Lourdes also wanted to escape by getting married, but she was afraid of her mother's reaction. Therefore, she secretly married a student from Brooklyn College, Javier. By the time she told her mother, there was nothing she could do about it.

> I tried to understand . . . I understood that she had to work to support her family. We moved in with her as teenagers. She didn't know how to deal with us. She was so strict that I couldn't talk to anyone. If I asked her if I could go out she said, "Okay, you go out at nine but [you] have to be back by eleven." Even if I had been thirty she would have acted the same way towards me. Maybe I rushed into my first marriage. The marriage lasted five years. I stayed in the marriage 'cause he's my husband.
>   They treated me like I was a child. My mother is into spiritualism. I was terrified of her. I thought she would do voodoo stuff. I was twenty-two years old. On September 28, 1969, I got married secretly but didn't tell her to this

day. I met my husband at Brooklyn College. He was in the Vietnam War. I was nineteen years old—he was more or less my age. He would cry in the middle of the night. It was scary. My mother did everything for my sister's wedding and nothing for mine. She rented a hall or community center for fifty dollars. I had to make my own wedding gown. I told the priest, I'm already married.

Even though Lourdes did not plan to have a child immediately after she was married, she did not use birth control because she decided that if she became pregnant it was okay.

When I married Javier I knew a little about birth control but not really. Yeah, I've heard about it, but maybe 'cause I didn't think much about sex. My sister had the coil. The pill makes you gain weight. You have to take it everyday. What about the last row of pink pills? The last row is so that you don't get mixed up about when to start again.

When I got married I didn't use anything. I was married so it was okay whatever happens. I didn't plan to have a child right away or anything like that. I figured if it happened, it happened; we never really planned it. Like today a lot of people would say, we're going to get married, five years from now we're going to get a house, and then seven years we're going to have a baby. I just got married and that was it. I was married at twenty-two, and we were still going to school. I thought well maybe twenty-two is a good age.

Lourdes did not have a good marriage with Javier. They broke up after their first son was born.

I married Javier in 1972. I may have married Javier because my mother was so strict. As soon as we got married my husband distanced himself from me and there was no more sex. Yeah, we had not been married one week and he started to act this way. I got pregnant one night when he came home drunk. I was a nervous wreck because he started making my life impossible. Since we got married his friends said now you'll have a chain around your neck. We argued a lot, so I had a miscarriage. I was bleeding. Pregnancy test was negative. If I had it, I lost it. I bled for forty-four days. They did a scraping. The fetus looked like a white sausage. It was so big.

In 1972, Lourdes had a daughter who died of crib death. In 1974, she had a son. Javier was abusive to Lourdes even when she was pregnant. A month after their son was born, he threw her out of the apartment.

I had my first son in 1974. We separated a month after Roberto was born. You would think a son, but no it didn't matter. He wanted to be a bachelor. He tried to hurt me when I was pregnant. He would hide my keys. He'd stay out and come home at 1 A.M. He would twist my arms, put my face against the wall. He threw me on the bed when I was seven months pregnant. This might have affected Roberto. At the end of our relationship he threw me out of the apartment. Later he tried to convince me to come back. He promised he would change, but I had already made up my mind. I moved out. I tried, tried, tried but when I said this was it, this was it. I left and he didn't let me take anything.

Although Lourdes did not have a good relationship with her mother or Javier, she felt her fortune changed for the better when she found and moved into a five-room apartment in the northern part of the neighborhood. The super of the building was a kind woman who had also experienced a lot of hardship in her life and treated Lourdes as if she were her surrogate daughter. In contrast, doña Margo was not supportive of her daughter. Even though doña Margo was not happy that Lourdes married Javier, she was angry with her when their marriage ended.

> After Javier and I split up, I met this wonderful woman, doña Ofelia. She was my main source of support when my children were little. She was the super of a building I went to see after Javier threw me out. Another couple saw the apartment before me, but she gave it to me. She helped me so much. She was so patient. She was like a second mother to me—always watching over me. We both suffered from headaches. She would say to me, sit here for fifteen minutes. God puts good people in your path. Roberto's father was mean. After we separated he kept calling me and saying: you're never going to make it in this world. He would call to tell me this instead of talking to his son.

After moving to the northern end of the neighborhood, Lourdes went to college and worked for several years before she met a Dominican man who fathered her two other children.

> A few years later I met the father of my other two children. I never married him. He would come over; we would talk—that was it. This went on for one and a half years. After one and a half years I said, wooo, this man never tried anything. I had sex with him one night and I got pregnant with Luisito. Second time got pregnant again with Lizzie. I only went to bed with him twice. Lizzie looks nothing like him. He lied about his age. He was four or five years younger than me.

When Lourdes was pregnant with Lizzie, the father of her child went to the Dominican Republic and married another woman. Even though she searched for him after he returned to New York to elicit his help for his children, he was a deadbeat father who did not recognize his children. This was a rough time for Lourdes and her children.

Lourdes's mother, doña Margo, was furious with her for having two children out of wedlock. She was so upset she did not talk to her daughter for a long time.

My mother never helped me. After I got pregnant she told me, don't show your face around here or I'll kill you. Luis and Lizzie were still wearing pampers. She was drinking Similac and he was drinking milk. After a while I started to see my mother and sister again, but only because I went to visit them—they never came to visit me.

Lourdes's bad relationships with men influenced her decision to get sterilized as a way of resolving her immediate problems. Equally important, she had achieved her desired family size, was familiar with la operación because her sister Gladys and her friends had already been sterilized, and it seemed like the right thing for her to do. Her doctor also recommended tubal ligation after her third live child because she had delivered her three children through caesarean section.

I was sterilized because I already had four children, and so I thought, I was like thirty-one, okay, I'll have it done. Who knew that the day I was going to give birth to Lizette, she would turn around and I would end up with a breech birth. The doctor I was seeing was on her way. The doctor who examined me told me my daughter was breech, and she said she was going to do a C-section no matter what. I had my first baby normally. The doctor did not want to put me to sleep. They tried to numb me from the waist down, but it didn't work. I had no pains but I knew I had contractions so that's why the doctor thought Lizette was in danger, and the doctor didn't want to wait. The doctor was impatient. They said just give her a few minutes. The doctor said I couldn't wait a few minutes. But then finally my legs got numb. My sister was with me for the whole thing. They didn't want to put me to sleep because if there was something wrong with Lizette they needed to consult with me.

At one point I was going to change my mind because I was having contractions for Lizzie, but I didn't feel anything so they thought she was in danger so they hooked me up to a machine. They asked me if there was anything wrong, did I still want them to sterilize me? At that moment I said just do it. I didn't think she wasn't going to make it so I said just do it.

After Lizzie's birth Lourdes returned to school. It was also hard to make ends meet with three small children. In order to keep her job as a nursery school teacher she had to go back to school and earn two master's degrees.

After Javier and I separated I kept on going to school. My minor was Puerto Rican Studies. I wanted to be a lawyer, physical education teacher, and an elementary school teacher. I majored in bilingual education. I went to work in a day care. I was the teacher. I worked there for two years.

In five years I was told I had to get a master's. I went to school full time and I earned a low salary of $175 every two weeks. I went to City College twice a week, from four to eight at night. I didn't get home till 11 P.M. My neighbor doña Gloria had one child, and my other neighbor doña Ofelia had the other two. I did this for two semesters. Doña Ofelia took care of me. I didn't have time to read, wasn't interested in reading. I don't know how I got A's and B's. I only read my notes. I wrote papers. I'd get up at 1 A.M.; I only slept four hours a night. All the kids slept with me. I gave them bottles, sang to them, that's it. Never had time to read a book. I am not saying I never read. That was for my first master. In order to get a raise I had to get a second master's in science. If I didn't, they threatened to lower my salary.

Lourdes needed childcare but could not afford it, and her mother, who could have been her greatest source of support, refused to help her. Lourdes was lucky that she found such strong support from the super of her building, doña Ofelia. Doña Ofelia encouraged Lourdes to go back to school, and she arranged childcare for her in the building. She personally took care of Lizzie and Luisito and convinced one of her other neighbors and lifetime friends, her next door neighbor doña Gloria, to babysit for Roberto, who was a bit older by now. In Lourdes's words, "doña Ofelia was a godsend because she was kind, supportive of my educational goals, and helpful in every way she could be." In addition Lourdes felt blessed because she had a wonderful coworker, Mrs. Crumb, an African American woman who offered to babysit for Lourdes's children whenever she needed a breather. Lourdes's story is a good example of the role that informal childcare networks based on systems of reciprocity among friends, neighbors, and coworkers play in enabling poor women to attend school, to work, and to provide each other with the support system they need.

After she was sterilized, Lourdes did not date again for several years. She worked full time during the day and went to school full time at night. Eventually she met Richard, an African American coworker. They dated for nine years. After the first two years of their relationship, she decided to have an operation to reverse her sterilization because Richard did not have any children and she wanted them to be a family. Lourdes admitted that she was never totally satisfied with their relationship. Yet she persisted with Richard because she did not feel she had many options.

You know what it was. I had the three kids. I didn't want to start again with somebody else. So I'm trying to stay with him because my kids already know him.

Our relationship didn't work out either. I now know he led me on. After one year, I should have said, what's going on? He would say we are engaged without an engagement ring. I don't like to lie. I like people to tell me the truth. Then, at the end, I had to put up with his flirting right in front of my face?! I had three kids. I don't want to start again with another man. Am I cheap or what? That is why I tolerated this.

Like hundreds of women who have undergone the sterilization reversal operation, Lourdes wanted to have a child with her new partner as a way of solidifying her relationship with him.

After I started seeing Richard I figured he doesn't have any children. I heard you could have a reversal—I was still in my thirties and they said it was microsurgery. You know being that I was with him and I had three, I thought that having one from him was like ours.

While Lourdes was with Richard she had a tubal reversal surgery, laparoscopy, to try and have another child. A laparoscopy consists of the reconstruction of the fallopian tubes after a woman has had a tubal ligation. However, like most women, Lourdes did not realize how complicated having a reversal operation would be, what it entailed, and how small her chances of having a full-term pregnancy were.

Lourdes's friend referred her to a doctor who had corrected her own infertility problem due o a fibroid tumor. Lourdes could not distinguish between an operation for a fibroid tumor and a reversal for a tubal ligation. According to Lourdes, the doctor reassured her that she and Richard would be able to have children again after the tubal reversal, but he did not explain the risks associated with the reversal surgery.

We talked about it, Richard was there, and he said, "Yes, we put back your tubes through microsurgery," and, yeah, yeah, yeah, you get pregnant, and that's it. Instead of microsurgery he performed a regular C-section. I thought that micro meant that the surgery was going to be small.

Because Lourdes was under the impression that microsurgery meant that the surgery would be minor, she was not psychologically prepared to cope with what turned out to be another major abdominal incision, equivalent to another C-section.

I said okay, micro being small, no problem, they're going to do a little incision . . . but no, maybe what they do inside is small, but on the outside it was another C-section. Because they cut so much of my tubes when they first did it, they had to attach a lot. I was thinking about an in vitro-fertilization, when they do the baby outside, but that costs a lot, and I could not afford it.

I was really surprised [*an ironic half laugh*] when I discovered that my whole C-section had been opened up again. It's ironic 'cause my other doctor told me I had to get operated on because it was dangerous for me to have another caesarean. This C-section was very painful because I did not have the bikini-cut, I had the long scar that makes it very painful to sit up. But being that I had the other two C-sections, I kind of knew how to get out of bed. The first time it was harder.

In addition to the pain Lourdes endured from the reopening of her previous caesarean scars, she was not prepared for the horrific pain she experienced from the test they performed before the surgery to make sure that she was still ovulating.

Somebody mentioned they had an operation to have another child and said I could actually do it. So, okay, then I had to go to the doctor and they had to test my ovaries. They had to cut a piece off each side. It was painful because they don't put you to sleep or anything like that. They put this long thing that cuts inside of you. They had those things, what do you call them, when you go every six months, what do you call them? Ahhhhh. They put the clamps in me and then they put that thing in there, then they had to cut a piece. I guess the ovaries on each side. OHHHHH my God, it was unbearable pain. I had to tell him to stop, stop. I don't know if they realize, but for certain things they should give you a local anesthesia, you know what I mean!

Lourdes had the sterilization reversal operation performed over the Christmas break so that she would only miss one day of work. She became pregnant five months after her reversal operation. However, she miscarried a few weeks later because she had an ectopic pregnancy.[2] Lourdes had three ectopic pregnancies in a year and a half. In her words,

I got pregnant five months later; everything was okay . . . at least in the beginning I thought everything was okay. I was excited because I was really going to have a baby. I was getting a little bit big and then all of a sudden, I am at work and I get a sharp pain—I go to the bathroom and I'm bleeding. Richard works there, too, so I say, "Richard I have a sharp pain and I am bleeding." So I go to the hospital, but I'm not thinking anything, you know. So I go to the hospital, and the pain is there and everything—then they find out it's an ectopic pregnancy. Okay, so now they have to give me another C-section. This was hard 'cause it was a C-section with all the pain but without a baby. They saved the tube. I don't know how they did it, but they took the baby out of the tube and the tube is still fine. Okay, then six months later I get pregnant again, and . . . the doctor started checking me—okay, you're pregnant—so now they were watching me. Then they start checking my blood, but the count is going down. So they wonder, you're pregnant, where is it? Is it in the tube again? Okay, your pregnant, I'm happy, where is it? So then that one I believe they did a scraping. That one just came out; I did not have to have surgery again. Another one they had to do a D and C. For that one I had to tell them I have a heart murmur. I had to tell them because for that one they had to give me antibiotics before anything. Even before I go to the dentist to have my teeth cleaned, I have to have antibiotics. They were surprised I had a heart murmur; they had to put an IV 'cause they didn't know, and they did not ask me that. After that I was afraid to try anymore, 'cause, that's three times. Okay, your pregnant, oh happy, where is it? That used to scare me. I would get pregnant, and the baby would start deteriorating in the tubes. I don't know. Maybe these tubes are like a hairline or whatever, and they start deteriorating. I don't know why it happened. It is so disappointing to go through all of this and you still can't have a child.

Lourdes's experience with the reversal operation was typical of other poor women. She became pregnant several times but was never able to carry the pregnancy to term. Because she was not initially aware that an ectopic pregnancy was one of the risks associated with having a tubal reversal, she kept trying to get pregnant again. After her third ectopic pregnancy and miscarriage, Lourdes finally gave up. She was sorry she had subjected herself to more surgery and the heartache it involved without the reward of having a child. "He said if we put your tubes back they were going to be like they were before. I do not remember him telling me about an ectopic pregnancy. I did not even know what that was. I never thought that anything would go wrong. I did not ask and they did not tell me. I figured they put the tubes back in, and, you know, you're fine."

Lourdes did not ask about the risks of the reversal operation, and her doctor did not provide her with the medical information she needed to make an informed decision. The doctor failed to inform Lourdes that the risk of ectopic pregnancies for women who have a reversal operation increases from 11.4 per 1,000 (for nonsterilized women) to 18.5 per 1,000 for women who attempt to have their tubal ligations reversed (Stead and Behera 2007, 205–206).

Even though Lourdes has a higher level of education than most of the women in this study, she thought that conception meant she was going to have a full-term pregnancy. Lourdes did not know how to investigate this procedure for herself. She believed what the doctor told her, trusted his knowledge and authority, and assumed that microsurgery meant minor surgery. Because of this confusion, she unwittingly subjected herself to a more significant and painful operation than she had expected. Had she been aware of the true scope of the surgery, she felt that she would not have chosen to have it.

Lourdes and Richard had a complex relationship. Although Richard and Lourdes did not break up immediately after her ectopic pregnancies, after a while he made it clear to her that he felt differently toward her by openly flirting with other women at their workplace. In time, Lourdes became a Jehovah's Witness and felt that her religion gave her the strength to leave him.

GLADYS: SECOND GENERATION

I met Lourdes's sister Gladys in 1981, when she was thirty-three years old. Gladys had a high school diploma. She married at the age of seventeen, and by the time she was twenty-five she had had seven pregnancies and four children. Gladys gave birth to twin boys when she was eighteen. Her second child was a girl who was born in 1972, and her last child was also a daughter born in 1981. Gladys was sterilized after she had four children and three miscarriages.

Although there were a number of factors influencing her decision, one of the primary reasons Gladys was sterilized was that her first husband, the father of her children, was an abusive man.

> We were married for seventeen years. Things weren't good from the beginning but got worse once I found he was with another woman. He wouldn't help me with the kids. Not only did he not help me financially, he hit me. That's when I went to workshops on abuse. I got up and said, "I'm sorry, you're not going to hit me again." My love started changing. He would deny it all the time. These workshops really opened my eyes.
>
> No more. It's hard. You have to do everything on your own. When I started working, that's it—I was on my own. Take care of my kids. Make sure my kids had everything that they needed. That was it. I left with my four kids. I lived in two and a half rooms with a kitchen to share. Okay. But my kids had food on the table.

Even though Gladys's mother, doña Margo, was aware that her daughter's husband was an abusive man, she did not want Gladys to leave him. A few other women in the first and second generations felt that it was better to stay with the husband whose faults you are aware of than to take a chance finding someone who might be worse than him, who, as doña Margo pointed out, might abuse your children.

> Yes, my mother said you can't leave him because he is your children's father and maybe you'll meet someone who will abuse your children. I said, I'm sorry, pero [but] I have to think of me because when my kids leave, who am I going to stay with? Am I going to be alone? You think their father was there for me? My son was fourteen years old and he had an accident. He was

fourteen and my daughter was nine. My other two boys were in the service. Remember, they were seventeen years old. My second husband was the exact opposite of the first. He was always there and he used to help me. I didn't have to shop for groceries, I didn't have to clean, and he didn't want me to do nothing. I was blessed because my second husband used to do everything for me. I told him I was going to be alone with my kids. He answered I did not have to be afraid. I'm your mother and your friend, whatever you want.

Like Gladys, many women in the survey cited problems with birth control as one of the reasons they were sterilized. For example, Gladys, like her sister Lourdes, was sterilized because the temporary methods of birth control she used before getting sterilized made her feel ill.

I took the pill for a month or so but stopped because it was making me sick. Then I had the loop. My husband never used condoms because lots of hombres Hispanos no le gusta usar condoms [Hispanic men don't like to use condoms]. Even now my husband who is so good to me in other ways won't use them.

Gladys's familiarity with tubal ligation predisposed her to la operación. She learned about la operación from her mother and friends.

A lot of friends of mine had abortions before, and as I said, I don't want to take no more pills and I don't want to have no more kids. The loop is not safe. The doctor examined me. I was getting my period. He said wait a minute let me check you again. So when he checked me again he said all right get dressed, get ready. So when I came home about an hour later, I went to the bathroom and I was bleeding. I felt uncomfortable. Then I had to go to the bathroom again. When I went to the bathroom the babies, they came out. That's when I called my mother. I was crying. They took me to the hospital. I still had a baby inside. The doctor examined me with those thongs scissors— those long things. He did a scraping that night. The next day I went home. That was, oh my God . . . I saw the baby, it was this big thing (gestured with her hand). Yeah, I was in shock, seeing that put me into another world.

Gladys's miscarriage reinforced her decision to get sterilized. Gladys's second husband was younger than she was and did not have any children of his own. In contrast to her first husband, he loved and respected her, and treated her well. He wanted her to have a reversal operation so that they could have a child together. However, Gladys secretly had Ricardo's sperm tested and found out that he was sterile. Because she did not want him to feel badly, she lied to him and told him she was the one who could not have children. However, had Ricardo been fertile, Gladys would have attempted (or at least would have considered) the reversal. She thought that because she had clips on her fallopian tubes rather than having her tubes "cut" like her sister Lourdes she could have this operation reversed whenever she desired. In her words, "My tubes were not cut. I have rings on them. The doctor said I could take them out anytime and have a baby. It's when they cut them that you can't get pregnant. They cut my sister's so much that when she wanted to have one she couldn't."

However, Gladys's chances of a successful post-reversal pregnancy were unlikely to have been significantly better than Lourdes's. The surgery she had involved cutting as well as clipping and is equally irreversible. This is an example of the way that colloquial terminology often obscures the actual details of medical procedures. Even though Gladys worked as a health aid in a grammar school, she was no more informed about sterilization than her sister.

LIZZIE, ROBERTO, AND LUISITO: THIRD GENERATION

Although Lourdes is an ambitious and upwardly mobile woman, her children, Lizzie, Luisito, and Roberto, have struggled. Lourdes worked long hours when they were young, and all three children grew up without a father. Under these circumstances, they had difficulties, particularly in adolescence. Lizzie and Luisito's father abandoned them when they were born. Both joined a gang, the Latin Kings, when they were thirteen and fourteen, respectively. Luisito only spent a year with the Latin Kings because, as Lourdes remarked, he was not cut out for a gang. He went back to school and studied for his GED.

In contrast, Lizzie remained with the gang and ran away from home when she was thirteen years old. Lourdes searched for her daughter for a year, and after she found her she put her in a juvenile delinquent's home. This was a difficult time for Lizzie and her mother. Lizzie was angry with her mother because she felt that by putting her in a home Lourdes used a double standard on her that she did not apply to her brother. However, on a certain level Lizzie recognized that their behavior was not equivalent. In her words, "I was cutting classes and my attitude was terrible. I don't think my mother could handle me anymore." After several months of being in the delinquent home, Lizzie moved in with her Aunt Gladys, who had accepted responsibility for her. Once again, we see the importance of family members taking responsibility for caring for children when arrangements in the child's nuclear family home are not working.

In time, Lizzie moved back into her mother's house and tried to make things right between them. She earned her GED and hoped to go to college and major in English. At the time I interviewed Lizzie, she and Lourdes were still trying to resolve their history. They both wanted to have a good relationship with each other but were not sure how to accomplish this.

Lourdes discovered that Lizzie had a boyfriend when she was thirteen. By this time Lourdes had converted from spiritualism to being a Jehovah's Witness, which influenced her approach to teaching Lizzie about birth control and sexuality. Lourdes recalls, "When we did our Bible study, we discussed things like that when the sister came. They talked to them about fornication. We went into certain things like peer pressure. When Lizzie was thirteen I found out she had a boyfriend. We talked about dating and marriage. That's basically the way we handled it."

Although Lourdes thought this had been a satisfactory sex education class, Lizzie told me she was not satisfied with it. When I asked Lizzie who she felt she could talk to about birth control and sex she responded, "My girlfriend, my aunt. Yes, I feel I can talk about sex, but not with my mother." She remembers having received sex education in junior high school and learning about sex by talking to her girlfriends and her ex-boyfriend.

Lizzie learned about birth control from her girlfriends. At the age of twenty-four she started taking Depo Provera, or "the shot" as she referred to it, as her primary method of birth control. A female health provider recommended it to her at the Health Insurance Plan of New York clinic she uses. Lizzie prefers the shot because she only has to take it once every three months. I asked Lizzie if she ever tried other methods of birth control and she said no, with the exception of the condom. She said she had never tried the birth control pill because she had a bad memory and would forget to take it. The only other contraceptive she has tried is the condom.

Lizzie's views about marriage, family size, and abortion differ from those of her mother and grandmother. Lizzie stated that her mother always told her to get married before having children. From her perspective, "My mom is old-fashioned. She always said get married and then have a kid." But Lizzie has her doubts.

I think it would be better that way, but you can't always get what you want. I watch my brother and his wife, and I wish I had what he has. They've been together for about three years. But then my mom had my brothers and me and she never married. It's hard to get that because most guys don't want to get married. So it's kind of hard. I would like to get married.

In talking about her parents' relationships, Lizzie commented:

It doesn't make a difference that she did not marry my father, because if she had, she would have gotten divorced. She raised us all by herself. She did an all right job. We got to meet our father and he was a real jerk. I still want to see him, but I don't know where he's at.

My father was a real jerk. He wouldn't see us. Mom took us to the store where he worked and she would make a scene. Every time she made a scene he would try and hide. He would tell people to tell us that he wasn't around when we had seen him. I was thirteen at the time. That's when I ran away with my ex-boyfriend, and that was it.

Although Lourdes clearly values a traditional family structure, and Lizzie clearly feels that one should not marry an unsuitable man, both take a pragmatic stance toward relationships and single motherhood. Their emphasis may differ, and these differences reflect generational change, but there are underlying similarities. Both would like to have (or to have had) a marriage with a good man. Yet both are, in some way, more oriented toward children, and they are not afraid to raise children on their own.

All of her girlfriends, Lizzie says, already have children. Many are troubled. "These girls are out of school and on welfare. The money they get, they spend it on drugs. They don't spend it on what they really need. I know that my friend, her kid's father is in jail. So how is he going to help her? And she's not helping her kids herself. She's outside partying." Lizzie helps her friends by cleaning the children, feeding them, playing with them. She knows that at least some of her friends envy her for having waited to have children. "Like when they ask me how many do you have, I say I don't have any kids yet 'cause, I'm not ready, they say you're so lucky."

Yet Lizzie does want to have children eventually. She would like to have one child, preferably a daughter. She contrasts this with her mother, who wanted a larger family of three children. Once she reaches her desired family size, Lizzie told me she would consider la operación. Like her mother, she believes that if she has her tubes tied she can have children again, but if she has them cut it is a permanent operation. Lizzie believes that her mother would like for her to have a child, and she feels that her mother would be supportive if she became pregnant because she wants another granddaughter. Her oldest brother Roberto also encourages her to have a child.

Lizzie has not dated very much but became involved with a young man who was jealous and possessive. He beat her up after she left him. Lizzie retaliated by having a couple of her friends beat him up. After that incident, Lizzie went to live in Florida for one year. She was motivated by two factors. She wanted to let things cool down in the home after her bad experience with her ex-boyfriend. And following in her mother's footsteps, she wanted to help her oldest brother, Roberto, who lived in Florida with his son.

Roberto, who is Lourdes's eldest child, moved to Florida five years before I met Lizzie because his girlfriend became pregnant and she relocated there. Roberto followed her because he wanted to be available to his son—to be the father that he did not have. When Roberto first moved to Florida, Lizzie accompanied her mother on several trips to visit him and help him set up a home. Even though his relationship did not work out with his girlfriend, Roberto stayed in Florida to be a part of his son's life. He found a job as a security guard. After several years the company decided to relocate to another state. He refused to move with them and was fired. Roberto was depressed when Lizzie went to visit him. Lizzie admired her brother's resolve to be a part of his son's life. She was determined to find a good man herself, someone with whom she could have a serious, lifelong commitment.

In 2006 Luisito was twenty-seven years old and had a single child with a lovely young woman of German descent, Lonnie. They moved in with his mother and grandmother in order to save for their own home. Luisito explained they had not planned to live there long, but with the high cost of real estate, even in the outer boroughs like Brooklyn, it was taking them longer than they had expected to save money for a down payment.

Luisito and Lonnie wanted to have another child, but Lonnie was a stay-at-home mom and Luisito did not earn enough money as a doorman to support a family of four. Lourdes felt pressured by the situation because she buys the baby diapers, baby food, and other necessities. She feels that as Luisito's mother she has to help them out. In a similar way that doña Margo supported her entire family, Lourdes pays for all of the food and rent for everyone.

Luisito plans to have a vasectomy, but he wants another child first. He and his wife laughed nervously when we discussed sterilization because of the fear some Puerto Rican men have about losing their virility if they have a vasectomy. They are familiar with the process because Lonnie's uncle had a vasectomy. In Luis's words, "If I had a son I would definitely have a vasectomy. Some men think it's going to take away their manhood but ahhh . . . [laughing]. Nah. I would do it."

Luisito, like his brother Roberto, considers himself a super dad. This means that he is involved in the daily care of his daughter. Indeed, Lizzie often spoke of how difficult it was to find a man who would be as good a father as her brothers are, and how she wished for the type of family Luisito had. Luisito is another example of a younger Puerto Rican man becoming involved in fertility decisions. He is willing to take action himself to ensure that he and his wife maintain their desired family size. Such individuals may be unusual, but they offer indications that some in the Puerto Rican community are beginning to question traditional gender roles.

By 2007 Luisito, Lonnie, and their daughter Esmeralda moved out of Lourdes's apartment. They now have their own apartment, and in addition to working as a full time guard, Luisito is exploring the music industry as a talent scout for reggaeton and hip-hop music. At this point, Lizzie lives alone with her mother. Although Lourdes and Richard broke up a long time ago, she takes care of him now that he has had a stroke.

SUMMARY AND ANALYSIS

The story of the Gomez family demonstrates the persistence of misunderstanding about reproductive surgery (particularly la operación and its reversal) across generations. It is also an example of the role that men play in influencing women's decisions about fertility and relationships.

Lourdes's story shares some common features with her mother's. She was sterilized but had the reversal operation mostly because she did not understand the risk of ectopic pregnancy and because she did not know how to ask the right medical questions. She also attempted reversal because of her idea of what "being a family" meant in the context of a relationship with a new partner.

Difficult relationships, however, in more direct ways can influence women's decisions to get sterilized. Lourdes was in several troubled relationships. Her marriage was troubled, and Lizzie and Luisito's father treated her unkindly. Lourdes was an excellent mother and person and consequently used sterilization as a last resort to gain control over her life.

Gladys, Lourdes's sister, is a successful example of a woman who has been a victim of domestic abuse and removed herself from that situation. She was sterilized after she had four children in this relationship. Even though she was raised in a home where sex was a taboo subject, she transcended that way of thinking and advocated for children and women.

Lizzie has not had any children but wishes to have one child if she can find a good man like her brothers in the near future. Although Lizzie also wants a stable and long-term relationship, she is ready to have a child on her own with her mother's help if she does not meet the right partner. Lizzie plans to get sterilized after she has one child.

Roberto and Luisito are sweet and gentle young men who love their families and their sons. They each have one child and are dedicated to them and their wives. In contrast to most of the men his age, Luisito is willing to consider having a vasectomy after he has another child.

The attitudes toward family demonstrated by Lizzie, Roberto, and Luisito have all clearly been shaped by their experience of abandonment by their fathers. The younger generation of the Gomez family seems determined not to repeat that experience with their own children, and this determination influences their approach to relationships and to fertility decisions.

Lourdes and Gladys used sterilization as a last resort to control their fertility after they achieved or surpassed their desired family size. Some women like Gladys see la operación as one way to gain a measure of control over their lives. For example, Gladys told me she felt good when she decided to get sterilized and leave an abusive relationship. However, although sterilization resolves the problem of unwanted pregnancies, it does not address larger issues in ther lives that are causing the problem. The stories of the second and third generations of the Gomez family illustrate the consequences of limited choices. Sometimes in exceptionally desperate circumstances a family will even resort to forcing one of its members to get sterilized. This is the case in the next chapter with the Morales family.

CHAPTER 6

The Morales and Rivera Families

TOUGH LOVE AND STERILE CHOICES

THE MORALES FAMILY

The story of the Morales family is a remarkable and unusual one. In fact, in all the years I have been doing research, this is the only time I have come across such a situation. Nilda and her husband, Enrique, with the aid of her parents, doña Caridad and don Guillermo, forced their youngest daughter, Millie, to undergo sterilization at the age of seventeen because she was a drug addict and was, in their view, having children irresponsibly. Millie's family arranged for her to get sterilized to mitigate the economic hardship of child rearing, substance abuse, and unwanted children. This family's story illustrates the power the Puerto Rican community's cultural beliefs about sterilization can have when a family in desperate straits uses sterilization because they do not perceive viable alternatives.

Doña Caridad: First Generation

Doña Caridad does not know the year she was born. She only recalls that she was born at the time of the small earthquakes. Her parents, like other women and men of their generation, had difficulty getting to town and so did not register their children's birth until several years later. Consequently, doña Caridad figured she was around sixty-four years old in 1981, making her approximately eighty-nine in 2006.

Like other women of her generation, she did not have access to birth control when she was a young woman. Consequently, after having four children by the age of twenty-six, she opted to have la operación for financial and health reasons.

In the old days women had thirteen or fourteen kids. There was no birth control except for la operación. Besides, they say birth control ruins your health. The Catholic Church wasn't against la operación. I had my tubes tied.

I got married when I was thirteen years old. I was very new.[1] My boyfriend was crazy, a very happy person. One day we had an argument. He got up on a mound near my window and started to sing, I'm going to take you with me. Since neither of us had any sense, I went with him. He took me to his aunt's house. She was alarmed to see me, but she let us stay.

My parents never let us go out alone, so I eloped. I knew my parents would not have given me their consent to marry him. In those days the older daughters had to marry before the youngest, and I was so immature. That marriage only lasted two months, because the war came and he was drafted. We split up because he was a ladies' man. He used to write to another woman who I knew. Besides, he drank rum, and my mother did not like him.

After we split up I started to work outside of the home. I worked as a maid in the home of a rich family, the Viñas. I moved in with them for several years, and I visited my parents on the weekends. One of those weekends I met Guillermo. I was nineteen years old. He saw me and fell in love. I did not accept him immediately because I was still a married woman. He visited me in my mother's home. My parents were very strict. Three years passed before we got together. When we got married we moved in with his sister.

Doña Caridad had difficult pregnancies. She was nauseous throughout each one.

After I married Guillermo I continued working. I ironed clothes for my neighbors and accompanied the sick to the hospital. I also cooked for them. Then I had my first daughter, Nilda. My second daughter was born one year later, Candida. Afterwards I had Mingo and then Fabian. I had one baby after the other. In total I had seven children, but only four lived. My life continued to change, you see. Sometimes I felt good, and sometimes I felt bad. We were so poor there was no work, no food, no medicine, life was tough. In order to work, my husband had to travel to the United States for a few months to work on a farm. He hated it. I'm not against birth control, but during that time there was only something for my husband to use, and neither of us liked it. On top of that I had *malas barriagas* [terrible pregnancies]. I use to get so sick I thought I was going to die. My husband's brother advised my husband to let me get sterilized; otherwise, as my husband said, "One of these days you are going to die giving birth." The doctor tied my tubes. Then the tubes became undone, and I became pregnant again. I had an abortion because I couldn't go through another pregnancy. After the abortion the doctor cut my tubes so that I would not have more children.

Doña Caridad and don Guillermo raised their children in Puerto Rico and lived there for most of their lives, except when they visited their children, who migrated to New York City.

Nilda: Second Generation

All of doña Caridad's children married and moved to the U.S. mainland. Of all her children, doña Caridad was especially close to Nilda. Following the same pattern as her mother in her first marriage, Nilda married Enrique, who was a womanizer, had a drinking problem, and was physically abusive. After Nilda left for New York, doña Caridad and don Guillermo visited them every year. Doña Caridad reminisces about how Nilda and Enrique met:

Nilda was fifteen years old when she visited New York for the first time. She spent the summer in my niece's apartment one summer. Even though she was young she wanted to work and knew how to sew, so her cousin arranged for her to get a job in a factory near where she lived. One day my niece took her to a party where she met Enrique. He pretended he was single, without any commitments, no other woman or children. When a neighbor called and told me and told that Nilda was in love, I made her come back to Puerto Rico at once. We didn't like Enrique from the beginning. He was too old for her. I advised her to forget him; her father even threatened to beat her if she did not break their relationship off, but she wouldn't listen to us. Enrique sent Nilda a letter to give to her father asking him for her hand in marriage. He kept writing to her for five years until he came to Puerto Rico, married her, and took her back to New York with him. I feel bad, bad, bad every time I remember that she told me she lost her first two babies because she fell in the snow. I only found out later he hit her because other people told me. He wouldn't dare hit her in front of me.

According to doña Caridad, Nilda had a hard life with Enrique indeed:

My daughter suffered with Enrique. He flaunted other women in her face. Once I was visiting her and he brought a woman to the apartment. It was early in the morning, and she was coming up the stairs behind him. I had looked down the stairwell and saw them. I closed the door so my daughter wouldn't see them, but it was too late. Nilda said to me, "Mami, get out of the way, you're always covering up for Enrique." She stepped out into the hallway and saw the other woman. She yelled, "Come on up, I'm waiting for you." You can't imagine how that woman turned around and ran. Enrique came upstairs and went to sleep; he had been working all night. That's how my daughter got AIDS; he kept hanging around other women until he got sick and made her sick, too. They both died. I'll never forgive him for that.

Nilda was a vivacious woman with a keen sense of humor. When we met in 1981 she was thirty-nine years old. She believed in birth control and had used several contraceptives. For example, during the first two years of her marriage, she used the pill but stopped after that because she felt it gave her varicose veins. She also used spermicidal cream and jelly. Nilda had several miscarriages before she was able to have her first daughter (prior to her marriage, she was not aware of an enlarged uterus that made it difficult for her to have children).

Her eighteen-year marriage with Enrique was turbulent. Whenever he drank, they would argue about his extramarital relationships, and he would hit her. Nilda's constant bickering and fights with Enrique about his infidelity aggravated her medical condition. It was only after her second miscarriage that her doctor discovered that the only remedy for her reproductive problem was complete bed rest during pregnancy. When she became pregnant first with Daisy and later with Millie, Nilda spent her entire pregnancy on the island with her parents until after she had the baby.

I was married at the age of twenty, *la desgracia* [my downfall], and sterilized at the age of twenty-five. I put up with my husband for eighteen years until he died of AIDS. He was a brutal man that had a drinking problem. When he drank we fought. He hit me, and I hit him back. On account of this, I miscarried twice. I had my first miscarriage because he refused to take me to the hospital when I told him I was in labor. By the time we arrived the baby had died.

I lost my last baby because we had an argument about a woman he was seeing and he beat me up so bad I ended up in the hospital. I told the doctor what happened and he felt bad. He said he was going to "cut my tubes," so that I would not have any more children from the bad husband that I have.

He told me to sign the consent form. When I asked him if I needed my husband to sign, he said no. I was in so much pain and in such a blind rage that I said okay without thinking about it. At the time I saw it as a way out of my problem and as a way to get even with my husband. Afterwards, I regretted it and cried. I would have liked to have another child; sometimes I still feel bad about this.

After the operation the doctor said to me, "I cut your tubes because I knew you did not want to have more babies. Your husband was a bad man." He thought he was doing me a favor. If it was now, and I had time to think about it, I wouldn't have done it. I would have tied them instead. I would have liked to have one more baby, at least a boy. I told my husband I did it and he accepted it because he knew it was his fault.

I would never tell a woman to have her tubes cut. I would advise her to have them tied instead. Or, to have an injection so that she does not get pregnant for a certain period of time.

A woman should not be operated on who is in a bad emotional state. They should give us a chance to think it over. I didn't go to the hospital with the intention of having my tubes cut. I did it because he recommended it, and I wasn't thinking straight. He didn't even give me time to talk to my husband. He told me I did not need his signature. He just gave me the paper and I signed it.

Nilda believed that a child was a gift a woman gave to her husband. Since her relationship was not working, it did not make sense to continue having more children with Enrique. But she regretted losing the opportunity to have other children in the future. Like most other women in this study, Nilda erroneously believed that if her tubes had been "tied" instead of "cut" she would have been able to have another child.

Nilda said she would have liked more children if her economic situation was better and if she had a good husband. Her ideal family size was four to five children. However, as Nilda told me, "If you have a lousy husband, you do not want to have more children because a child is a gift. The more children you have the more you have to put up with."

Nilda found out that the baby she lost was a boy and she told her husband because she knew it would hurt him since he wanted a son so badly. After this experience, Nilda continued living with Enrique. Their lives were turbulent and she was not happy.

Nilda's problems worsened when Millie, her youngest daughter, reached adolescence. She and her husband spent a lot of time at work, and there was no one around to supervise Millie or Daisy. When Millie was about thirteen years old she started to spend time with the wrong crowd, cut classes, stay out all night, and take drugs. Millie was out of control, and Nilda and Enrique could not handle her. Nilda and Enrique initially tried to solve the problem by sending Millie to Puerto Rico to live with Nilda's parents, doña Caridad and don Guillermo. They hoped that by separating Millie from her friends she might change. In doña Caridad's words: "Enrique called me and said Millie was going crazy and that I'd better take her before he broke her head. I told him it was his fault because he was so bad. They sent her to me."

It was not easy for doña Caridad and don Guillermo to help Millie, but after spending several months in Puerto Rico she stopped taking drugs. In doña Caridad's words,

Millie was confrontational when she arrived. She'd throw her clothes out of the window and get dressed downstairs. She even tried to push me around. I told her, Millie, you have to change. I can't slap you, but my son Pablito has a bad temper. You have to respect me, I'm your grandmother, and I love you. I kept working with her, and slowly she stopped taking drugs. Six months later her father calls me to say he misses Millie, and if she is better he wants her back home. Reluctantly, I sent her back and within two weeks she was on drugs again. I went to New York to see if there was anything I could do, but I could not get her to come back with me because Millie would disappear for long periods of time.

The situation worsened. In the next two years Millie became pregnant twice and gave birth to two baby girls, whom she gave to her mother to raise for her. Nilda tried to help her daughter get her life back on track, but the more she struggled with her the more Millie rebelled. At her wits' end, Nilda decided to have her daughter sterilized so that she could not continue to have children. Originally, Nilda took Millie to a hospital in New York to inquire if they would sterilize her there, but the doctor refused because Millie was a minor (sixteen years old). After several doctors turned her down, Nilda sent Millie to Puerto Rico to get sterilized.

In the beginning her grandparents did not want to sterilize Millie; they hoped to help her get out of her drug habit. However, when Millie continued to take drugs and fool around with men, they decided that la operación was the only solution. They took Millie to the same doctor who had sterilized doña Caridad, Millie's grandmother, when she was a young woman. According to doña Caridad:

We took her to get sterilized. If we hadn't she'd have five or six kids by now and what would we do? By the time she came to Puerto Rico she already had two daughters she had left with her mother. Who knows how many more children she would have if we hadn't had her operated on? I told Millie that she could not continue to have babies under these conditions. She did not listen to us and kept on running around with men. She would stare me in the face and scream, "Tu no me mandas [You can't tell me what to do]." We struggled for months with her.

I spoke to my husband, and he said, "Let's go see the doctor and see what we can do." My old doctor's name was Cordoni. When I saw the doctor, I gathered my courage and told him what was happening with our granddaughter. "Our granddaughter is living with us," I said, "and I'm going to bring her here to see what you can do." He asked me how my granddaughter was. Because she was underage, her mother had to sign a form. He told us to bring her to his office tomorrow early the next morning.

My husband got up at one that morning and told me to help dress Millie, "I'm taking her to the clinic." We hadn't said anything to Millie. She came home late that night as usual and was sleeping off a drugged stupor. I struggled to dress her; she fought me. I told her that if she didn't calm down, I was going to tie her up. She stopped fighting me. After my husband saw how upset Millie became when I was trying to dress her, he told me, "You stay home. I'll go alone, because if you're there when we get to the clinic, she won't want to go in."

The time passed by, one o'clock, two o'clock, three o'clock . . . my husband left for the clinic at about three because it was far away from where we lived. By the time they arrived at the clinic, the doctor was waiting. My husband told her she had to get operated . . . Even though she was a minor she did not have to sign anything because I had signed and her mother had signed. I think she was seventeen years old, I'm not sure.

The doctor did not refuse to operate on her. He was the same doctor who had operated on me when I was young—he knew we were a good family and doing the best we could for Millie. Everything was arranged. Later Guillermo told me, "I took her and by six in the morning she was in the operating room. They gave her an injection. Millie was calm."

I don't know if they tied or cut her tubes. Daisy should know. I don't know if she can have more children. But imagine, what else could we do? She already had two children and would have had more. If she had another baby, I would have taken it, but my husband said, "No, a crazy girl like her can't keep having babies and abandoning them." Daisy, her sister, adopted her two daughters. Millie had to accept that because she was a disaster. She was in such a bad state that she often even peed on herself. *Ay mija* [my daughter], I can't even begin to tell you what we went through with her.

Millie: Third Generation

I met Millie when she was seventeen years old in 1981. In 2006 she was forty-two. I met Nilda when Millie was seventeen and trying to get her sterilized in New York. This conversation took place in 2005, when Millie was forty-one.

I was seventeen when I was sterilized [*nervous laugh*]. I was operated on in Puerto Rico. I was confused. I went because I knew myself that I had to do it, because it was back to back I was getting pregnant, and I wasn't ready for that. I had two girls already, two years apart, and I didn't want to get pregnant again. Melody was a surprise, but not Melissa. I knew I was going to get pregnant with Melody. I didn't even know I was pregnant. When I had the baby it was too late. I realized that that wasn't going to happen either. I couldn't keep having kids. That was too soon, and I wasn't ready to have another kid. The father and I had broke up.

The first time my mother took me to the hospital in New York to get sterilized, the doctor told me I was underage. As a matter of fact, I think I went to a couple of doctors and they didn't want to operate me. Even though the doctors here refused to sterilize me, my mom didn't give up.

My grandparents took me to a private doctor in Puerto Rico, and they did it. I guess I knew I was going to get sterilized when I went to Puerto Rico. My mother talked to me about this when I was still in New York. I agreed to do it because I knew I was too young to be having kids. I wasn't ready to be having kids as it was. So I was, no way . . . you know, if they had not done that to me, God knows how many kids I might have [nervous laugh].

The doctor told me he was going to tie my tubes. They didn't tell me nothing else. I didn't ask. Like, nowadays, I say, wow, how could I have been so dumb and not asked, you know. Now, in order for me to find out, God knows, you know. Supposedly they just tied my tubes, not cut them. I asked the doctor, and he said that after so many years of tubes being tied something goes wrong and you have to do another operation. He told me, I forgot what he told me exactly, but he told me that after a while, so many years tied, you might need something else, a treatment.

Ricardo and I met in 1999 in a drug rehabilitation program. His father is Italian and his mother is Puerto Rican. He loves spaghetti and meatballs. He's so hard sometimes, but I love him.

I want another baby. I don't know, I just want a baby. I want a boy. My boyfriend already has a baby, but we want one together. I want my own baby and 'cause he wants a baby too. Both of us want a baby. Now I am forty-one. I feel more ready. I feel ready, but I'm insecure.

I do not regret that I was sterilized at seventeen. In a way, I'm thankful because God knows how many kids I would have now. I'm not angry at my mother or grandparents. Definitely not. I'm grateful, very grateful. I didn't raise my own daughters. Now, I want a baby. Sometimes I be lonely, but then I think about it—why am I going to bring a kid into this world, and it's like I'm so confused. But I do want one—that's for sure—but I don't know if I could have one. I hope I could.

I want to have another operation to have a baby, but I'm scared 'cause what if I can't have one. I say what if something goes wrong in the [reversal] operation. I'm scared to have that operation. I haven't set a date yet, but I'm planning to. I went to a clinic and he referred me to a hospital. He just told me he can't answer my questions because he knows there can be complications after so many years.

I don't think it will affect my relationship with my Ricardo if I can't have a baby, although he loves kids. He says we can adopt one, but it wouldn't be my baby. It's not the same. It wouldn't be mine and Ricardo's. Sometimes I think I'll wait for my grandchildren. I'm not thinking of having a baby for two years, but I'm scared to find out what kind of operation they did to me . . . you never know.

I remember how I was sterilized. My grandfather said, nah, that we were going to the doctor to get my operation. My mother told me, look, you are going to Puerto Rico to get your tubes tied because she don't want me to have no more kids. I was okay with that. I didn't have no problem with it.

Funny thing I didn't know my mother was sterilized. I didn't know that. I went to a private doctor. I guess if they hadn't taken me to a private doctor in Puerto Rico, they wouldn't have done it, because they figure young girls change their minds when their lives changes. I don't know why, but that shouldn't be that way. I think they should operate young girls depending on their reasons. I don't regret it.

Daisy had two miscarriages. She can still have a baby, so much new technology. Something is wrong with her uterus. She had used contraceptives, but I'm pretty sure she could still have a baby. Her baby was born and he passed away. That was sad. I'm sure if she goes to a good doctor, I'm sure she can have a baby, even if she has to be the whole nine months in the bed.

I want a baby real bad. Ricardo wouldn't mind having a girl, but I want a boy. I thought my girl Melodie was going to be a boy. Even if I had a boy now I'd still want another child. 'Cause the husband wants a baby. That's the reason I really, really want . . . I want a baby but that's more of a reason for me. 'Cause I know he wants one. It's not that I want a baby, 'cause he wants a baby. I want to give him a baby, 'cause I know he wants a baby so bad.

Millie clearly has complicated feelings about her sterilization. On the one hand, she claims to have been supportive of the decision and accepts her family's solution to what they saw as an untenable situation. But when she talks about her current relationship, she, like many of the other women in this study, emphasized the importance of a couple having a child together to cement the relationship and build a family. Her phrase "I want to give him a baby" echoes her mother's description of a baby as a gift to the father. Furthermore, since Millie's sister Daisy adopted and raised her two daughters, Millie has never really had the opportunity to be a mother. Like Lourdes, Millie is willing to reverse her sterilization in order to have another child now that her life situation has changed. Although she had trepidations that the reversal may not be successful, she is not informed about the risks of having an ectopic pregnancy either.

Daisy: Third Generation

Daisy is five years older than Millie. She is the dutiful daughter who remained emotionally close to her mother and secured a good job right after high school. Her super-responsible role in the family, along with her proximity of residence, provided her sister Millie with strong family support. Daisy lived with her parents until her early twenties, when she met and married Freddie. She moved to an adjacent neighborhood in order to stay close to her mother.

Daisy was married at the age of twenty one. She had her first child at the age of twenty-three. Daisy inherited her mother's fertility problems and, although she had a baby of her own, the child died a year later. She also had two miscarriages after her baby died. She did not have a problem using other methods of birth control, but she had only used Depo Provera because it was convenient and she was not aware of any risks. She had a supportive and happy relationship with her husband, and they did not have difficulty talking about birth control.

Daisy and Freddie officially adopted Millie's girls, and they raised them as if they were their own. When the girls were young, Daisy worked full time and her mother, Nilda, helped raise them as well. Daisy is an advocate of tough love, and she took this approach to dealing with her troubled younger sister. After Millie was sterilized, she returned to New York to live with her family. Sterilization, of course, had not solved Millie's emotional problems, and she stole from her own family. They pressed charges, and Millie went to jail for a few years. This was a tough decision Daisy and Nilda had to make, but they did not see another alternative.

After Millie did time in jail and stabilized in a drug rehabilitation program, she and her boyfriend Ricardo found an apartment within walking distance of Daisy's family so that she could see the girls every day. This traditional residential pattern (proximity of residence) strengthened the bonds between them by facilitating visiting and childcare. To this day, Millie continues to see her daughters and Daisy frequently. Doña Caridad travels to New York occasionally, although less frequently than she used to because of her age, and Millie and Daisy visit their grandmother in Puerto Rico whenever they can. They are a tight-knit family who love and look after each other. Some changes have taken place since 2006. Daisy and Freddie separated in 2006, and doña Caridad was placed in a nursing home because she became senile.

The Rivera Family

Clara is Nilda's first cousin. Nilda's mother, doña Caridad, is the sister of doña Esperanza, Clara's mother. Clara is doña Esperanza's oldest daughter. The Morales and Rivera families are tight-knit, with a strong sense of family obligation that has persisted across three generations. Their stories offer an opportunity to consider how the experience of giving birth has (and has not) changed over the generations, and to consider the impact of poverty—both in Puerto Rico and in New York City—on women's birthing experiences.

Doña Caridad and doña Esperanza are half sisters. In 1981 doña Caridad was sixty-four and doña Esperanza was sixty-seven. At the time of this interview in 1991 Dona Caridad was seventy-four and doña Esperanza was seventy-seven.

Doña Caridad and doña Esperanza grew up very poor in a small coastal town near San Guillermo, which is located on the northeastern part of the island of Puerto Rico. Their mother was a midwife, and their memories of childhood offer insight into the situation women in childbirth faced around 1914. Doña Caridad recalls: "My mother doña Esmeralda was a dedicated midwife. Even though she herself was extremely poor, she delivered babies whether she was paid or not."

Doña Esperanza recalls that the women in their community trusted Esmeralda more than they did the doctors. She said that once a doctor told a woman that her baby had died in her stomach, and her mother corrected him and told the woman the baby was fine. Doña Esperanza's mother was right. As doña Esperanza said, doña Esmeralda knew a lot about pregnancies because she also aborted unviable fetuses. Doña Esperanza continues,

> Mother suffered from hunger. Sometimes they came to get mami late at night and she had to leave at that hour. If they paid her, fine, and if not it was okay, too. My mother was very accommodating—day or night. She worked with pay or without it.
>
> My mother also took rotted kids out of women's bellies. My mother helped these women and these women trusted her more than they did the occasional doctor that came around. Mami also straightened babies in women's bellies before they had them.

Doña Esmeralda's background as a midwife was unusual because unlike other midwives she had received some training in a hospital. As doña Esperanza recalls,

> Mami took some classes at a health center. She used to examine urine samples. One time mami examined a woman. A doctor in the same clinic examined her, too, and my mother said to the doctor, *Mira* [look], I am telling you that this woman does not have a lump of meat inside, or cyst inside of her, she is pregnant. My mother knew. When nine months were up, they called her and that woman had a beautiful baby in her belly [*laughter*].

Doña Esperanza: First Generation

Doña Esperanza claimed that when she married, she and her husband were so poor they had no place to live. They moved in with her godmother when she was eight or nine months pregnant:

> I married when I was twenty years old. Initially, I had to live in someone else's house because we had no place to live. When I was pregnant with my first son, Roberto, I had to sleep on a hammock. I had this ball of stomach, and it felt like that baby wanted to come right out of me. Between that pregnancy, living in so much poverty it ruined my health. After I had Edward and Clara,

mami and my stepfather gave me a little shack they had bought. If it hadn't been for that *ranchito* [shack] I don't know what we would have done.

Like other women of her generation, doña Esperanza cooked, cleaned, and hauled water through the end of her third trimester of pregnancy and had her baby at home.

My labor pains started when I had come up a hill with a bucket of water. My husband called my mother. I wasn't scared, but I felt kind of bad. My mother came, but she had to leave late because I did not give birth and she had no one to take care of the children. I laid down at about six in the morning. I slept sitting up, otherwise I felt asphyxiated. I was home alone because since I did not have the baby my husband had to go to work. When my water broke, I stood up, covered myself, and went to the window and called out to my godmother next door. It's a miracle that the baby didn't fall to the floor. My godmother, who was looking out for me, heard me immediately and ran for help. When my mother arrived, the baby girl had already arrived. I laid down and I felt this pain that lifted me up to the sky and back down again. By the time she arrived my little girl was born. I couldn't move because I guess I had pushed too hard and the baby was born, but the pains continued. When mami arrived, she felt my stomach. She screamed, "Stay still, you have one more in your belly" [*doña Esperanza laughs*]. My Lord, I did not know what was happening since the second one didn't hurt. Then mami gave me a squeeze and a tug and pushed the other baby out.

According to doña Esperanza, the second of her twins was born in a thin sac. She said some people thought that was good luck, but doña Caridad thought it signaled bad luck for her sister. Doña Esperanza admitted it must have been bad luck, because both babies died within the week. "The boy died first and then the little girl. After I had the babies, they took me to the hospital with a fever."

After the twins doña Esperanza had five more viable pregnancies, practically one after the other, but she also had a turbulent relationship with her husband. As she told me, he was a *mujeriego* (a womanizer). Doña Esperanza left her husband before the forty-day abstinence period, *la cuarentena* (forty-day postpartum ritual), was over because she heard that her husband had betrayed her while she was pregnant. In her words,

We got back together and broke up again several times, and each time I got pregnant. I finally left him for good when I was pregnant from my last son, Eduardo, because I found out he had another woman and family. I had to work full time to take care of my children and help my mother, so I went to work as a maid in a rich woman's home. My mother was with them [her children] during the day, and I spent the evenings with them. It became too expensive for me to travel back and forth like that everyday, so the *señora* gave me a room with my own bed and dresser. She treated me like I was her own daughter. My kids lived with my mother, and I visited them Saturday and Sunday. I came back to work late on Sunday. Doña Caridad helped my mother raise my kids while I worked. We have both raised a lot of kids in our lives, and we're still doing it.

Clara: Second Generation

Doña Esperanza's daughter Clara was born and raised in Puerto Rico. She lived with her parents her entire life. In contrast to her mother, who married at the age of twenty, Clara married at twenty-nine, a relatively late age for a woman of her generation. Therefore, she had her first baby immediately. She and her husband were very poor and could not afford a regular apartment in which to live, so when they first came to New York, they moved to a room in the basement of a tenement on Manhattan's Upper West Side. Later they moved to a public housing project in Brooklyn.

I came to New York for the first time to visit my brother and his wife when I was in my mid-twenties. My brother lived in a seven-room complex where he rented one room. I came with my nephew Eddie, who was only seven years old at the time. I slept on the couch with my nephew and cooked in the owners' kitchen.

I met my husband Antonio that summer. He lived with his stepfather, mother, and sisters. My brother and Tonio were friends, and I met him when he came to visit my brother one day. We had a long courtship. I was so shy I didn't even look at Tonio. He use to bring me *novelitas*, short stories and like that. Sometimes we would go to the movies, but we were never alone together. My brother would accompany us because he knew Tonio was a very decent fellow.

After that summer I returned to Puerto Rico, and I was there for three years. We did not write to each other during that time. I never asked him for his address, and he did not ask me for mine. During that time my brother moved to New Jersey. One day he bumped into Tonio, who said he had been trying to find him to get my address. It was a happy surprise to receive a letter from him. We kept on writing to each other, and when Tonio saved enough money, he gave my brother my airfare, so that he would send for me. I came to New York to work and see Tonio. My brother now lived in New Jersey, so I was only able to see him on Saturdays, because we both worked during the week and my brother lived far from Manhattan. We continued visiting each other in that way until we were married.

When Clara was a newlywed, she did not use birth control because she, as well as her family, expected her to have a baby right away. However, after she had her first baby, she went to a family planning clinic.

I didn't use birth control because it was my first time married, and other women said birth control was bad for your health. They said the pill gave you cancer. I got pregnant in three months. That was the tradition then. When you married you had your first baby right away. It was only after I gave birth for my first child that I went to a family planning clinic. Yo no me quería llenarme de muchachos [I did not want to have one child after the other]. They prescribed the pill, but they made me sick, so the doctor fitted me with an IUD.

After we were married we lived in a basement with my in-laws. It was so uncomfortable. We lived in a small room with one bed, a tiny kitchen on the side, and the bathroom was located outside of the room, in the hallway. They eventually moved out and we had the place to ourselves. A year after I came to New York my mother moved here, too. She was living with another family member at the time. Before I gave birth we were robbed. That day I went out, and when I returned I found they had taken the few things I owned, an iron I received as a wedding gift and fifty dollars I had saved with great sacrifice. They even took the baby's clothes. All I had left was my wedding ring, and they didn't take that because I was wearing it.

That evening we were expected at my in-laws for dinner. I love rice with gandules [peas] and pork, and Tonio's mother had prepared a special meal for us. Even though they live kind of far, we took the subway and went to 118th Street on the east side of Manhattan where they live. We had to climb two flights of stairs because there was no elevator. When I reached the first flight I felt a pain, but I didn't say anything to Tonio. There was some confusion about when the baby was supposed to be born. One doctor said in March and the other April. It was a cold March day, and when we arrived it was snowing. When I sat down to eat, I felt a sharper pain this time. I didn't say anything to anyone. I went to the bathroom, and when I realized I was bleeding I told my mother-in-law and my mother, who was also there. My mother said to me, "Oh my God, I think you're on the verge of having the baby."

If they had not hurried and taken me to Metropolitan hospital I would have had the baby right there. A few doctors examined me, and I started to bleed even more. Those doctors were brutes. Then they told me they didn't have a bed for me, and they called an ambulance and took me to Flower [another hospital]. As soon as I arrived, they gave me an enema and they left me naked on the bed. When I looked, there were two doctors. I almost died. I was all by myself in a room with those doctors, Virgen Maria [Virgin Mary].

They had put me in a white robe, but they had to take it off because the robe was full of blood. I tried to cover myself, but I was in advanced labor pain that, ahhh, after a while, I didn't even care who saw me. Then a nurse came and put a robe on me and left me alone again.

After the enema I had to go to the bathroom, and I couldn't stand up from the bathroom afterwards. I was finally able to come back to bed and two doctors came in and put an IV in my arm. Before they wheeled me out, they put a phone in my hand and I started to say hello, and after that I don't know what happened until the following day. I didn't know if I had a boy or a girl. All I know is that I woke up vomiting. The nurse told me to get up and wash myself, but I was so dizzy that I could hardly stand. I kept falling sideways. I took a shower that same day, but I felt dizzy the whole time and no one helped me. After this experience, I was afraid of going back to the hospital when I was going to give birth again.

In the course of this research I have come across different versions of Clara's story. I found that many women, especially those in the second generation, were afraid of going to a hospital in the early stages of their labor because they feared they would be subjected to endless painful and humiliating pelvic examinations. They resisted this treatment by waiting until the last minute to go the hospital to give birth.

Clara learned from her experience. Even though she had heard that birth control was bad for a woman's health, after her first baby she went straight to a family planning clinic:

My daughter Gloria was four years old before I became pregnant again with Tony junior. I became pregnant with Junior when we moved into these projects. I felt more at ease here because we were doing a little better now than when I had Gloria. My mother was also able to move in with us and help me with the baby. I had also found a better hospital to go to when I had my second baby. It was the same hospital where they operated me from my *vesícula* [gall bladder].

I used the birth control pill after Tony was born for six years. Then the counselor suggested that I use the IUD again, since the first time I used it I had no problems with it. I used the IUD for two or three years. The nurses told me I needed to have it checked, but I never did. I mean I used to go to my yearly exam, but then one day they told me that they were sending women from that hospital to 55th Street, and I told them I was not going to go so far away.

Clara's second birth experience was a qualitatively better experience than her first birth because she was more at ease—her living conditions improved and she found a better hospital at which to give birth. Although this birthing experience was superior to the first, once again, she was not sure of many facts—for instance, the logistics of the birth—because the doctor did not discuss the details of the birth with her or ask whether she wanted full anesthesia.

The only problem I had when the baby was born was that they did not put me to sleep completely like when I had Gloria. This time when I got my labor pains I knew what was happening to me because I had gone through this with Gloria. We called a cab and were there quickly. The nurses wheeled me in immediately because I was bleeding. They took the bobby pins out of my hair. They put me in a white robe, and I can't remember if they gave me an enema. Then they laid me on a gurney, and they put that mask on my face. I didn't feel any pain, but this time I was surprised that I was still awake. They then gave me an injection and I could feel them working on me. I could hear the nurse talking but in a very deep voice. The nurse kept wiping my forehead with a cool cloth. And then I saw my baby boy screaming. They even let my husband be there while the baby was born. They made him put on a white robe like the doctors wore. Tony junior was born on the same day as Tonio senior. My husband wanted a boy. I would have been happy with another girl. I always thought the baby was going to be a girl. The only problem I had after the baby was born was that I bled a lot and that made me feel weak.

After we had our first baby we moved to a furnished room. Later we were able to get an apartment when the projects were built. We've been living here ever since. My husband Tonio still works as a janitor in a school, and I stay home with my mother who is very old now. She moved in with us when we moved to the projects in Brooklyn.

Like other women, Clara would have gotten sterilized if she had not reached menopause at a fairly early age:

I never got sterilized because I stopped having my period when I was about forty-one years old. It kept getting shorter and shorter and I would only get it sometimes until I did not get it again. If I hadn't lost my period so early I would have gotten operated on. At the time they had a law that you had to have five children to get sterilized. That law has changed today.

When we moved into the projects, Tonio was the only one working and he didn't earn a lot of money. When we moved to this apartment all we had was a mattress. At that time he didn't even have a job. Before he got a job as a janitor he worked in a bodega and hardly earned anything at all. Luckily neither one of us wanted to have many children, because we couldn't have afforded them.

Gloria: Third Generation

Gloria is Clara's and Tonio's only daughter. Even though Clara was a stay-at-home mom, she started to work when Gloria was twelve to help her husband save up enough money to pay for Gloria's Catholic high school.

> My parents were good-humored people, but they were unbearably strict when I was growing up in the projects. They were always afraid and wanted to know where I was. They did not let me hang out with my girlfriends or date boys. My friends made fun of me, and I never got to go to the parties my friends went to. I was sick of Catholic school, sick of the nuns telling me what to do. When I met Raphael, he was my way out. I realize now I shouldn't have dropped out of high school, but I was so fed up. He was older than me and seemed so confident. He made me feel so special. My poor family really freaked out when I left school and moved in with him.

Against her parents' and her grandmother's wishes, Gloria dropped out of high school in the eleventh grade after she met Raphael, who was ten years her senior, and moved in with him. This was a difficult period for Gloria's parents and her grandmother, doña Esperanza, who wanted more for Gloria than this man could offer her. Gloria's relationship with Raphael was rocky and lasted only a year. After Gloria left him, she enlisted in the army and was stationed in Kentucky, where she earned her high school degree. In the interim she met Deepak, who was also in the army; they fell in love and were married. Deepak was South Asian. His mother opposed their marriage because Deepak was from Pakistan and she had selected a Pakistani bride for him, but Deepak married Gloria instead. They have a daughter, and Gloria was sterilized after one child because neither of them wanted more children.

> I made a serious mistake dropping out of high school. I didn't like school. My parents and the nuns were so strict that they were making me nuts. When I met Raphael I just went crazy because I thought I loved him and we had fun together. We were okay for the first six months but then he got lazy, pulled his macho stuff and expected me to do all of the housework. When I did not respond like he wanted me to, he started getting home late and acting funny, and I realized one day what was going on when a woman started to call our apartment. So, I left him and joined the army.
>
> I was stationed in Kentucky, and then they moved me to Maryland, and later Virginia, where I met Deepak, my daughter's father. He is from Pakistan, a great guy. We got married and spent a few years stationed in Hawaii. After we served our term in the army, we decided to move back to Kentucky because life is cheaper there. We had a little girl, bought a house, and that is where we plan to stay for now. I had my tubes tied right after my daughter

was born. We have good insurance coverage and hospitalization, so if we change our minds in the future and decide to have another child we can. Right now we want to have a good life, and it's hard if you have a lot of kids. Deepak is a good father, and we want to give our daughter all of the opportunities we didn't have. I miss my family, but they come to visit once in a while and we visit them. Maybe when my parents are older and don't want to live in New York anymore, they'll consider moving to Kentucky with us.

As for many poor young men and women, the army was a vehicle of upward mobility for Gloria. Gloria and Deepak were able to reap some of the benefits of the army without incurring the risks because the United States was not at war when they joined. They are unusual because they both married outside of their ethnic group and made Kentucky their home. Deepak did not object to Gloria getting sterilized because he was familiar with this surgery since his mother had been sterilized in Pakistan after she had five children. Moreover, it is also unusual for Latinas and Pakistanis to get sterilized with one child since they generally feel it is not good for a child to grow up by themselves. However, their attitudes may reflect changing trends among women and men in the third generation.

SUMMARY AND CONCLUSIONS

These three generations of women, doña Caridad, Nilda, and Millie, illustrate how poverty, the lack of access to temporary methods of birth control, women's limited knowledge of birth control, domestic violence, men's infidelity, and the cultural acceptance of sterilization itself (even when used as a last resort) have led women in each generation to undergo sterilization. What I have described as the forced sterilization of Millie was a unique instance in my experience. However, in this case, as well as in cases where parents have encouraged women to undergo voluntary sterilization, Millie's parents thought they were doing their best for her and for the family by preventing her from having children in what they saw as an irresponsible way. Generations of women beforehand, then, did not see anything wrong with sterilization because they themselves had been sterilized. This was part of their cultural repertoire. Thus, women in Millie's family saw sterilization as an effective means, if as a last resort, to get through a crisis.

Apparently, Millie's family did not perceive any other way of coping with Millie's drug problems. Had they possessed the wherewithal and knowledge, they could have sought the help of a therapist or drug rehabilitation program in Puerto Rico, particularly when Millie was still underage. They could have requested the state to assist them in supervising Millie. And they could have gone to a family planning clinic that offered counseling and other birth control alternatives with low rates of user failure. For example, since Millie already had two children, a counselor could have recommended that Millie use a Lippies Loop (IUD) to prevent her from becoming pregnant again while not removing her future ability to choose if and when she wanted to have another child.

In fact, as this case study shows, Millie did want to have a baby many years later. To this day, she wrestles with contradictory feelings about it. On the one hand, Millie would like to have a baby with Ricardo to create a stronger bond between them and to fill up her own life. On the other hand, she is aware of her own personal and social limitations and expresses some doubt about whether more children would be sensible within the overall context of her life.

As with other women whose experiences this study recounts, it is not likely that Millie will be able to have her own child after she has her tubal ligation reversed. Yet, like her grandmother and mother, Millie does not have full medical knowledge about the situation facing her. For instance, she is not aware of the increased risk of ectopic pregnancy after tubal ligation is reversed. Millie also continues to make an erroneous distinction between the "tying" and the "cutting" of the fallopian tubes. If she continues on this path, she may experience the same heartache and medical problems other women have endured. Take, for instance, the case study of Lourdes; as previously described, Lourdes had several ectopic pregnancies before finally deciding to stop trying to have a child with Richard.

Doctors play an important role in this family's story. Nilda's doctor recommended sterilization to her when she was vulnerable and at the peak of an emotional breakdown. She had just lost her baby through domestic violence. Because Nilda did not have time to think things through, she regretted the hasty decision she made for years to come.

Millie's doctor's behavior was equally problematic. Her doctor sterilized her even though he was aware she was a minor. It appears that this doctor was acting on his own personal biases and also out of loyalty to her family. He agreed with Millie's family that she was a drug addict who needed to be stopped from having more children. Yet, curiously, after the tubal ligation his concern ended, even though Millie's emotional problems—which entailed long-term repercussions of la operación—did not.

Both these doctors appear to have taken a paternalistic approach toward their patients. Assuming that Nilda's doctor had good intentions, Nilda nevertheless would have been better served if the doctor had referred Nilda for counseling before sterilizing her. Instead, he only offered her sterilization as a solution to her problems so that, in her words, "She would not have more children with that bad man." In Millie's case, it is troublesome that a doctor would even sterilize a minor, all the more so without referring her and her family to counseling or trying to help them find another alternative.

Not only did Nilda and Millie's male doctors play a major role in their sterilization process, but Millie's story also illustrates the extent of her grandfather's
active involvement. It is remarkable that Millie's grandfather, don Guillermo,
became so involved in an area that has traditionally been considered a women's
domain, illustrating the extent of the entire family's concern. Her grandfather
literally took her, by himself, for her operation. He was involved in the planning and discussions with the doctor and with his wife. In the first generation's
era, some men played a more active role in the sterilization process, not only
by influencing their wives' decisions but also through exercising legal requirements. For example, up until the 1950s, women needed their husband's permission to get sterilized. Men had to sign their wives' consent forms; otherwise,
doctors would not conduct the operation. Don Guillermo not only played an
important role in the sterilization process of his granddaughter; he was also
instrumental in deciding when doña Caridad was sterilized. Finally, Nilda's
husband, Enrique, certainly influenced her decision to get sterilized—albeit
in an entirely negative fashion—through her life with him of marital infidelity
and domestic abuse.

Even though the Rivera family thought the Morales family acted harshly
with Millie, they thought that sterilizing her was understandable given that
Millie was a drug addict and having children irresponsibly. Doña Esperanza
and doña Caridad's own story highlights the destitute lives of poor women
in Puerto Rico and the difficult conditions under which they gave birth.
However, despite their hardships, it is clear that their mother's relationships
with these women were based on trust, respect, and dignity. In contrast, even
though Clara, doña Esperanza's daughter, had both of her children in a hospital in the mainland United States, her first birthing experience was alienating
and humiliating. Consequently, after her first birth, she avoided going to the
hospital until the last moment, like many other poor women in New York at
that time. Having access to quality health care, then, is necessary but not sufficient; as with all the women in this chapter, caring relationships are just as
important.

PART III

Reproductive Rights and an Integral Model of Reproductive Freedom

CHAPTER 7

Ideologies and Inequities
in the Health Care System

Each semester I give a lecture to my undergraduate classes on sterilization and Puerto Rican women in New York City. And each semester, without fail, several Latina students in my classes mention that they are sterilized. I explore this topic gingerly with them in order to find out the circumstances under which they were sterilized and to further educate them. One of the tools I use is the film *La Operación*. Although it provides an excellent historical overview of the development of sterilization in Puerto Rico, the film is problematic because it presents most Puerto Rican women as victims of sterilization abuse. As this study makes clear, however, this is not the experience of the majority of Puerto Rican women. To avoid making the sterilized students in my class feel like victims, I prepare them by presenting a more complex and nuanced analysis beforehand. For example, I distinguish between victims of sterilization abuse and women who are proactive in their fertility decisions (i.e., those who make the best fertility decisions they can under difficult conditions). Even though I argue that Puerto Rican and other poor women are not in a position to exercise full reproductive freedom, I have learned that most women seek sterilization in an attempt to maximize their individual and social circumstances. While some Puerto Rican women are victims of sterilization abuse, not every sterilized Puerto Rican woman is a victim in the classical sense.[1]

At the beginning of my lecture, I ask my students to raise their hands if they believe that a woman can still have children after she has been sterilized. In my predominately Latino class of thirty to thirty-five students, almost all but one or two raise their hands. I am always struck by the high level of misinformation among Puerto Ricans, Dominicans, and other Latinos on this important topic. These misconceptions are not unique to the students in my classes. They are reflected in the attitudes of white, black, and Latina women citywide (Carlson and Vickers 1982) and of Puerto Rican women in the neighborhood where my research took place (Lopez 1983, 1993, 1998).

In a survey I took of 128 women in this neighborhood, I found that Puerto Rican women make a distinction between the "tying" and "cutting" of the fallopian tubes. Ninety percent of them believed that if their tubes were "tied" they could become pregnant again, but if their tubes were "cut" they would not be able to have more children. Despite all of the information available today, my students, the women in this study, and most Puerto Rican/Latina women in New York City at large, continue to make a distinction between the "tying" and "cutting" of the fallopian tubes. One of the most difficult dilemmas I faced during my fieldwork was when sterilized women told me they were going to have children again, and I knew that in all probability they would not be able to do so.

In trying to tease out the meaning of the distinction that Puerto Rican women make between the tying and cutting of the tubes, I asked two questions. One was "Did you have your tubes cut or tied?" Fifty percent (48 out of 96) said their tubes were cut; the other half said they were tied. The widespread misinformation about the likelihood of pregnancy following sterilization had significant consequences for those women who opted to have their tubes "tied," many of whom planned to have more children.

As for the women who said their tubes were cut, their decisions did not have the same deleterious effect on them, since at the time of their surgery they did not want more children. In their cases it is very possible that the women who opted to have their tubes cut would have done so even if they had possessed full and accurate medical information.

Although at first glance it may appear that the women are satisfied they had their tubes cut, when I asked, "If you had to do it all over again would you still get sterilized?" these same women qualified their responses in a way that showed they chose sterilization at least in part because they did not feel they had viable options. Once again, half of these women (n = 24) said they would still get sterilized again; the other half said they would not. First, those women in the survey who said they would *not* opt for sterilization if given a second chance regretted their decision at a later point when, for example, one of their children died, they remarried (e.g., Nancy), their economic situation improved, or they wanted a son (e.g., Nilda). But what is more striking is that many of the women who said they would get sterilized again qualified their response by saying that if their life conditions improved they would not seek the procedure. Thus, women's awareness of the limitations of their situation brings up an important point: for many women, sterilization as fertility control is not an optimal choice but more often an act of last resort under restrictive circumstances.

SOURCES OF MISINFORMATION

The origins of Puerto Rican women's misinformation can be traced back to the Pomeroy method, the first sterilization procedure performed in Puerto Rico, in the early 1940s. It consisted of the ligation of fallopian tubes and had a high rate of failure because in some cases the tubes would become unligated, resulting in pregnancy. Many women may have heard stories from (or about) older generations of women who were sterilized, then became pregnant, with the Pomeroy procedure. Doña Caridad, for example, told me she became pregnant after she had her tubal ligation in Puerto Rico in 1945.

After 1960 doctors no longer simply ligate the tubes: they cut, burn, clamp, and virtually obliterated them. Despite the development of this more effective procedure, in the past twenty-five years countless women and men have told me they either know or have heard of someone who had a child after sterilization. Although it is the exception rather than the rule for a woman to give birth after having la operación, it does still occur on rare occasion.[2]

There are several reasons for high rates of misinformation among Puerto Rican women. One is the language that health care providers use to describe tubal ligation in hospitals and clinics. For example, euphemisms like "band-aid" operation or the "bikini cut" blur and minimize the permanency and magnitude of surgery. The sterilization counseling information session run by Mrs. Gonzales, described earlier, provides an example of the ways that health care professionals may also adopt colloquial terms of "tying" and "cutting" of the tubes to discuss la operación with their patients. These professionals may or may not realize that their use of colloquial language mystifies rather than explains the nature of the procedure. Examples like this do, however, suggest that simply adopting colloquial language when explaining medical procedures to prospective patients will not in itself guarantee informed consent.

In the late 1980s, misinformation emerged in the community about tuboplasty. Puerto Rican women widely believed that even if their fallopian tubes were "cut," they would nevertheless be able to have more children with this sterilization reversal procedure. Lourdes's story demonstrates that this belief is often reinforced by doctors who tell women they will be able to have a child again with tuboplasty. The reality is that, following the operation, there is only a 25 to 30 percent chance of conception, and a conception does not always lead to a full-term pregnancy (Bower 1995). The risk of an ectopic pregnancy among women who have had a reversal operation is ten times higher than those who have not. However, the precise risk depends upon the sterilization procedures used and may be much higher in individual cases. For example, women who had a bipolar tubal coagulation (both tubes burned) before the age of thirty had a probability of ectopic pregnancy twenty-seven times higher than women of similar age who underwent a postpartum salpingectomy, a form of tubal ligation (31.9 versus 1.2 ectopic pregnancies per 1,000 procedures) (Petersen et al. 1996; Zurawin 2006). Yet the women in my study were generally not aware of this risk, nor were they aware of the potential danger of ectopic pregnancy. In addition, their physicians had not informed them that the success of the tuboplasty also depends on the type of sterilization procedure the women originally had, as well as on the doctor's experience and skill in reconstructing a woman's fallopian tubes.

I found that, overall, the women in this study were not educated about sterilization technology per se. For example, out of the ninety-six sterilized women, none could identify the type of sterilization procedure they had received. The majority of these women were also sterilized before they were thirty years old. Obviously, this has implications if a woman wants to have her tubal ligation reversed, as both the age at the time of sterilization and the procedure used affect the chances of successful tuboplasty.

POOR PUERTO RICAN WOMEN'S EXPERIENCES IN THE HEALTH CARE SYSTEM

The limited knowledge about sterilization, other reproductive surgeries, and birth control demonstrated by the women in my survey and case studies has been perpetuated by their experiences with doctors, hospitals, clinics, and the health care system. Their experiences with general medical care and with specialized reproductive care have been shaped by inequality.

Although the United States has the most advanced medical technology in the world, the exorbitant cost of health care and private insurance and the lack of effective public insurance mean that access to high-level care is not equitably distributed.[3] For example, individuals without good health insurance cannot obtain certain medical treatments, even if they are available. Because the women in this study are poor, do not have adequate insurance, and cannot pay out of pocket, they generally use municipal (public) hospitals for their general health care needs. Seventy percent of all of the women in the survey paid for their health services through Medicaid. The remainder had Medicare but no secondary health insurance. All of the women in the five case study families (fifteen women) had health care coverage either through Medicaid or Medicare or both. Two out of the five older women had Medicare but did not have secondary health coverage. They had to pay their doctor bills out of pocket, an expense they could not afford.

Although medical providers in municipal hospitals are, for the most part, well-intentioned people who work exceedingly hard, the quality of medical care they provide is compromised because municipal hospitals have fewer resources than private hospitals. Consequently, institutional constraints translate into inferior quality medical services for the poor. Sometimes these constraints stem from the lack of state-of-the-art medical technology. It is also reflected in the shortage of staff, resources, and inadequate training of some of their personnel (Caro et al. 1988; Lopez 1988). The women in this study recognized these limits and they referred to the primary hospital in their neighborhood as the slaughterhouse, or *el matadero*.

The problem with inadequate health care stems not only from institutional constraints but also, and just as important, from the negative attitudes of some health care providers. For example, in addition to the poor quality of care generated by institutional constraints, major medical studies found that racism and some medical providers' negative stereotypes of African American and Latino communities adversely affect the quality and types of medical treatments they administer (Physicians for Human Rights 2003; Smedley et al. 2003). *Unequal Treatment* (2003), a landmark study by the National Academies Institute of Medicine on the inequities of the health care system, found that even when controlling for insurance, health care facility, and severity of condition, racial and ethnic minorities receive lower-quality care than whites. According to the doctors who conducted this study, the disparity in treatment derives in part from medical providers' negative stereotypes of their poor patients of color. The Physicians for Human Rights report further concludes:

> [Ethnic inequities and] disparities are embedded in two aspects of the nation's larger social and health care structures: the persistence of negative racial and ethnic stereotyping and bias, reflected in repeated national surveys, and the inequities of a system that leaves more than 40 million Americans without health insurance. (Physicians for Human Rights 2003)

Due to a history of racism, colonialism, and inequality (slavery and colonialism), most African Americans and Latinos today are in a more economically disadvantaged position in comparison to most whites. Even though both blacks and whites have fought to eradicate segregation, and African Americans have made many social strides, social injustices still exist. The Physicians for Human Rights (2003) also found multiple national surveys corroborate the persistence of negative racial and ethnic representations of people of color in the general population. "In a 1990 national survey, for example, 29 percent of white respondents characterized blacks and Hispanics as 'unintelligent'; 44 percent said blacks were 'lazy'; and 33 percent said the same of Hispanics; 56 percent and 42 percent, respectively, said blacks and Hispanics 'prefer welfare,' and 50 percent and 38 percent, respectively, believed blacks and Hispanics were 'violence prone.' In 1995 a similar study reported almost identical responses, including a judgment by 60 percent of white respondents that 'most blacks just

focus on individual issues obfuscates structural issues

don't have the motivation or willpower to pull themselves up out of poverty'" (Physicians for Human Rights 2003, 9). Therefore, these researchers concluded that some doctors may share these biases against poor people of color and it may affect their medical treatment.

> Racial and ethnic disparities in medical care are widespread, occurring across the full spectrum of disease categories and medical and surgical procedures. The evidence is robust, beyond reasonable doubt, of a pervasive and troubling finding in the health care system, and a cause for deep concern. (2003, 1)

WOMEN'S GENERAL HEALTH CARE

With the prevalence of racial and economic disparities in the health care system, it is not surprising that municipal hospitals and clinics, the primary sources of health care for the poor, are characterized by fewer resources: less modern facilities and space, less state-of-the-art medical equipment, and a shortage of health care providers as compared to private hospitals. They also tend to have a larger patient-to-doctor ratio, a longer waiting period for patients to see a health provider, rushed doctor-patient visits, and inconsistency of care. All of this, along with some doctors' and health care providers' negative attitudes and biases toward poor women of color, hinders doctor-patient communication and generates mistrust among patients toward health care providers in general and doctors in particular. Most important, as a consequence, the quality of health care is adversely affected (Caro et al. 1988; Lopez 1988).

Municipal hospitals/clinics are so crowded that patients sometimes must stand while they wait to see a doctor because there are not enough chairs for everyone to sit. Some of the women in this ethnography and the survey experienced this firsthand. The lack of space involves a shortage not only of chairs but also of beds and rooms. Sick patients must often wait on stretchers in hospital corridors in a noisy and sometimes chaotic environment for forty-eight to seventy-two hours or longer until a bed opens up. The hospital corridors are noisy and brightly lit so that it is disorienting and impossible for the sick to get any rest.

The shortage of health care providers and the large patient-to-doctor ratio mean that patients must wait many hours to see whichever doctor is available. Poor women who lack medical insurance typically do not have general practitioners—they tend to use hospitals for general and nonemergency treatment, thus putting even more pressure on both women and municipal facilities. After waiting for hours to see a doctor in a dingy waiting room with tired and hungry children, some of these sick patients claimed that most doctors only spend a few minutes with them. Patient-doctor visits are rushed, which exacerbates the problem caused by already limited communication between doctors and patients, particularly for those who do not speak English, because there are not enough translators to meet patient needs. For example, Tata, a fifty-year-old mother of three, said the following:

> When I have to go to the hospital I get up at five in the morning so that I can dress myself and the kids and have enough time to travel and get there early. I don't get home till three or four. I spend at least an hour registering and running around the hospital, standing on long lines to drop an envelope or to pick up a slip. Then I have to wait to see the doctor. They don't have any respect for our time. They think we have all day and can spend hours waiting. It is always a frustrating experience and hard on women with small children.

Women also offered complaints about the quality of doctors' interaction with them in the local hospital. For example, more than half of the women in this survey claimed they did not mind waiting, even though they had to wait long periods of time, because they understood that doctors were busy. However, the biggest complaint lodged by women in this study was that doctors did not listen to them. Julie, a thirty-nine-year-old mother of one, explained:

> I walked into the doctor's office and he never looked up at me. I tried to tell him what my problem was but before I opened my mouth he started writing. It was upsetting and I asked him to wait until I had told him what my problem was before he started to write. He was very rude and did not respond or look up. When he finished writing he stood up and left. I felt humiliated. The nurse came in with the prescription. I was so angry that when I got home I tore up the prescription. There is no excuse for a doctor to treat a patient like this.

Clara, a forty-two-year-old mother of two, felt resentful because when it was her turn to see a doctor, he spent half his time with her talking on the phone to someone else. This concerned Clara because she questioned how a doctor could diagnose her if he was not fully paying attention to what she said.

> The first problem is that the doctor is with a patient and the phone rings— it's the doctor's wife. Now, I assume if he is taking care of the patient that brief moment is for the patient. This usually happens to me. It never fails. Then he takes care of his wife—do you think he is going to remember what I was saying to him before she called. I don't think so. Other times people are entering and walking out of the office.

When doctors do not listen and do not make eye contact, women consider this behavior rude and disrespectful. To these women this is an indicator of how the doctors feel about them, and their feeling that doctors are indifferent to their concerns makes them less likely to ask questions about the treatment they receive.

In addition to rushed visits, one of the worst problems in public hospitals/ clinics today is inconsistency of care. This is especially problematic because doctors are not familiar with the medical histories of the patients they see, nor are they accountable for individual patients. In my estimation, inconsistency of care is one of the leading problems in municipal and private hospitals today. (There is inconsistency of care in private hospitals, too, but because of the shortage of staff and general lack of resources, the situation is worse in public hospitals). Inconsistency of care leads to serious problems such as poor communication, misdiagnoses, and prescribing the wrong medication (Doescher et. al 2000). Consuelo, a thirty-year-old mother of three, claimed the physician who cared for her misdiagnosed her:

> I have a sensitive stomach. I had gone to the hospital with abdominal pains twice in the same day and each time had seen a different doctor. My sister-in-law accompanied me; she was my interpreter since I don't speak English. The first doctor said I had gas. Because the abdominal pain persisted I went to the emergency room. A doctor examined me. He did not take any tests, the way he was supposed to, and simply prescribed some medication. The medicine was something like Mylanta, a white liquid. After a few hours I went back to the hospital writhing in pain. This time they prescribed some pills, and I almost died. When I took the pills I became dizzy and started to throw up. They had to rush me to the hospital in an ambulance. It turned out that the problem was with my appendix. The doctor had to operate on me immediately.

Patients' rushed visits, misdiagnoses, inconsistency of care, and poor communication between patients and doctors lead to patient mistrust of doctors. This mistrust, often developed over years of experience with public health, has significant implications for women's reproductive health care. For example, Elsie, a thirty-two-year-old mother of one who had a hysterectomy, does not trust doctors. She felt that her hysterectomy could have been prevented if her doctor had only listened to her. Instead, she claims that he ignored her complaints until it was too late.

> I went to the doctor to discuss a problem I was having that was causing me to lose my urine involuntarily. They told me it was all in my head. This went on for about two years. Then finally I went to a doctor who told me that what had happened was that my womb had collapsed on top of my bladder, and that was what was causing me to lose my urine. If those other doctors had

listened to me and found my problem on time I might not have had to have a hysterectomy.

Years of negative experiences with the health care system affect the expectations women have of medical care and make them less likely to challenge a system—or the individuals within it—that fails to meet their needs. Medical studies have found that blacks and whites have different experiences and expectations of doctors (Blendon et al. 1995). My interviews revealed that the women in this study had low expectations of doctors and did not fully trust them. For example, Celeste, a thirty-one-year-old mother of two, felt most physicians did not care about her and that most doctors were in the medical profession for the money.

There are doctors that study medicine not because they want to cure anyone but because there are big bucks in it for them. I've consulted with doctors who have told me that I have an infection when I know I do not. They have prescribed medication to me when I know I don't need it. Some doctors even have a small drug store in their clinics where they can sell you whatever they have prescribed. They are really slick . . . not only do you pay for the visit, but they can charge for the medicine as well.

Other women like doña Hilda, were aware and sensitive to class differences. For example, she was aware that patients with insurance and higher income received better medical treatment than she did:

When you're on Medicaid the treatment that you receive in the hospitals/ clinics is different than the treatment private patients receive. Private patients are taken care of faster than Medicaid patients. When you are on Medicaid you have to wait until the paying patients are taken care first. They are also treated better. The quality of medicine they get is also better because the doctors want Medicaid patients to keep coming back. For doctors Medicaid is big money.

Despite this mistrust, patients are often reluctant to challenge doctors. In the United States, doctors have considerable social prestige and medical authority (Starr 1982). Consequently, they exercise a significant amount of influence over their patients, especially when they are ill. Although the rich and poor are equally susceptible to this influence, which has been described as the "medical mystique," the poorest and least educated are more vulnerable because they do not always have access to other sources of medical knowledge that will enable them to make more informed decisions. For example, when doctors told doña Hilda and doña Margo that they needed to have a hysterectomy because of a fibroid tumor, they did not know how to cross-check this information. They did not understand what a second opinion was, which is why they mistook what the interns who examined them told them as a second opinion. Furthermore, they were not part of a middle-class network that included health care professionals. Finally, they did not know how to look up medical information on a computer or in a library.

This is not to deny that I have met many wonderful doctors who elicit their patients' participation in the healing process. Stories of negative experiences with the health care system, however, far outweigh positive experiences in this study, and one might argue that they have a more significant impact in influencing women's perceptions of their options for reproductive care.

Rude and insensitive attitudes among health care providers were not confined to doctors. The women in this study sensed negative attitudes at every level of the hospital, from doctors to clerks. Some claimed that hospital clerks treated them even more disrespectfully than doctors. The message to these poor women was that they were not important. According to Sonia, a twenty-one-year-old mother of two:

> Clerks are not friendly in this hospital. Almost all of the clerks are Afro-American and they don't speak any Spanish. They never smile or are polite. I stand there waiting to register and in front of me they are talking about their personal business as if I were not even there. They don't even have the courtesy to say, "I'll be right with you." I have sometimes stood and waited for at least ten minutes before I am taken care of. They think I don't have anything better to do than to waste my whole day here. If you say anything to them they make you wait longer. They have no respect for us because we are poor Latinas.

Ironically, even though most clerks in municipal hospitals are women of color who have the least amount of power as compared to other staff in hospitals/clinics, some of their attitudes reflect the institutional mentality and the larger structural inequities in these institutions.

Some of the women in the study also had problems with nurses and nurses' aids. Clara, a thirty-four year old mother of two, was in the hospital because she broke her arm. She claimed she went out of her way not to bother the nurses because she was aware of how busy they were. However, she recalls how many hours she had to wait for a nurse to come after she rang the buzzer.

> When I stayed in the hospital the nurse's aid would throw the food in front of me, even though she knew that I could not pick it up, or eat properly because my right arm was in a cast. For breakfast they would bring me a hardboiled egg without peeling it. They would not help me get to the bathroom. Sometimes I would ask one of them to help me and they would keep walking as if

they had not heard me, or they would say they'd be right back and wouldn't
return. I didn't want them to baby me. All I wanted was for them to help me
with a few basic things I could not do for myself. I don't speak much English. Most of the nurses were black. Maybe if there had been a Spanish nurse
around she would have helped me.

WOMEN'S REPRODUCTIVE SURGERIES

Institutional constraints, medical providers' negative ethnic and racial stereotypes, and sexism not only preclude poor women of color from receiving
certain treatments for their general health care but also limit their reproductive freedom by influencing the kinds of recommendations they receive about
reproductive surgery. It is not my intention to stereotype or scapegoat doctors,
but as I noted earlier, surveys taken in the United States show that there are
still stereotypes of poor women of color as lazy and irresponsible. These views,
in combination with the insidious stereotypes that were propagated of Puerto
Rican and African American women as "welfare queens" in the 1960s, may have
influenced some doctors to recommend unnecessary reproductive surgeries
such as hysterectomies and caesareans. This is reflected in the fact that that
poor minority women have higher rates of hysterectomies and caesareans than
white women in general.[4] In addition, women on Medicaid have a higher rate
of tubal ligation in municipal hospitals than they do in private hospitals (New
York City Department of Health 1982). The more prevalent orientation toward
hysterectomy and tubal ligation in municipal hospitals is most likely influenced
by a convergence of factors, including economic and cultural factors, but the
result is an approach that tends to disempower patients, who may be assumed
to be unable or unwilling to control their own fertility (Hartmann 1995).

Hysterectomies and caesareans are controversial. In some cases, these procedures are necessary and save women's lives. The problem arises, however,
when doctors recommend these procedures unnecessarily because of their personal biases or, in the case of caesareans, to accommodate doctors and hospital
administrators' schedules (Lowe 2003, 281).

FIBROID TUMORS AND THE CANCER SCARE

Studies have shown that poor racialized women have higher rates of hysterectomy than white women. For example, a study on hysterectomy and race conducted in 1993 (Kjerulff et al. 1993) found that the average annual age-adjusted
hysterectomy rate was higher for black women (49.5 percent per 10,000) than
for white women (41.2 per 10,000). Moreover, for 65.4 percent of the hysterectomies in black women, the principal diagnosis was uterine fibroids compared

to 28.5 percent for white women. A fibroid tumor is part of the uterine wall that gets twisted into a knot and grows separately. Fibroid tumors shrink and disappear on their own when a woman goes into menopause because their growth is stimulated by estrogen. Whether or not a woman requires surgery depends on the location of the fibroid, its size, the amount of bleeding, and whether she has more than one fibroid tumor. Surgery is necessary in cases when a woman has multiple fibroid tumors and excessive bleeding. However, even in cases where fibroid tumors cause a medical complication, there are alternatives to a hysterectomy.[5] Depending on what part of the uterus the fibroid tumor is located, the doctor can perform a myomectomy, which consists of removing the fibroid tumor and leaving the uterus intact. According to Wallach and Vlahos (2004, 393):

> Uterine fibroids are benign gynecologic tumors that are treated because of the symptoms they create: abnormal uterine bleeding, pelvic pain, and pressure on the surrounding viscera. From a clinician's perspective, medical devices that are used to treat uterine fibroids should be proven safe and effective in reducing these symptoms. As well, patient selection for the use of these devices should take into consideration the patient's age, desire for future fertility and potential short term and long term complications that could add a reduced quality of life such as pain from adhesions, reduced ovarian reserve and weakening of the uterine wall.

Dr. Wallach's conclusion is corroborated by the federal government's fact sheet on fibroid tumors: "Fibroid tumors are almost always benign, or not cancerous, and they rarely turn into cancer (less than 0.1 percent of cases)" (U.S. Department of Health and Human Services 2006).

The stories of women in my study are illustrative of the experiences of many poor women of color and poignantly demonstrate the ways that racism, classism, and sexism intersect in the health care system to constrain poor women's reproductive freedom.

Eighteen women in my survey had hysterectomies. Of these women, two indicated that they received a hysterectomy in order to sterilize them for birth control purposes, and three did not know why they had this surgery. In my case study families, doña Hilda, doña Margo, and Carmen were clearly victims of hysterectomy abuse. Doña Hilda and doña Margo both felt they had unnecessary hysterectomies because of a fibroid tumor that was not causing a medical complication. Their doctors told them that if they did not have a hysterectomy, they might develop cancer, which is contradicted by the medical information provided by the federal government's fact sheet on uterine fibroids. Doña Hilda and doña Margo did not know about this fact sheet, and they did not have other sources of medical information. Moreover, the doctors did not explain any alternative treatments or provide them with sufficient information to allow them to make an informed choice about their treatment. Doña Hilda and doña Margo were frightened into thinking that if they did not have the hysterectomy they would get cancer. I would argue that this medical practice used against poor women is unethical and constitutes reproductive abuse.

Other studies have investigated the question of why doctors perform hysterectomies when a fibroid tumor can also be removed with a myomectomy. One possible explanation for this is that municipal hospitals are teaching hospitals, and interns need bodies to learn how to perform hysterectomies and other kinds of surgeries (Egbert and Rothman 2003; Kjerulff et al. 1993). Others have argued that hysterectomies are expensive operations and noted that Medicaid reimburses hospitals/clinics for them (Physicians for Human Rights 2003). Others feel that once a woman has had children, she no longer needs a uterus (Price 2008). Finally, some doctors share the stereotype with fellow citizens that poor women, especially women of color, are a burden on the state and tax payers, and they may feel that they are doing society—and possibly even the women themselves—a favor by operating on them so they do not have more children. Carmen (second generation), doña Rosario's daughter, is not certain why her doctor performed an unwanted and unnecessary hysterectomy on her. She wanted a tubal ligation, and he performed a hysterectomy instead. Carmen felt violated, outraged that a doctor would remove her uterus without her knowledge or consent. She told me she has never recovered from this trauma.

The Link between Caesareans and Tubal Ligations

The high (and increasing) rate of caesarean sections performed—many of which may well be medically unnecessary—is a medical practice that contributes to the high rate of tubal ligation in the United States. Henderson (1976) pointed out the positive correlation between caesarean births and tubal ligations in New York City and Puerto Rico. According to her findings, a doctor typically recommends tubal ligation after a woman has three caesarean births. Other studies have found that the exceedingly high rate of caesareans in Brazil is also leading to a high rate of tubal ligations in that country (Diniz and Chacham 2004; *Depenbrok v. Kaiser Foundation Health Plan, Inc.* 1978; Hopkin 2000; Potter et al. 2001). In fact, another study found in 1995 that poor nonwhite women in the United States are more likely to have a caesarean than more well-to-do whites. These authors concluded that "among women who resided in substantially non-English speaking communities, who delivered high-birth weight babies, or who gave birth at for-profit hospitals, cesarean delivery appeared to be more likely among non-whites and was over 40 percent more likely among Blacks than among whites" (Braveman et al. 1995, 625).

Lourdes's story illustrates this trend. Her doctor recommended a tubal ligation after she had her third caesarean delivery because he did not think it wise for her to have more abdominal surgery. Ironically, later Lourdes had a reversal steilization in which the doctor opened her caesarean incision for a fourth time.

Evelyn's case was different. She elected sterilization herself because she did not want to be subjected to another caesarean.

> I was sterilized because I did not want to have another caesarean. I had both of my children through caesarean section. For my first child I remember that my doctor wrote on my medical chart, "high danger." I wondered what he meant by that. I figured that since this was my first child I was considered high danger. I think doctors put that on the charts of all women who are having their first child. My sister had her first child naturally, normally, but for the last baby they performed a caesarean section on her. The problem is doctors don't wait for women to give birth normally. They wait a few minutes, but if the baby is not born right away they pull out their knives.

Lourdes makes the point that caesareans are convenient for doctors. As Henderson (1976) points out, a consequence of women having so many caesareans is that they become candidates for sterilization. Given this factor, it is not surprising that as the rate of caesareans have increased, so have tubal ligations worldwide.

Negative Birthing Experiences

One of the primary reasons the women in this study went to hospitals when they were pregnant was to receive prenatal care, give birth, and to get sterilized. These were not always positive experiences. Indeed, stories of negative birthing experiences were common among women of the first and second generations, especially among those who migrated to New York between the 1950s and 1960s and did not speak English. Despite the problems in municipal hospitals today, the third-generation women were generally more adept at negotiating the health care system, in part because they were fluent in English but also because they learned from their mothers' and grandmothers' experiences and are more aware of how to advocate for themselves and their families.

These negative experiences contributed to some women's decisions to opt for sterilization. Chicky, a twenty-five-year-old mother of two, explains her decision to get sterilized.

> I had three miscarriages, and in the last one the baby died inside of me. I went to Bellevue hospital and they told me I could not go home because my baby was dead inside of me. I became so frightened I went home. I told

an Italian friend of mine, and she told my husband to take me back to the hospital. When the doctor saw me, he said, "She goes home, now I don't put injections, I don't put nothing." He was going to take the baby out in cold blood. I told him I went home because I got scared and I wanted to bring my husband. He responded, "I don't care." He laid me down and with a scissor he took out the baby. I was awake while he was taking these pieces of meat out of me. He did the operation in cold blood. I screamed like a dog on that table. My husband didn't do anything. After all I had been through. That experience influenced my decision to get sterilized.

Chicky's story is so chilling it almost seems exaggerated. Even if she exaggerated in part, it is consistent with other unpleasant experiences she has had in the hospital. Her story highlights the mistrust that many of the women in my study expressed toward doctors, and it also illustrates her experience of the doctors' lack of sympathy and regard for her as a person. The important point here is that this traumatic experience, in combination with other problems, contributed to her decision to get sterilized.

Ana also had a terrible experience in the hospital with her first baby. She migrated from Puerto Rico in the early 1950s. She was twenty-two years old when she had her first child. Ana told me that a nurse slapped her face when she was lying on a stretcher in labor because the nurse said she was making too much noise:

For my second child I waited till the last minute to go to the hospital because they treat pregnant women so badly when they are there. I was nervous when I went to the hospital to have my first birth. It was painful and sometimes I just had to scream out in pain. They don't like that in hospitals. They think you're being overly emotional, that is because they are not the ones going through labor pains.

You lay there for hours in pain. Occasionally someone comes over and checks you to find out when the baby is coming. There was a very rough nurse who kept coming over to check me. In order to examine you they have to put part of their hand inside of you. I begged her not to keep doing that to me because it hurt a lot. She would just say *cállate*, shut up in Spanish and in English. She hurt me so much that I really screamed. She slapped me across the face then. I couldn't protect myself at that moment, but I swore to myself I would find her.

Nora described a similar experience. Her nurse's comments reflect racial and class bias:

When you are in labor you get nervous. The nurses hear you screaming and they get annoyed. They examine you so many times and pinch you and even hit you in the face. When I was on a stretcher a woman hit me in the face. Right before I gave birth a woman came over to examine me again. I had already been examined several times. I told her the examination hurt. The nurse screamed at me in English, "Shut up—is that why you have so many kids. Deal with the pain." I told the nurse please, miss, I can't stand the pain. I am going to get sterilized after I have my child.

In the 1950s, Julie, twenty-one and having her first child, also had a traumatic experience. Her case points to class bias on the part of the nurse assigned to her. She gave birth by herself on a stretcher in a hospital corridor and, by her account, no one paid any attention to her until her baby was born.

I went to the hospital with labor pains. The nurse put me on a stretcher in the corridor with other women who were going to have babies too. I started to have sharp pains almost immediately. I screamed for help, but they ignored me. The pains kept coming faster and faster, I knew I was going to have the baby, but no one would listen. I had my first daughter alone on that stretcher. When the nurse finally realized what was happening, she started screaming at me that I could not have the baby on the stretcher. It was horrible, and I never wanted to go through that again.

Cindy, a twenty-six-year-old mother of two, also had a very unpleasant experience when she gave birth. The doctor forgot to remove her placenta. After he performed an episiotomy on her without anesthesia, he removed the sutures without anesthesia to remove the placenta. Cindy believes that he would not have treated a patient with private insurance that way.

When I had my daughter, after they wheeled me down on the cot, they had to take me back to the delivery room. The doctor touched my stomach and told me the placenta was still inside of me. Oh my God, I had the cold sweats, I don't want to remember this day. After they took those stitches in cold blood, he had to cut them again to take out my placenta. I screamed so loud they could hear me in heaven. I bet they did not give me anesthesia because I am on Medicaid.

These women's stories highlight the medical mystique and abusive treatment that some of the women in the first and second generations were subjected to in public hospitals. Practices in municipal hospitals have, fortunately, changed for the better in some ways since the 1950s. For example, today a medical provider would not have the audacity to strike a patient. However, they did this with impunity with older immigrants like doña Zoraida because they were more vulnerable, did not speak English, did not have an advocate, and were not aware of their rights. Finally, it is hard to imagine that a doctor would remove a middle-class woman's sutures right after she gave birth and had been sewn up without giving her an anesthetic because he forgot to remove her placenta. It is also unimaginable that a woman would give birth by herself on a stretcher and that all of the health providers would ignore her cries for help. These women's experiences are testimonies to the problems that poor women have had with health care. Their only way to resist was to wait until the last minute to go to the hospital to give birth and get sterilized (often postpartum) after achieving their desired family size so that they would not continue to be subjected to such abuse.

In sum, the experiences of the working-class Puerto Rican women in my study with the health care system were often highly negative. A range of factors, including institutional barriers in public hospitals/clinics, combined with a medical culture that perpetuates negative stereotypes of poor women of color, bureaucratic indifference, inequitable distribution of access to medical procedures, the pressure doctors face to see a large volume of patients in municipal hospitals, and the "medical mystique" that affects doctor-patient interactions, contribute to a lack of access to quality health care services, which in turn circumscribes poor women's reproductive freedom. Studies have demonstrated that doctors in municipal hospitals recommend tubal ligation, caesareans, and hysterectomies to poor women of color more frequently than middle or upper class white women. Lack of access to quality health care services limits poor women's fertility options, predisposing them to higher rates of unnecessary reproductive surgery. This is compounded by Puerto Rican women's cultural predisposition toward and misconceptions of la operación.

This combination of forces constrains poor women's reproductive freedom. However, within this framework of institutional constraints and problematic treatment by health care providers, these women insist on dignity and respect. They resist the problematic treatment they receive and refuse to go along with it, exercising reproductive choice within the limited options open to them.

CHAPTER 8

Toward an Integral Model of Reproductive Freedom

A discussion of the ideology of choice is fundamental to any analysis of sterilization. As I noted in the introduction, the ideology of choice is the basis of the fundamental ideal underpinning American society: that we live in a free society, that as individuals we have an infinite number of options from which to choose, and that because all individuals are presumed to be created equally, regardless of race, class, or gender, we all therefore must have equal opportunity to choose. In addition, as individual free agents, we are purportedly capable of making good choices to increase our options by envisioning appropriate goals (Solinger 2001). The implication of this argument is that if individuals fail, there must be something wrong with their choices and therefore something inherently wrong with themselves.

Although I believe that most Puerto Rican women are proactive in making reproductive decisions, I have deliberately not framed their fertility decisions within a paradigm of choice. The ideology of choice is rooted within a binary construct. The misguided assumption that Puerto Rican women who opt for sterilization are making a free choice to pursue their own goals led me to question whether the ideology and language of choice clarified or confused the understanding of Puerto Rican women's fertility behavior. In this formulation of individual choice, a distinction needs to be made between decisions based on a lack of viable alternatives versus optimal reproductive freedom.

At the root of the logic that Puerto Rican women are making voluntary decisions is the fallacy that because women make decisions, and because decision making is a proactive process, women are exercising free will and enjoying reproductive freedom, regardless of their social conditions. As I use the term more positively, however, reproductive freedom means being able to choose from a series of safe, effective, convenient, and affordable methods of birth control. It means that both women and men have viable alternatives from which to choose, and that the best possible social and political conditions exist that allow women to decide, free from coercion or violence, if, when, and how many children to have (Colón et. al. 1999; Hartmann 1995; Lopez 1998; Petchesky 1984, 1998, 2003; Roberts 1997; Solinger 2001). When a woman's "choice" is between sterilization and continuing to have children under adverse, impoverished conditions, she is not exercising full reproductive freedom—even if she is making a decision. This key contradiction highlights the failure of the oppositional or binary model of agency versus victimization to capture the nuances and contradictions of Puerto Rican women's experiences with la operación. Even though many Puerto Rican women make individual decisions to get sterilized, their fertility options are limited by multiple personal, social, cultural, and historical constraints.

The opposite explanation—that all Puerto Rican women who get sterilized are victims—is equally troublesome and must also be addressed. While, indeed, women have been victimized by forces beyond their control, one must question the limitations of any interpretation that denies subjectivity and argues that women are entirely products or even victims of their social conditions. This view is as simplistic and mechanistic as the ideology of choice that attributes full responsibility to the individual and denies the influence of objective social forces. Although this perspective is changing, some researchers (CESA 1976; CARASA 1979; Mass 1976) have assumed, ipso facto, that if a woman is sterilized she must be a victim of the medical establishment or of her race, ethnic, class, and/or gender status. Again, while there are clear cases of women as victims of sterilization abuse, this position takes the significance of social conditions and social factors to an extreme. It does not recognize agency, personal responsibility, and cultural or personal meaning—in other words, that people can and do make decisions in whatever situation they find themselves.

The women in this study do not see the issue of sterilization and reproductive decision making in a binary way. They talk about the choices they have made, but also about the constraints they experience. The women claimed they wanted to be sterilized as a way of taking control of their bodies or lives, but noted that if they had viable options they would not have necessarily opted for sterilization. On the one hand, all of the women in this study were familiar with la operación, recommended it to family and friends, felt that women should not have children too quickly, and talked about "shutting down the factory" euphemistically as a way of putting an end to their fertility. On the other hand, many of the same women also complained about getting sterilized because they could not afford to have more children; believed that a woman could have children after having her tubes "tied"; had regrets about their sterilization; made futile attempts to reverse their tubal ligations; underwent

unwanted hysterectomies; had problems with birth control, unplanned pregnancies, and abortions; and talked about sexual double standards where they
as women were expected to have primary responsibility for birth control, child
care, and domestic work. They also described their negative experiences in the
health care system, and they were acutely conscious of the discrimination and
negative attitudes directed at them within institutions like municipal hospitals
and society at large.

Thus, many cultural and social forces shape women's (and men's) views
about reproductive rights, and the women in my study were often very aware
of these forces. For them, the binary of choice and victimization fails to capture the nuances of their reproductive experience. I argue that one can better
understand their experience through what I have termed an integral model
of reproductive freedom. This approach to understanding fertility control,
including sterilization, reveals the lived experience of women and offers a
more sophisticated understanding of the complex influences shaping reproductive decisions.

Developing an Integral Model of Reproductive Freedom

The integral model does not focus on a binary of choice and constraint, but
provides a more nuanced analysis of how and why women make decisions. In
order to understand Puerto Rican women's fertility decisions from an integral
perspective, we need an analysis of reproductive freedom that considers the
four major realms affecting women's fertility experiences: personal, cultural,
social, and historical. In addition, we need a synthesis that incorporates and
transcends the individual by connecting the different realms of analysis in
a dialectical way without reducing any of these to one unit of analysis. This
avoids conceptualizing women's realities in a linear and hierarchical mode. For
the purposes of analysis and discussion, I have listed the personal, cultural, and
social factors that influence and limit women's fertility options into different
categories, although I am aware that in everyday life these forces converge and
are inseparable. It is never one single factor that leads to a woman getting sterilized, but myriad forces operating simultaneously.

Personal

This level of analysis reflects women's personal orientations or motivations;
their desire to gain control over their lives for the sake of their own and or
others' happiness and well-being. The Puerto Rican women in this study cited
a number of reasons why they underwent sterilization: children are expensive;
they wanted to do other things with their lives in addition to having children; they desired fewer children in order to take better care of the ones they

already had; they achieved their desired family size; they had problems with birth control; they did not know how to use birth control effectively; they felt responsible for birth control and child rearing; they became ill when they were pregnant; they had hysterectomies because they feared they would develop cancer; and they were unhappy with their partner due to domestic violence, substance abuse, and/or consistent interpersonal conflict and did not wish to continue to have more children with this individual. The respondents always had more than one reason for getting sterilized.

I also found that the way women approach la operación is related to their gender awareness, to the ways they think about themselves as women, and their ideas about relations between women and men. More specifically, it is also related to their self-esteem and gender entitlement—that is, to what extent they feel it is their right to control their body, to insist on mutual responsibility for birth control, to have an abortion, to get sterilized, and to take care of their overall individual needs. While none of the women asked the men to consider having a vasectomy, which would represent a healthy sense of entitlement with respect to their own well-being, many women nevertheless told me, "This is my body and I will do with it as I please." This was not just an isolated phrase, but a positive assertion of healthy self-entitlement in its own right that many repeated to me when talking about their reproduction. Although they positively embraced their right to control their fertility, their sense of gender entitlement did not transcend their person.

Cultural

Cultural factors also play a significant role in setting the parameters for women's reproductive freedom. In this study, women's reproductive decisions were framed by the way in which women and their community perceived la operación, as well as by their medical and popular knowledge of birth control and sterilization procedures. Furthermore, Puerto Rican culture influences women's internalization of the value of family, and their ideas about the ideal or desired family size, appropriate gender roles, and definitions of motherhood and fatherhood, so that culture influences gender awareness. This culture is shaped by the ongoing colonial relationship between the mainland United States and Puerto Rico, by Catholicism, and by family histories of migration.

Puerto Ricans are a family-oriented community. They are loyal to their family and they love children. This is reflected in doña Hilda's statement that "a home without children is a home without joy." With few exceptions, most women seek sterilization because they take family members' needs as well as their own into account. Women often framed their decisions to undergo sterilization within an idiom that stressed the value of family and motherhood. For example, I found that many of the women in this study, such as Sonia (third generation) and Evelyn (second generation), reported that they could be better parents if they had more energy for each child rather than spreading themselves thin with a larger family. Even those women, such as Evelyn, who claimed to make the decision on their own without consulting with anyone else were sterilized because of their sense of responsibility for others. A smaller number were sterilized because that is what their husbands wanted.

Cultural definitions of what it means to be a woman in the Puerto Rican community are based on the ability to have children. This is why it is considered a tragedy when a woman is naturally infertile or she has surgery that ends her fertility, such as a hysterectomy, even if she has already had children. Carmen's story offers an example of this cultural understanding of hysterectomy. The Puerto Rican community stigmatizes women who have hysterectomies because of the cultural interpretation that a woman who has had her reproductive organs removed is *hueca*, or empty inside. In other words, the loss of a woman's reproductive organs symbolizes the loss of femininity and sexuality.

Women in the second generation often stressed the importance of having a child with the significant man in their lives in order to solidify the couple's bond, suggesting that having children is fundamental to the definition of the family unit.[1] This was an important issue women considered in making fertility decisions, and it is one of the reasons why making the decision to undergo sterilization on the basis of a misunderstanding about the reversibility of the process reveals constraints that limit women's reproductive freedom.

The ideal or desired family size varies among the Puerto Rican women in this study intergenerationally. Both ideal and actual family size are influenced by cultural factors, and by the economic value of children, the historical period in which people live, and their environment. As doña Caridad and doña Rosario's stories illustrate, the immigrant generation of women grew up in rural Puerto Rico at a time when women had large families. In contrast, their daughters and granddaughters, who grew up in urban areas and in different social and historical circumstances, desired significantly fewer children.

Culture is important. It is a source of values, meaning, and knowledge for individuals as well as communities. The women in this study have retained a strong Puerto Rican cultural identity in New York, and this identity is often centered on family. New York Puerto Rican culture continues to influence the way women's individual and gender awareness develops.

Social

Puerto Rican women also face objective social and economic constraints that shape their life experiences and influence their fertility options. One of the strengths of the integral model is that it sheds light on Puerto Rican women's reproductive experiences from a race, class, and gender perspective, which influence their socioeconomic status, social mobility, educational status, and employment history. Race, class, and gender also influence the perception of Puerto Rican women by society at large (e.g., the insidious stereotype of the welfare queen), which is demonstrated by women's experiences with the health care system. The Puerto Rican women in this study are aware of and resentful of being portrayed as having babies to get on welfare. Socioeconomic constraints are evident in women's daily lives, and these pressures of living with racism and poverty influence women's reproductive decisions. For example, Evelyn was motivated to undergo sterilization because she was concerned about the peer influence to which her children were exposed in a high crime neighborhood. Other women were influenced to limit their fertility because of the lack of government-sponsored child care services. Many women claimed they could not afford to have more children because their salaries were so low they could not pay for child care for more than one child.

Class and race limit Puerto Rican women's reproductive freedom. Even though all women (and men), regardless of class or race, are limited by the contraceptives available on the market, poor women's reproductive options are more constrained because their lack of access to quality health care services and medical insurance narrows the quality of counseling and birth control options made available to them. For example, the women in this study were not familiar with the diaphragm, a barrier method, because the clinics they used were overcrowded, understaffed, had a disproportionate ratio of patients to providers, and lacked the privacy for counselors to show women how to use the diaphragm properly. In addition, counselors tended to stereotype low-income Puerto Rican women by assuming that they would not use a diaphragm because they were incapable of planning or that they were confined by puritanical cultural taboos that prohibit women from touching themselves.

One of the consequences of lack of access to quality health care services and poor birth control counseling is that a large number of the women in this study did not use contraceptives correctly. For example, Sonia, Nancy, Lourdes, and Evelyn became pregnant while using the pill. There are also cost issues associated with birth control. The women in this study, like many poor or working-class Americans, did not usually have adequate medical insurance. The escalating cost of birth control, such as the patch, is reducing the birth control options of the women in the granddaughters' generation.

The experiences of the women in all three generations illustrate the social constraints that influence reproductive decisions: poverty, which limits the financial and social options for caring for additional children; dangerous neighborhoods lacking in infrastructure, which result in a poor environment for children; and poor health care, particularly reproductive care.

Historical

In order to understand the extent of and limits to women's reproductive freedom in any community, it is essential to consider a historical perspective.
The history of the colonial relationship between Puerto Rico and the United
States, the development of the island's birth control movement in the midst of
imported Malthusian and eugenic ideologies of overpopulation on the island,
and the promotion of sterilization and migration as part of Puerto Rico's
unofficial population control strategies continue to have ramifications for the
reproductive freedom of Puerto Rican women in New York City today. As this
ethnography has illustrated, at various times in Puerto Rican history the politics
of population control on the island played a part in making sterilization the
only method of fertility control available. The historical realm also sheds light
on why Puerto Ricans migrated to the United States in the 1950s and the ways
in which changes in the New York City economy affected their migration and
reproductive experiences in the United States (Briggs 2002; Rodriguez 1989).

An integral model also sheds light on the historical differences between
poor whites and racialized minorities. In the United States, the Puerto Rican
community shares a similar status to African Americans, Native Americans,
Inuits, and indigenous peoples of Hawaii. As a consequence, Puerto Ricans,
like these other racialized minority groups, are more likely to be poor, have
one of the highest rates of high school attrition, and have a high rate of unemployment. One cannot fully comprehend the marginalization of Puerto Ricans
without taking into account Puerto Rico's dependent neo-colonial relationship
to the United States and its influence on Puerto Rican culture.

AN INTEGRAL ANALYSIS

By analyzing the intersection of personal motivations and gender awareness,
cultural influences, social structural constraints, and historical experience,
one can better understand the interplay of agency within constraint in the
lives of Puerto Rican women in New York. This analysis demonstrates the rich
variety of individual experiences, even when women face similar constraints
and live in the same community. Although the experiences of the women in
each of the following three stories were influenced by each of the four realms
(personal, cultural, social, historical), an integral analysis of their decisions
shows that these factors combine in different ways for different individuals.

Evelyn: Second Generation

Evelyn's story highlights the key role that individual desire and determination
can play in reproductive decisions. A binary framework evaluating Evelyn's

case study would likely reduce her to the individual unit of analysis and see her as a free agent exercising full reproductive freedom. She did indeed assert agency and expressed herself in carrying out the action that she felt was best. However, simply describing such a process as "choice" glosses over the influence of the social and cultural forces in her life.

After Evelyn had two unplanned pregnancies, she felt that she had achieved her desired family size. At the time, she was with a man who did not feel that birth control is a shared responsibility and who refused to use condoms. Evelyn was familiar with la operación, and so she decided to get sterilized.

On a daily basis Evelyn confronted difficult social conditions that contributed to her decision to get sterilized. She lived in a high crime neighborhood, where she was robbed. As a result she was afraid of letting her children play with their friends on the street, for fear that they would be a bad influence on her children.

By virtue of her cultural background as a Puerto Rican woman, Evelyn was more familiar and comfortable with sterilization as a means to address her reproductive needs. As a consequence of her impoverished situation, Evelyn felt that even if she had not achieved her ideal family size of two children, she could not afford to have any more children. By including the cultural and social aspects of Evelyn's life, it is evident that, while she clearly expressed and acted on her personal desire to have the operation, sterilization was not simply a matter of Evelyn's agency or choice. Within the social constraints of her world, scarce financial resources, a dangerous neighborhood in which to live and raise children, a lack of access to proper birth control information, two unplanned and problematic pregnancies, the medical condition she suffered while pregnant, two caesarean deliveries, a patriarchal relationship, and familiarity with an available solution to her problems, sterilization, are all indisputable parts of Evelyn's life which contributed to her decision.

The Robles Family: First, Second, and Third Generations

The Robles family provides several examples of the transmission of cultural beliefs about la operación through family relations and illustrates the coexistence of individual agency with social constraints and oppression. Doña Rosario, the first-generation matriarch, had ten children. She was the first woman in her family to get sterilized. Even though she adored her children, she felt she had more children than she desired. At times she was so poor she could barely feed them. Like other women in the immigrant generation, doña Rosario grew up during the early part of the twentieth century, when sterilization was practically the only method of fertility control offered to women in Puerto Rico. She was able work the political system, embedded in Puerto Rican cultural life, that unofficially offered women sterilization in exchange for a vote. Doña Rosario adopted sterilization as a successful method of birth control, and over time she transmitted her knowledge of sterilization as birth control to other women in her family. Thus, sterilization became a culturally familiar practice.

Nancy, doña Rosario's youngest daughter, was sterilized because by the age of twenty-five she had had three pregnancies and four children. Ideally, Nancy wanted to have just three children. However, after I got to know Nancy, it became apparent that her social constraints, cultural factors, and gender awareness played a considerable role in her decision to get sterilized. When I met Nancy she was living below the poverty line. She had problems with birth control due to her lack of knowledge of how to use the pill effectively. She struggled with her patriarchal husband, who refused to help her with the housework and children when he was home because he felt that, as he was the provider for the household, those were Nancy's responsibilities. When Nancy sought a solution, she turned to the culturally familiar option of la operación, which was recommended by her mother and other female relatives to whom she felt close. This cultural influence transmitted through her family relationships in combination with her resentment toward her sexist husband played a significant role in her seeking la operación to avoid more unwanted pregnancies. Although Nancy was a strong, vibrant woman with a solid awareness of gender issues and a healthy sense of entitlement, it is hard to argue that she exercised full reproductive freedom given that her social structural constraints and cultural practices shaped her understanding of her options, leading her toward sterilization.

In the Robles family, doña Rosario, her daughters Nancy and Carmen, and her granddaughter Sonia all felt that la operación was an effective way to deal with their reproductive needs. After all, each one of them, along with other women in their extended family, had been operated on and it worked for them. The Robles women were a close knit family. They loved and supported one another emotionally and economically. Doña Rosario was a role model to her daughters and granddaughter. Although her children and grandchildren meant the world to her, she felt that in New York women should not have so many children because of financial reasons, as well as for the woman's sake. Doña Rosario felt that women have other options today; they can work, go to school, and be independent. Therefore, she encouraged her daughters and her granddaughter to empower themselves by taking care of themselves, which in her mind begins with having control over their bodies.

Doña Hilda and Doña Margo: First Generation

The stories of doña Margo and doña Hilda, both first generation women, exemplify the powerful influence that social-structural constraints, particularly the lack of access to quality health care services, have on working-class Puerto Rican women's reproductive options. An integral perspective of their stories of hysterectomy abuse enhances the traditional understanding of "victim" by accounting for women's cultural beliefs as well as social structural inequities. Their stories also complicate the traditional understanding of "victim" in discussions of hysterectomy abuse.

From the standpoint of an agency/victim binary framework, both doña Hilda and doña Margo would be seen as nothing more than victims of hysterectomy abuse. Both had medically unnecessary hysterectomies after developing fibroid tumors. In both cases, the women's doctors did not provide them with clear medical advice or options to the recommended surgery. Because they were poor women, they lacked the knowledge and skills to negotiate the healthcare system and so did not seek second opinions. In addition, their stories illustrate a medical institution that disempowers its patients, discouraging them from asking questions, challenging diagnoses, or seeking further medical information elsewhere. A combination of significant social-structural constraints and lack of access to medical information meant that neither woman was likely to consider alternatives to a hysterectomy.

However, from an integral perspective, even though they are victims of hysterectomy abuse, both doña Hilda and doña Margo exercised some degree of personal agency—as do all women—and actively shared cultural values with other Puerto Rican women. Within the constraints of her world, doña Hilda took her doctor's warning seriously and decided to take care of herself by having the hysterectomy. From the standpoint of culture, she internalized the view that a fibroid tumor, which she called a *guiste* (cyst), could lead to cancer, a belief she shared with other Puerto Rican woman. Even though she did everything she could to take care of herself, she still suffered at the hands of an inequitable medical system, but in the process she was actively seeking a good medical outcome for herself and made decisions on the basis of constrained options and her own beliefs.

Doña Margo saw her medically unjustified mastectomy as a natural outcome of her work as a spiritual healer with women. Given her considerable fear of cancer, she agreed to have a hysterectomy and a mastectomy. Upon receiving news that she did not have any malignant tumors following the surgery, rather than getting angry at being victimized, she was relieved she did not have cancer and saw these experiences as opportunities to be cancer free. Taking into account how women make sense of and find meaning in what happens in their lives restores a sense of their agency within these constraints. It does not deny that these women are victims of an inequitable medical system.

These examples illustrate how an integral model of reproductive freedom can help resolve two problematic issues: the ideology of choice and the dualistic bind of agency versus constraint. But again it is not enough to focus only on choice or on social constraint. Reproductive decision making is more complicated, and it is shaped by a sense of one's self, both as an individual and as a woman. Gender awareness, as well as cultural beliefs, social constraint, and historical influences combine to provide a richer understanding of the lived experiences of reproduction.

At the fourth world conference on women in Beijing in 1995, reproductive rights were declared as human rights. The integral model resonates with the notion of human rights in that it calls for optimal reproductive freedom. In order to realize reproductive freedom, we need to take into account personal, cultural, social, and historical forces. As noted earlier, reproductive activists have defined reproductive freedom as a woman's right to choose if, when, and with whom she will have children, free of violence and coercion. This definition includes having the right social conditions to be able to choose (e.g., comprehensive health care that provides but does not focus exclusively on sterilization and abortion and also addresses women's, men's, and children's general health issues). Rosalind Petchesky (2003, 18–19) emphasizes the significance of women having the right social conditions to be able to take advantage of their reproductive rights.

> [But] how can a woman avail herself of this right if she lacks the financial resources to pay for reproductive health services or the transport to get to them; if she is illiterate or given no information in a language she understands; if her workplace is contaminated with pollutants that have an adverse effect on pregnancy; or if she is harassed by parents, a husband or in-laws who will abuse her or beat her if they find out she uses birth control?

Based on my work with the women in this study, I would now add to the definition of reproductive freedom the necessity of women's and men's self and gender awareness. In other words, reproductive freedom is not only about having viable options and the right social conditions, but also the kind of self-awareness and sense of entitlement that enables each individual to make the best decision. To the list of important questions raised by Petchesky, who herself recognizes the importance of self and gender awareness, I would add: How can a woman avail herself of reproductive rights if she believes that men are to be obeyed, or that a person of authority must always be right, or that she couldn't possibly go against what her mother, sisters, and elders think about things? Would reproductive rights be sufficient in such a case?

Are Puerto Rican Women's Reproductive Experiences Unique, Universal, or Both?

Puerto Rican women's reproductive experiences are both unique and universal. They are unique because as early as the beginning of the twentieth century

Puerto Rican women became the first subjects for implementing Malthusian ideologies of overpopulation. Puerto Rican women and men were citizens of the first nation in Latin America that used sterilization and migration as a means of population control. In contrast, the overpopulation argument was not applied to other Third World women until the 1960s (Hartmann 1995). Another factor that makes Puerto Rican women's experiences unique is that sterilization was implemented on the island as early as 1937, decades before it was legally made available in the mainland birth control market. In the 1950s Puerto Rican women also became the subjects of U.S. pharmaceutical laboratory tests for the pill, the Internal Uterine Device (IUD), and Emko contraceptive foam. These birth control technologies, along with sterilization, were developed at the expense of Puerto Rican women.

Puerto Rican women's reproductive experiences are also universal. Like other women around the globe, Puerto Rican women want to control their fertility and demand the reproductive and human right to decide if, when, and under what conditions they will have their children free of violence and coercion. However, along with other women worldwide, Puerto Rican women (and men) have not been offered better social conditions that include comprehensive health care that provides viable contraceptives along with tubal ligation. Instead, like other Third World women, they were blamed for the overpopulation problem and targeted for population control via sterilization, which became a euphemism for birth control in the Third World.

Sterilization as a reproductive technology is, in and of itself, neither good nor bad. The problem is that it has been used as population control instead of birth control (Hartmann 1995). This was especially true for the first generation of women because they grew up in Puerto Rico during the early part of the twentieth century, when the Puerto Rican/U.S. government policy encouraged sterilization of Puerto Rican women for population control purposes. Simultaneously, Puerto Rican women accepted sterilization because they wanted to control their fertility and attain a modicum of control over their lives. Even though the state's intentions may have been completely unrelated, or even diametrically opposed, to women's objectives, given the gaps in Puerto Rico's birth control movement in that era, women's desire and need for birth control intersected with the state's goal and facilitated the acceptance of sterilization. Until 1968 the Puerto Rican and U.S. government did not provide federal funding for temporary methods of birth control. Yet la operación had been consistently available to women since 1937, and over time it became part of Puerto Rican culture. My integral analysis helps one understand how sterilization, an imposed method of fertility control in Puerto Rico, was transformed into part of Puerto Ricans' cultural belief system. This occurred not just as a hegemonic, internalized source of oppression, but as a deliberate or conscious act that women used for their own needs, especially when they had no other birth control options.

Conclusion

I have shown Puerto Rican women's agency within constraints through the integral model of reproductive freedom and how they have created personal and cultural meaning out of la operación; for example, they use it to improve their lives and to take care of their families. Puerto Rican women have shown tremendous courage, ingenuity, and fortitude in the face of considerable obstacles. Nevertheless, just because Puerto Rican women exercise some agency does not mean they have full reproductive freedom; and just because they do not have full reproductive freedom does not mean they are all victims. This holds true for all women. In this ethnography, poor women's reproductive options have been shown to be more circumscribed than middle-class women's; however, even though middle-class women tend to exercise more reproductive freedom than poor women, neither do they necessarily exercise optimal reproductive freedom.

The challenge that remains for Puerto Rican women, indeed all women, is one that no longer can be framed in binary terms of agency or victimhood: the need for all women and men to work for optimal reproductive freedom. This means optimizing all aspects of human activity—personal, cultural, and social.

For optimal reproductive freedom to exist for everyone, we would need to live in a world where socially responsible women and men with a high degree of self- and gender awareness actively participate in birth control and domestic and child rearing responsibilities. In this way, such responsibilities would not continue to fall unevenly on women, but would be shared by both sexes. A gender-aware and equitable society would provide decent affordable housing, education, health care, and childcare for everyone, enabling men and women to fulfill themselves through education, leisure, and meaningful work. An optimal society would welcome different types of sexualities and family forms. It may even develop new family organizations where the everyday work of cooking and cleaning is shared and more adults are encouraged to share in the child-rearing process.

An integral perspective grew out of my desire to reconcile the contradictions between what women said about why they were sterilized and what I knew about them. The challenge was to provide a space where Puerto Rican women's voices could be heard and situated within the broader framework of the cultural, social, and historical experiences. The integral model of reproductive freedom is an interpretive strategy that enables a researcher to see the complexity of social phenomena, a way of reconciling the individual, cultural, social, and political elements in lives of individual groups as they are lived. In this way, it is a tool for analysis. But it is more than that. It also includes an image of social justice toward which we can strive. As a daughter of this neighborhood, I have the Puerto Rican women in my study to thank for that—because their participation in helping us to see and to understand their social worlds opens up new vistas of human possibility. By letting me into their lives and allowing me to share my life with them, the brave and resilient Puerto Rican women, and their families with whom I worked, opened up their hearts and shared intimate stories that enabled me to understand the complexity of their lives and the meaning of something highly personal, to them, to me, and perhaps to every woman as well.

Appendix: Genealogical Charts

The Velez Family

First Generation
Doña Hilda
Mother

Age: 1981: 59
2006: 84
Number of Children: 2
Reproductive Status: Hysterectomy

Second Generation
Evelyn
Daughter

Age: 1981: 25
2006: 50
Number of Children: 2
Reproductive Status: Sterilized

Third Generation
Frankie
Grandson-in-Law

Age: 1981: 4
2006: 29
Reproductive Status:
Considering a
vasectomy

Third Generation
Cookie
Granddaughter

Age: 1981: 3
2006: 28
Number of children: 1
Reproductive Status:
Not sterilized

Third Generation
Gabriele
Granddaughter

Age: 1981: 4
2006: 29
Number of children: 0
Reproductive Status:
Not sterilized

Fourth Generation
Frankie Jr.
Great-Grandson

Age: 2006: 9

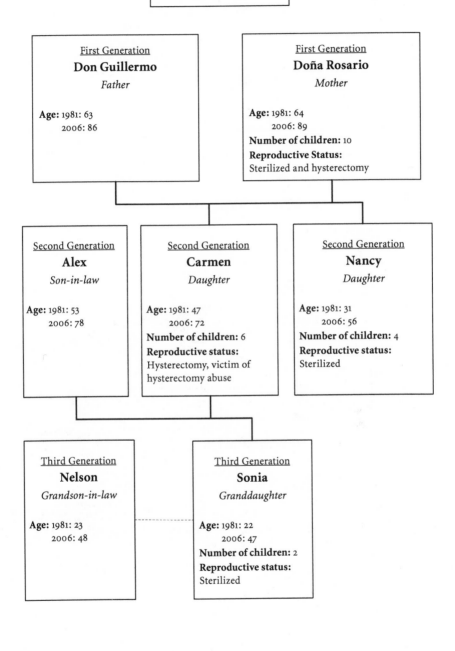

The Robles Family

First Generation
Don Guillermo
Father

Age: 1981: 63
2006: 86

First Generation
Doña Rosario
Mother

Age: 1981: 64
2006: 89
Number of children: 10
Reproductive Status:
Sterilized and hysterectomy

Second Generation
Alex
Son-in-law

Age: 1981: 53
2006: 78

Second Generation
Carmen
Daughter

Age: 1981: 47
2006: 72
Number of children: 6
Reproductive status:
Hysterectomy, victim of
hysterectomy abuse

Second Generation
Nancy
Daughter

Age: 1981: 31
2006: 56
Number of children: 4
Reproductive status:
Sterilized

Third Generation
Nelson
Grandson-in-law

Age: 1981: 23
2006: 48

Third Generation
Sonia
Granddaughter

Age: 1981: 22
2006: 47
Number of children: 2
Reproductive status:
Sterilized

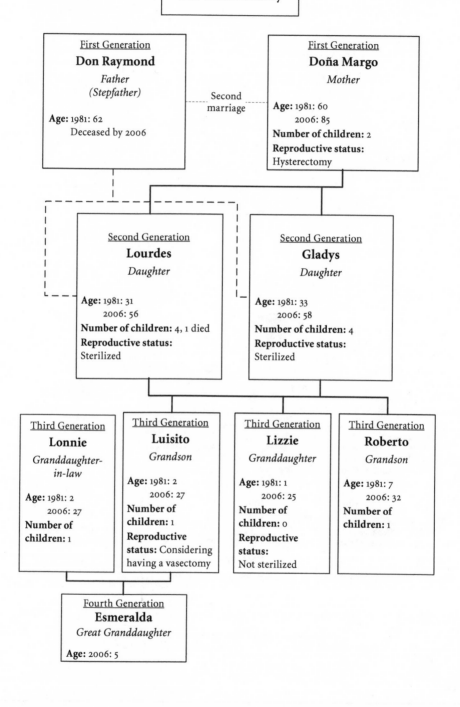

The Gomez Family

First Generation
Don Raymond
Father
(Stepfather)

Age: 1981: 62
Deceased by 2006

Second marriage

First Generation
Doña Margo
Mother

Age: 1981: 60
2006: 85
Number of children: 2
Reproductive status: Hysterectomy

Second Generation
Lourdes
Daughter

Age: 1981: 31
2006: 56
Number of children: 4, 1 died
Reproductive status: Sterilized

Second Generation
Gladys
Daughter

Age: 1981: 33
2006: 58
Number of children: 4
Reproductive status: Sterilized

Third Generation
Lonnie
Granddaughter-in-law

Age: 1981: 2
2006: 27
Number of children: 1

Third Generation
Luisito
Grandson

Age: 1981: 2
2006: 27
Number of children: 1
Reproductive status: Considering having a vasectomy

Third Generation
Lizzie
Granddaughter

Age: 1981: 1
2006: 25
Number of children: 0
Reproductive status: Not sterilized

Third Generation
Roberto
Grandson

Age: 1981: 7
2006: 32
Number of children: 1

Fourth Generation
Esmeralda
Great Granddaughter

Age: 2006: 5

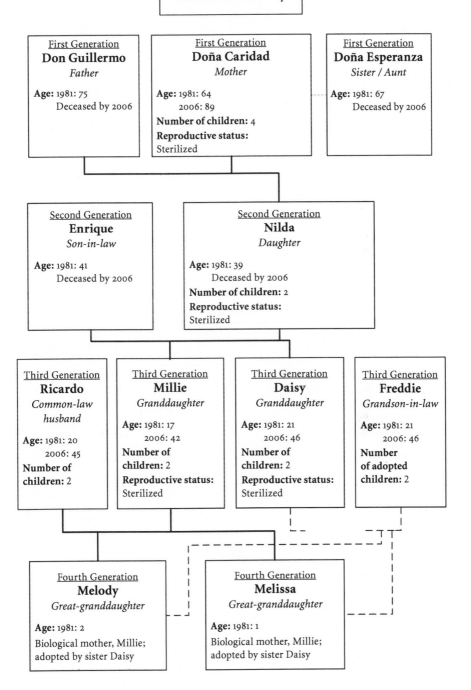

The Morales Family

First Generation
Don Guillermo
Father

Age: 1981: 75
Deceased by 2006

First Generation
Doña Caridad
Mother

Age: 1981: 64
2006: 89
Number of children: 4
Reproductive status:
Sterilized

First Generation
Doña Esperanza
Sister / Aunt

Age: 1981: 67
Deceased by 2006

Second Generation
Enrique
Son-in-law

Age: 1981: 41
Deceased by 2006

Second Generation
Nilda
Daughter

Age: 1981: 39
Deceased by 2006
Number of children: 2
Reproductive status:
Sterilized

Third Generation
Ricardo
*Common-law
husband*

Age: 1981: 20
2006: 45
**Number of
children:** 2

Third Generation
Millie
Granddaughter

Age: 1981: 17
2006: 42
**Number of
children:** 2
Reproductive status:
Sterilized

Third Generation
Daisy
Granddaughter

Age: 1981: 21
2006: 46
**Number of
children:** 2
Reproductive status:
Sterilized

Third Generation
Freddie
Grandson-in-law

Age: 1981: 21
2006: 46
**Number
of adopted
children:** 2

Fourth Generation
Melody
Great-granddaughter

Age: 1981: 2
Biological mother, Millie;
adopted by sister Daisy

Fourth Generation
Melissa
Great-granddaughter

Age: 1981: 1
Biological mother, Millie;
adopted by sister Daisy

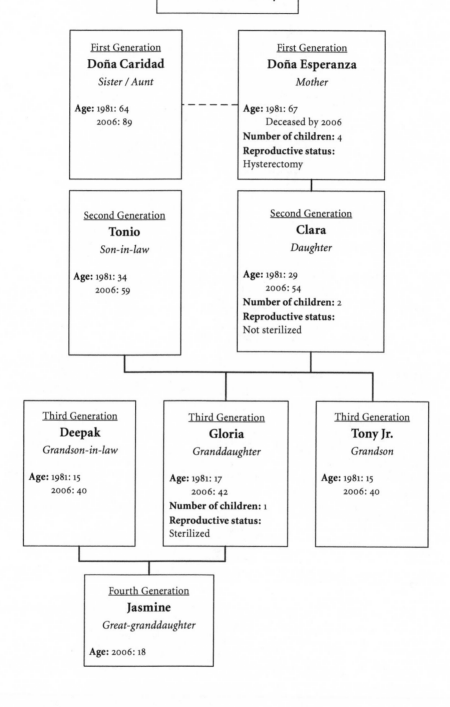

The Rivera Family

First Generation
Doña Caridad
Sister / Aunt

Age: 1981: 64
2006: 89

First Generation
Doña Esperanza
Mother

Age: 1981: 67
Deceased by 2006
Number of children: 4
Reproductive status:
Hysterectomy

Second Generation
Tonio
Son-in-law

Age: 1981: 34
2006: 59

Second Generation
Clara
Daughter

Age: 1981: 29
2006: 54
Number of children: 2
Reproductive status:
Not sterilized

Third Generation
Deepak
Grandson-in-law

Age: 1981: 15
2006: 40

Third Generation
Gloria
Granddaughter

Age: 1981: 17
2006: 42
Number of children: 1
Reproductive status:
Sterilized

Third Generation
Tony Jr.
Grandson

Age: 1981: 15
2006: 40

Fourth Generation
Jasmine
Great-granddaughter

Age: 2006: 18

Notes

1. Tubal ligation is the medical procedure that terminates women's reproductive capacity. It consists of cutting and suturing the fallopian tubes in order to permanently block the flow of sperm to the egg cell and to prevent the egg from entering the uterus. A hysterectomy is a form of sterilization generally implemented for medical reasons rather than birth control. There are two types of hysterectomies, partial and full. A partial hysterectomy is when the fallopian tubes are removed. A full hysterectomy is when a woman's fallopian tubes and uterus are removed.

2. Nancy had remarried by the year 2006; however, her household income could still be considered below or close to below the poverty level. For example, in the year 2006, the U.S. governement determined that the official poverty line was $20,444 for a family of two adults and two children. In 2008, New York Mayor Bloomberg tried to redefine the poverty level for the same family as $26,138 (Rauh 2008).

3. In many cases, a developing country in need of aid agrees to lower its rate of population growth in order to receive funds or to be forgiven a loan. The sad reality is that in many Third World countries sterilization continues to be used as population control because those governments do not offer women and men viable birth control alternatives (Hartmann 1995).

4. As a graduate student I reformulated the oppositional framework. However, I am now aware that many other social scientists have critiqued this model. My study is an example of why the binary model does not work.

5. To ensure confidentiality, all of the interviewees' names have been changed.

CHAPTER 1 — THE BIRTH CONTROL MOVEMENT IN PUERTO RICO

1. In 1933 Germany passed laws that led to the sterilization of 200,000 Jews and others in Nazi concentration camps. Hitler modeled the laws on those developed by the U.S. Eugenics Record Office (Gaag 1998).

2. Yet, oddly enough there are more statistics available on tubal ligation in Puerto Rico than in the continental United States.

...se is a calculation that shows the population growth
...and deaths without taking into account immigration

...nong Puerto Rican women declined in the late twentieth century. See Colón et al. 1999, 63.

5. Schoen argues that even though this eugenic law was passed in Puerto Rico, the majority of the sterilizations that took place were elective. According to her work, she only found ninety-seven sterilization operations were undertaken in Puerto Rico for eugenic reasons (Schoen 2005, 213, 206).

6. The pharmaceutical industry played a powerful role in the history of Puerto Rico's birth control movement. For example, according to Briggs the pharmaceuticals in Puerto Rico were so influential that when Rockefeller refused to fund birth control research in Puerto Rico the pharmaceuticals did (Briggs 2002, 124).

7. See Alice Colón-Warren et al. (1999) for an excellent analysis of the history of abortion in Puerto Rico. See also Azize-Vargas and Avilés (1997).

CHAPTER 2 — GENDER AWARENESS ACROSS GENERATIONS

1. Prior to the industrialization of Puerto Rico, life was harsh. In the 1940s, the average life expectancy was 46.0 years as compared to 63.6 for residents of the U.S. mainland (CRS Report 2006, 3; Puerto Rico Health n.d.). In general, the poor were malnourished and suffered from poor health. The most common illnesses in Puerto Rico prior to 1940 were anemia, tuberculosis, hookworm, and typhoid fever. One of the primary reasons the second generation women accepted sterilization was because of their poverty and the high rate of maternal mortality. Because poor women were malnourished and suffered from chronic anemia and other debilitating health problems, frequent consecutive pregnancies made them more vulnerable to certain health conditions.

2. The Catholic Church and the *Independentistas* adamantly opposed birth control and frequently forced these clinics to close down. In addition, in the early 1940s corporate millionaire Clarence Gamble temporarily monopolized the birth control market in order to promote his own methods. As historian Briggs (2002) notes, this gap in the birth control market led a significant number of Puerto Rican women to accept sterilization because it was the only effective method available on the market at this time.

3. Doña Rosario's example shows how embedded la operación had become in Puerto Rico's cultural politics. Puerto Rican women sought out these politicians, and corrupt officials—who abused their power by offering la operación as a bargaining chip for political favors—garnered enough votes to remain in office. A similar situation occurred in Brazil. See A. Caetano and J. Potter, "Politics and female sterilization in northeast Brazil," Population and Development Review 30:1 (March 2004): 79–108.

4. Statistics from the garment industry, where many Puerto Rican women in New York were employed, illustrate this transition. Between 1947 and 1958 a total of 54,000 jobs were lost in the garment industry. In the succeeding decade 72,000 jobs were lost (Ortiz 1996, 62), resulting in total job losses between 1960 and 1970 of 137,000 jobs (40 percent). As these jobs diminished, Puerto Rican women experienced a sharp decline in labor force participation, dropping from 35 percent to 24 percent. In contrast, the participation of American white females only dropped from 29 percent to 28 percent in the same period (Ortiz 1996).

5. Joseph Lasalle, People's Firehouse, Brooklyn, pers. comm., August 12, 1980.

CHAPTER 3 — THE VELEZ FAMILY

1. Doña Hilda refers to Eddie as her husband because he is the father of her daughter, Evelyn. However, as she states, she did not marry him, because by her standards they were not in a functional relationship.

CHAPTER 4 — THE ROBLES FAMILY

1. In the 1950s and 1960s, Puerto Ricans commonly bought jobs. The employer charged them the first week of pay for the job. *[handwritten: └ this is weird?]*

CHAPTER 5 — THE GOMEZ FAMILY

1. For a discussion of the reciprocity system and a process equivalent to children by rearing among African Americans in the United States, see Stack (1997).

2. An ectopic pregnancy occurs when the egg is fertilized in a woman's fallopian tube and starts to grow there. If this condition is not detected immediately, the fallopian tube explodes, which can be deadly.

CHAPTER 6 — THE MORALES AND RIVERA FAMILIES

1. By the term "new" doña Caridad meant that she was young and naive.

CHAPTER 7 — IDEOLOGIES AND INEQUALITIES IN THE HEALTH CARE SYSTEM

1. Unlike China, which has an official and blatantly coercive population control program, Puerto Rico's is unofficial and more subtle. Puerto Rican women's experiences with la operación are more varied. Although some women have been subjected to sterilization abuse, most women use it as a way of empowering themselves by taking control of their bodies. Some get sterilized after they have achieved their desired family size, and others use it as a coping mechanism to try and gain a modicum of control over their lives, especially after they have surpassed their desired family size.

2. Tubal ligation has a failure rate of 1/10 of 1 percent (Bower 1995; Zurawin 2006). Although this is a very low percentage, pregnancies can occur, according to Bower, due to surgical error, equipment failure, or the natural processes in which the body reestablishes itself.

3. Despite the fact that the United States has excellent health care, individual medical care is fragmented unless a doctor or social worker coordinates it. Since the majority of the poor receive inconsistency of care theirs is even more fragmented than individuals who have private doctors.

4. The trend in caesareans is changing. Other studies show that the rate among educated women and middle-income women, in the United States and worldwide, has increased (Colon et al. 199, 62; Groom 200; Moaveni 2006). This is due to a combination of doctors' scheduling convenience and women's desire to avoid labor.

5. Alternative treatments are available for fibroid tumors. Nonsurgical treatments include hormones and pain relief medicine. Taking gonadotropin-releasing hormone can cause fibroids to shrink.

CHAPTER 8 — TOWARD AN INTEGRAL MODEL OF REPRODUCTIVE FREEDOM

1. This belief in the importance of having children to cement a relationship is not as prevalent in the third generation.

References

Abramovitz, M. 1988. *Regulating the lives of women: Social welfare policy from colonial times to the present*. Boston: South End Press.

Acuña-Lillo, E. 1988. The reproductive health of Latinas in New York City: Making a difference at the individual level. In *A community at risk: The health of Puerto Ricans*, 2:4, 7–15.

Alvarado, C. R., and C. Tietze. 1947. Birth control in Puerto Rico. *Human Fertility* 12 (1): 15–18.

Arras, J. D., and J. Blustein. 1995. Reproductive responsibility and long-acting contraceptives. *Special Supplement, Hastings Center Report*, 25, ser. 1, S27–S29.

Ayala, C. J., and R. Bernabe. 2007. *Puerto Rico in the American century: A history since 1898*. Chapel Hill: University of North Carolina Press.

Azize-Vargas, Y. 2000. The Emergence of feminism in Puerto Rico, 1870–1930. In *Unequal sisters: A multicultural reader in U.S. women's history*, ed. Vicki L. Ruiz and Ellen Carol Dubois, 268–275. New York: Routledge.

Azize-Vargas, Y., and L. Aviles. 1997. Abortion in Puerto Rico: The limits of colonial legality. Reproductive Health Matters 5 (9): 56–65.

Barnes, J. E. 2000. The two faces of Bushwick. *New York Times*, February 27.

Benjamin, B. C. 2003. Hysterectomy: A primer. http://www.students.haverford.edu/wmbweb/topics/hysterectomy.html.

Blendon, R. J., A. Scheck, K. Donelan, C. Hill, M. Smith, D. F. Beatrice, D. Altman. 1995. How whites and African Americans view their health and social problems. *Journal of the American Medical Association* 272 (4): 341–46.

Bonilla, F., and R. Campos. 1986. *Industry and idleness*. New York: Centro de Estudios Puertorriquenos.

Bower, K. 1995. Tubal Ligations: Some questions and answers. http://www.cc/i.org/nfp/tubal.phb.

Bowser, R. 2003. Self-Perpetuating mythology: The degenerate black patient. http://academic.udayton.edu/health/03access/bias01.htm.

Braveman, P., S. Egerter, F. Edmonston, and M. Verdon. 1995. Racial/ethnic differences in the likelihood of caesarean delivery, California. *American Journal of Public Health* 85 (May): 625–630.

Briggs, L. 2002. *Reproducing empire: Race, sex, science, and U.S. imperialism in Puerto Rico*. Berkeley: University of California Press.

Brown, G. F. 1995. Long-acting contraceptives: Rationale, current development, and ethnical implications. *Special Supplement, Hastings Center Report*, 25, ser. 1, S12–S15.

Browner, C. H. 1993. New feminist scholarship on reproduction and women's health. *Signs: Journal of Women in Culture and Society* 18 (3): 698–703.

Browner, C. H., and C. F. Sargent. 1990. Anthropology and human reproduction. In *Medical anthropology: A handbook of theory and Research*, ed. T. Johnson and C. F. Sargent, 215–29. Westport, CT: Greenwood Press.

Bruni, F. 2002. Persistent drop in fertility reshapes Europe's future. *New York Times*, December 26.

Canino, G. J., M. Rubio-Stipec, R. Shroat, and H. R. Bird. 1987. Sex differences and depression in Puerto Rico. *Psychology of Women Quarterly* 11:443–459.

CARASA. 1979. *Women under attack: Abortion, sterilization abuse, and reproductive freedom*. New York: Photo Comp Press.

Carlson, J., and G. Vickers. 1982. Voluntary sterilization and informed consent: Are guidelines needed? Manuscript available from United Methodist Church, 475 Riverside Drive, New York, NY 10115.

Caro, F., E. Marshall, A. Carter, D. Kalmuss Darabi, and I. Lopez. 1988. *Barriers to prenatal care: An examination of the use of prenatal care among low-income women in New York City*. New York: Community Service Society.

CDC on Infant and Maternal Mortality in the United States: 1900–49. 1999. *Population and Development Review* 25 (4): 821–826.

CESA. 1976. *Workshop on sterilization abuse*. Bronxville: Sarah Lawerence College.

Chancer, L. 1998. *Reconcilable differences: Confronting beauty, pornography, and the future of feminism*. California: University of California Press.

Chandra, A. 1998. Surgical sterilization in the U.S.: Prevalence and characteristics, 1965–95. *Department of Health, Vital Statistics* 23 (20): 1–33.

Chase, A. 1980. *The legacy of Malthus: The social costs of the new scientific racism*. Urbana: University of Illinois Press.

Chavkin, W., and E. Chesler, eds. 2005. *Where human rights begin: Health, sexuality, and women in the new millennium*. New Brunswick, N.J.: Rutgers University Press.

Chesler, E. 1992. *Women of valor: Margaret Sanger and the birth control movement in America*. New York: Simon and Schuster.

Cofresi, E. 1951. *Realidad poblacional de Puerto Rico*. San Juan: Universidad de Puerto Rico.

Cohen, H. 1982. Arson on the Hudson. *City Limits* (May): 8–10.

———. 1983. What the city arson study said and didn't say. *City Limits* (October): 11–12.

Collins, P. H. 1991. *Black feminist thought: Knowledge, consciousness, and the politics of empowerment*. New York: Routledge.

Colón, A., A. Dávila, M. D. Fernós, and E. Vicente. 1999. *Políticas, visiones y voces en torno al aborto en Puerto Rico*. San Juan, Puerto Rico: Universidad de Puerto Rico.

Colón-Warren, A. 1991. Reestructuracion industrial, empleo y pobreza en Puerto Rico y el alantico medio de los Estados Unidos: La situation de las mujeres puertorriquenas. *Revista De Ciencias Sociales* 3 (June): 135–188.

———. 2003a. Mujeres, familias y trabajas en Puerto Rico: Discusiones en la investigacion social. *Revista de Ciencias Sociales* 12:68–101.

———. 2003b. Puerto Rico: Feminism and feminist studies. *Internacional perspectivas on gender research* 17 (5): 664–690.

Colón-Warren, A., and E. P. Larrinaga, eds. 2001. *Silencios, presencias, y debates sobre el aborto en Puerto Rico y el Caribe Hispano.* San Juan: Universidad de Puerto Rico.

Committee for Abortion Rights and Against Sterilization Abuse. 1979. *Women under attack: Abortion, sterilization abuse and reproductive freedom.* New York: Committee for Abortion Rights and Against Sterilization Abuse.

Cook, R. 1993. International human rights and reproductive health. *Studies in Family Planning* 24 (2): 73–86.

Cook, R., J. Kickens, and M. F. Fathall. 2003. Reproductive health and human rights. New York: Oxford University Press.

Cooney, R., and A. Colón-Warren. 1996. Work and the family: The recent struggle of Puerto Rican females. In *Historical perspectives on Puerto Rican survival in the United States*, ed. Clara E. Rodriguez and Virginia Sanchez-Korral. Princeton: Marcus Wiener.

Correa, S., and R. Petchesky. 1994a. Exposing the numbers game: Feminists challenge the population control establishment. *Ms.* 5 (2): 10, 13, 15–17.

Correa, S., and R. Petchesky. 1994b. Reproductive and sexual rights: A feminist perspective. In *Population policies reconsidered*, ed. G. Sen, A. Germain, and I. C. Chen. Cambridge: Harvard University Press.

Crespo-Kebler, E. 2001a. Ciudadanía y nación: Debates sobre los derechos reproductivos en Puerto Rico. *Revista de Ciencias Sociales* 10:57–84.

———. 2001b. Liberación de la mujer: Los feminismos, la justicia social, la nación y la autonomiá en las organizaciones feministas de la decada de 1970–1979. In *Documentos del feminismo en Puerto Rico: Facsímiles de la historia. Vol. 1, 1970–1979*, ed. L. Rivera and E. Crespo-Kebler. San Juan: Editorial de La Universidad de Puerto Rico.

Crossette, B. 2002. Population estimates fall as poor women assert control. *New York Times*, March 10.

Dávila, A. 1990, April. Esterilizacion y practica anticonceptiva en Puerto Rico. *Puerto Rico Health Sciences Journal* 9 (1): 61–67.

———. 1994. Las practicas reproductivas ante las políticas de poblacion: Regulaciones de la fecundidad y tendencias demograficas entre las mujeres Puertorriquenas. Paper presented in October at the Demography Program, School of Public Health, Brandeis University, Waltham, MA.

Davis, A. 1981. *Women, peace and class.* New York: Random House.

Depenbrok v. Kaiser Foundation Health Plan, Inc. 1978. 79 CA3d 167. http://online.ceb.com/CalCases/CA3/79CA3d167.htm.

Diniz, S. G., and A. S. Chacham. 2004. "The cut above" and "the cut below": The abuse of caesareans and episiotomy in Sao Paulo, Brazil. *Reproductive Health Matters* 12 (23): 100–110.

Dixon-Mueller, R. 1993. *Population policy and women's rights: Transforming reproductive choice.* Westport, CT: Praeger.

Doescher, M. P., B. G. Saver, and K. Fiscella. 2000. Racial and ethnic disparities in perceptions of physician style and trust. *Archives of Family Medicine* 2000 (9): 1156–1163.

Dresser, R. 1995. Long-term contraceptives in the criminal justice system. *Hastings Center Report, Special Supplement,* 25, ser. 1, S15–S18.

Duany, J. 2002. *The Puerto Rican nation on the move: Identities on the island and in the United States.* Chapel Hill: University of North Carolina Press.

Earnhardt, K. C. 1982. *Development planning and population policy development in Puerto Rico: A case study and a plan for population stabilization.* San Juan, Puerto Rico: Editorial de la Universidad de Puerto Rico.

Egbert, L. D., and I. L. Rothman. 2003. Relation between the race and economic status of patients and who performs their surgery. *New England Journal of Medicine.* http://content.nejm.org/cgi/content/abstract/297/2/90.

Ehlers Bachrach, T. 1991. Debunking marianismo: Economic vulnerability and survival strategies among Guatemalan wives. *Ethnology* 1 (30): 1–6.

Ehrlich, P. R. 1968. *The population bomb.* New York: Ballantine books.

Laraque, F., E. Grahman, and K. Roussillon. 1995. *Sterilization in New York City, 1995.* New York: New York City Department of Health, Bureau of Maternity Services and Family Planning.

Fathalla, M. F. 1996. A woman-centered agenda for the twenty-first century. *Advances in Contraception* 12 (4) (December): 331–334.

Fernos, M. D. 2001. El aborto en la política de control poblacional en Puerto Rico. In *Silencios, presencias y debates sobre el aborto en Puerto Rico y el Caribe Hispaño,* ed. Alice E. Colón and Elsa Planell Larrinaga. San Juan: Projecto Atlantea, Intercambio Academico Caribe Universidad de Puerto Rico.

Foster, R. 1994. The Cairo Conference: The stakes, the players. *International News* 5 (2): 12–13.

Fox Piven, F., and R. Cloward. 1979. *Poor people's movements: Why they succeed, how they fail.* New York: Random House.

Freedman, L. P., and L. S. Isaacs. 1993. Human rights and reproductive choice. *Studies in Family Planning* 241:18–30.

Gaag, N. 1998. Of woman born: A history of reproduction, contraception, and control. *New Internationalist* (303). http://www.newint.org/issue303/history.htm.

Garcia, A. M. 1982. *La Operación.* Directed and produced by Ana Maria Garcia with Latin America Film Project. New York: Cinema Guild.

Gil, R. M., and C. I. Vasquez. 1996. *The Maria paradox: How Latinas can merge old world traditions with new world self-esteem.* New York: G. P. Putnam Press.

Ginsburg, F. D., and R. Rapp 1995. *Conceiving the new world order: The global politics of reproduction.* Berkeley: University of California Press.

Goleman, D. 2007. *Social intelligence: The revolutionary new science of human relationships.* New York: Bantam.

Gonzalez, J. 2000. *Harvest of empire: A history of Latinos in America.* New York: Penguin Books.

Gordon, L. 1990. *Women's body, women's right: Birth control in America.* New York: Penguin Books.

Gould, S. 1996. *The mismeasure of man.* New York: W. W. Norton and Co.

Grady, D. 2004. Trying to avoid second caesarean, many find choice isn't theirs. *New York Times*, November 29.

Groom, K., S. Paterson Brown, L. G. Quadros, K. Eftekhar, P. Steer, M. Pai, N. Sabrine, M. P. O'Connell, W. Lindow, J. M. Belizán, F. Althabe, F. Barros, S. Alexander, and C. Nuttall. 2000. Caesarean section controversy. *British Medical Journal* 320 (7241): 1072–1074.

Hansen, K. V. 2005. *Not-so-nuclear families: Class, gender, and networks of care.* New Brunswick, NJ: Rutgers University Press.

Hartmann, B. 1995. *Reproductive rights and wrongs: The global politics of population control.* Boston: South End Press.

Hayt, E. 2003. Surprise, mom: I'm against abortion: Parents expecting young people to take the liberal view, as in the past, learn otherwise. *New York Times*, March 30.

Henderson, P. M. 1976. *Population policy, social structure and health system in Puerto Rico: The case of female sterilization.* Ann Arbor, MI: University Microfilms International.

Hernandez-Alvarez, J. 1976. *Return migration.* New York: Greenwood Press.

Herrnstein, R. C. M., and C. Murray. 1994. *The bell curve: The shaping of American life by difference in intelligence.* New York: Free Press.

History Task Force/Centro de Estudios Puertorriquenos. 1979. *Labor migration under Capitalism: The Puerto Rican experience.* New York: Monthly Review Press.

———. 1982. *Sources for the study of Puerto Rican migration.* New York City: Hunter College.

Hopkin, K. 2000. Are Brazilian women really choosing to deliver by caesarean? *Social Science and Medicine* 51 (5): 725–740.

Jukelevics, N. 2004. *Once a cesarean, always a cesarean: The sorry state of birth choices in America* 123 (March/April): 1–10. http://www.mothering.com.

Kaufman, J., Z. Zhirong, Q. Xinjianj, and Z. Yang. 1992. The quality of family planning services in rural China. *Studies in Family Planning* 23 (2): 73–84.

Kasarda, J. D. 1993. Inner-city concentrated poverty and neighborhood distress: 1970–1990. *Housing Policy Debate* 4 (3): 271. http://www.fanniemaefoundation.org/program/hpd/pdf/hpd_0403-Kasarda.pdf.

Kent, M. 1987. Survey report: Puerto Rico. *Population Today* 15 (2): 4.

Kevles, D. J. 1985. *In the name of eugenics: Genetics and the uses of human heredity.* Berkeley and Los Angeles: University of California Press.

Kjerulff, K. H., G. M. Guzinsi, P. W. Langenberg, P. D. Stolley, N. E. Moye, and V. A. Kazabjijian. 1993. Hysterectomy and race. *Obstetrics Gynecology* 82 (5): 757–764.

Kjerulff, K. H., P. Langenberg, and G. Guzinski. 1993. The socioeconomic correlates of hysterectomies in the United States. *American Journal of Health* 83 (1): 106–108.

Krase, K. 1996. Sterilization abuse: The policies behind the practice. *National Women's Health Network, Network News* 1 (4).

Lai Y. M., J. D. Lee, C. L. Lee, T. C. Chen, Y. K. Soong. 1995. An ectopic pregnancy embedded in the myometrium of a previous cesarean section scar. *Acta Obstet Gynecol Scand* 74 (7): 573–576.

Laraque, F., E. Graham, and E. and K. Roussillon. 1995. *Sterilization in New York City 1995.* New York: Bureau of Maternity Services, New York City Department of Health.

Laureano-Cartagena, S. M. 1994. Sterilization in Puerto Rico: From massive and imposed to wanted and not available. In *We speak for ourselves: Population and development*, 100–105. Washington, DC: Panos Institute.

Leacock, E. 1971. The culture of poverty: A critique. New York: Simon and Schuster.

Leon, L. E. 1996. *Sterilization and depression: A study of Puerto Rican Women living in New York*. Ann Arbor, MI: University Microfilms International.

Lewis, O. 1966. *La vida: A Puerto Rican family in the culture of poverty*. New York: Random House.

Lewontin, R. C., S. Rose, and Kamin L. J. 1984. *Not in our genes: Biology, ideology, and human nature*. New York: Pantheon.

Linder, F. E., and R. D. Grove. 1943. Vital statistics in the United States, 1900–1940. Washington, D.C.: Government Printing Office.

Lindemann Nelson, H., and J. Lindemann. 1995. Feminism, social policy, and long-acting contraception. *Hastings Center Report*, 25, ser. 1, S30–S32.

Loaiza, E. 1995. Sterilization regret in the Dominican Republic: Looking for quality-of-care issues. *Studies in Family Planning* 26 (1): 39–48.

Lock, M., and A. P. Kaufert, eds. 1998. *Pragmatic women and body politics*. Cambridge UK: Cambridge University Press.

Lombard, P. 2006. *Eugenic sterilization laws. Image archive on the American eugenics movement*. http://www.eugenicsarchive.org/html/eugenics/essaysandtext.html.

Lopez, I. 1980. Sterilization in Puerto Rico: Coercion or personal choice? *Genes and Gender* 2:84–98.

———. 1983. Extended views: Social coercion and sterilization among Puerto Rican women. *Sage Relations* 8 (3): 27–40.

———. 1985. Sterilization among Puerto Rican women: A case study in New York City. Ph.D. diss., Columbia University, New York.

———. 1988. Barriers to the timely use of prenatal care among non-white women in New York City. *Special Health Issue, Estudios Puertorriquenos Bulletin* (Fall): 72–77.

———. 1993. Agency and constraint: Sterilization and reproductive freedom among Puerto Rican women in New York City. *Urban Anthropology and Studies of Cultural Systems* 22 (3–4): 299–343.

———. 1998. An ethnography of the medicalization of Puerto Rican women's reproduction. In *Pragmatic women and body politics*, ed. M. Lock and P. A. Kaufert, 240–259. Cambridge, UK: Cambridge University Press.

Lowe, N. K. 2003. Amazed or appalled, apathy or action? *Journal of obstetric, gynecological, and neonatal nursing* 32 (3): 281–282.

Lykes, B. M., A. Banuazizi, L. Ramsay, and M. Morris, eds. 1996. *Myths about the powerless: Contesting social inequalities*. Philadelphia: Temple University Press.

Marks, J. 2003. *What it means to be 98% chimpanzee: Apes, people, and their genes*. Berkeley: University of California Press.

Marreo, S. A. 1977. Puerto Rico: The kept woman of the United States. Master's thesis, Columbia University.

Mass, B. 1976. Emigration and sterilization in Puerto Rico. *Population target: The political economy of population in Latin America*. Toronto: Latin America Working Group.

May, E. T. 1995. *Barren in the promised land: Childless Americans and the pursuit of happiness*. Cambridge, MA: Harvard University Press.

Moaveni, A. 2006. Iran's Caesarean Section Craze. http://www.time.com/time/printout/0,8816,1537543.html

Mooney, J. 2004. Neighborhood on the verge? *New York Times*, January 25.

Morgan, L. A. 1981. The Hispanic female headed households. MS. Puerto Rican Legal Defense and Education Fund.

Moskowitz, E. H., B. Jennings, and D. Callahan. 1995. Long-acting contraceptives: Ethical guidance for policymakers and health care providers. *Hastings Center Report, Special Supplement*, 25, ser. 1, S1–S8.

Moynihan P. 1965. The Negro family: The case for national action. Washington, D.C.: Office of Policy Planning and Research, United States Department of Labor.

Mullings, L. 1978. The new ethnicity: Old wine in new bottles? *Reviews in Anthropology* 4:614–624.

Nash, J., and H. Safa, eds. 1986. *Women and change in Latin America: New directions in the study of sex and class*. South Hadley, MA: Bergin and Garvey Publishers.

Navarro, M. 2004. For younger Latinos, a shift to smaller families. *New York Times*, December 5.

Negro-Muntaner, F., and R. Grosfoguel, eds. 1997. *Puerto Rican jam: Essays on culture and politics*. Minneapolis: University of Minnesota Press.

New York City Department of City Planning. 1981. Proposed seventh year community development program: Application and budget. Unpublished report. May.

New York City Department of Health. 1982. Sterilizations reported in New York City in 1978. Department of Biostatistics, unpublished data.

Ortiz, A. 1996. En la aguja y el pedal eche la hiel: Puerto Rican women in the garment industry in New York City, 1920–1980. In *Puerto Rican women and work: Bridges in transnational labor*, ed. Altagracia Ortiz. Philadelphia: Temple University Press, 55–81.

Paniagua, M. E., M. E. Tayback, J. L. Janer, and J. L. Vasquez. 1973. Medical and psychological sequelae of surgical sterilization of women. In *Foolproof birth control: Male and female sterilization*. Boston: Beacon Press.

Pantelides, E. A., and S. Bott, eds. 2000. *Reproducción, salud, y sexualidad en America Latina*. Buenos Aires: Editorial Biblos.

Parrilla-Bonilla, A. 1975. Puerto Rico: Un caso de genocidio por la manipulación poblacional imperialista. *Desarrolla Indoamericano* 9 (28): 19–22.

Pessar, P. 1995. *A visa for a dream: Dominicans in the United States*. Boston: Allyn and Bacon.

Petchesky, R. P. 1981. "Reproductive choice" in the contemporary United States: A social analysis of female sterilization. In *And the poor get children: Radical perspectives on population dynamics*, ed. K. L. Michaelson, 50–87. New York: Monthly Review Press.

———. 1984. *Abortion and woman's choice: The state, sexuality, and reproductive freedom*. New York: Longman.

———. 1995. From population control to reproductive rights: Feminist fault lines. *Reproductive Health Matters* 6:152–161.

———. 2003. *Global prescriptions: Gendering health and human rights*. New York: Zed Books.

Petchesky, R. P., and K. Judd, eds. 1998. *Negotiating reproductive rights: Women's perspectives across countries and cultures*. London and New York: Zed Books.

Petersen, Herbert B., X. Zhisen, and J. Hughes. 1996. The risk of ectopic pregnancy after tubal sterilization. *American Journal of Obstetrics and Gynecology* 174 (4): 1161–1168.

Physicians for Human Rights. 2003. The right to equal treatment: An action plan to end racial and ethnic disparities in clinical diagnosis and treatment in the United States. A report by the Panel on Racial and Ethnic Disparities in Medical Care convened by Physicians for Human Rights, Boston.

Potter, J., E. Berquo, H. O. Ignez, I. H. Perpetuo, L. Fachel Ondina, and K. Hopkins. 2001. Unwanted caesarean sections among public and private patients in Brazil. *Prospective study* 323 (November): 1155–1158.

Powderly, K. E. 1995. Illustrations from American history. *Hastings Center Report, Special Supplement* 25, ser. 1, S9–S11.

Presser, H. B. 1973. *Sterilization and fertility decline in Puerto Rico.* Westport, CT: Greenwood Press.

———. 1978. Contraceptive sterilization as a grassroots response: A comparative view of the Puerto Rican and United States experience. In *Behavioral-Social aspects of contraceptive sterilization*, ed. S. H. Newman and Z. E. Klein, 25–48. Lexington, MA: Lexington Books.

Price, A. 2008. Do I Really Need That Hysterectomy? http://www.beckysingleton.com/doctor5.htm.

Puerto Rico Health. N.d. http://www.city-data.com/states/PuertoRico-Health.html.

Ramirez de Arellano, A., and C. Seipp. 1983. *Colonialism, Catholicism, and contraception: A history of birth control in Puerto Rico.* Chapel Hill: University of North Carolina Press.

Ramos-Bellido, C. G. 1977. *The politics of birth control in Puerto Rico.* Ann Arbor, MI: University Microfilm International.

Rauh, G. Bloomberg attempts to redefine poverty. *New York Sun*, July 14, 2008. http://www.nysun.com/new-york/bloomberg-attempts-to-redefine-poverty/81790/

Ringheim, K. 1993. Factors that determine prevalence of use of contraceptive methods for men. *Studies for Family Planning* 24 (2): 87–99.

Rivera-Batiz, F. L., and Santiago, C. E. 1996. *Island Paradox: Puerto Rico in the 1990s.* New York: Russell Sage Foundation.

Roberts, D. 1997. *Killing the black body: Race, reproduction, and the meaning of liberty.* New York: Pantheon.

Robertson, J. A. 1995. Norplant and irresponsible reproduction. *Hastings Center Report, Special Supplement*, 25, ser. 1, S23–S26.

Robles, R. R., R. E. Martinez, M. Vera, and M. Allegra. 1987. Health care Services and sterilization among Puerto Rican Women. Paper presented at the 115th annual meeting of the American Public Health Association, New Orleans, October 18–22.

Rodriguez, C. 1989. *Puerto Ricans: Born in the USA.* Boston: Unwin and Hyman.

———. 2005. Commentary: Forging a new, New York: The Puerto Rican community, post-1945. In *Boricuas in Gotham: Puerto Ricans in the making of modern New York City*, ed. G. Haslip-Viera, A. Falcon, and F. Matos Rodriguez, 195–218. Princeton: Markus Wiener.

Ross, L. 1994. Sterilization and 'de facto' sterilization. *AMICUS Journal* 29 (Winter). http://www.ncbi.nlm.nih.gov/sites/entrez?

Rothberg, D., and S. Kelly, eds. 1998. *Ken Wilber in dialogue: Conversations with leading transpersonal thinkers.* Wheaton, IL: Quest Books.

Saidi, M. H., and C. M. Zainie. 1980. *Female sterilization: A handbook for women.* New York: Garland Press.

Salvo, J., M. G. Powers, and R. S. Cooney. 1992. Contraceptive use and sterilization among Puerto Rican women. *Family Planning Perspectives* 24 (5): 219–223.

Sanabria, C. 2000. The Puerto Rican organized workers' movement and the American Federation of Labor, 1901 to 1934. Ph.D. diss., City University of New York.

Sanchez-Korral, V. 1994. *From colonia to community: The history of Puerto Ricans in New York City.* Berkeley: University of California Press.

———. 2005. Building the New York Puerto Rican community, 1945–1965: A historical interpretation. In *Boricuas in Gotham: Puerto Ricans in the making of modern New York City,* ed. G. Haslip-Viera, F. Matos-Rodriguez, and A. Falcon, 1–20. Princeton: Markus Wiener.

Sanhueza, H. and R. Jaimes. 1975. Contraceptives Progress in Latin America and the Caribbean. Proceedings of the IPPF/WHR Second Regional Medical Seminar held in Medellin, Columbia, November 25–26. International Planned Parenthood Federation, Western Hemisphere Region.

Santana-Cooney, R., and Colón-Warren, A. 1996. Work and family: The recent struggles of Puerto Rican women. In *Historical perspectives on Puerto Ricans' survival in the United States,* C. E. Rodriguez and V. Sanchez Korral, 69–85. Princeton, NJ: Markus Wiener Publishers.

Sassen, S. 1988. The mobility of labor and capital: A study of international investment and labor flow. New York: Praeger.

Satterhwaite, A. P. 1965. Experience with oral and intrauterine contraception in rural Puerto Rico. In *Public Health and Population Change,* ed. M. C. Scieps and J. C. Ridley, 474–480. Pittsburgh: University of Pittsburgh Press.

Schoen, J. 2005. *Choice and coercion: Birth control, sterilization, and abortion in public health and welfare.* Chapel Hill: University of North Carolina Press.

Scrimshaw, S. C. 1970. *The demand for female sterilization in Spanish Harlem: Experiences of Puerto Ricans in New York City.* Paper presented at the 69th Annual Meeting of the American Anthropological Association, San Diego, November 19.

Shah, M. A. 2003. Soaring caesarean section rates: A cause for alarm. *Journal of Obstetric, Gynecological, and Neonatal Nursing* 32 (3): 283–284.

Sidel, R. 1978. *Urban survival: The world of working-class women.* Boston: Beacon Press.

Silvestrini-Pachecho, B. 1986. Women as workers: The experience of the Puerto Rican women in the 1930s. In *The Puerto Rican woman: Perspectives on culture, history, and society,* ed. Edna Acosta-Belén. New York: Praeger.

Smedley, B. D., A. Y. Stith, and A. R. Nelson. 2003. *Unequal treatment: Confronting racial and ethnic disparities in health care.* Washington, DC: National Academies Press.

Solinger, R. 2001. *Beggars and choosers: How the politics of choice shaped adoption, abortion, and welfare in the United States.* New York: Hill and Wang.

Stack, C. 1997. *All our kin: Survival in a black community.* New York: Harper and Row.

Starr, P. 1984. *The social transformation of American medicine.* New York: Basic Books.

Stead, L., and S. R. Behera. 2007. Ectopic pregnancy. *Journal of Emergency Medicine* 32 (2): 205–206.

Steinbeck, B. 1995. Coercion and long-term contraceptives. *Hastings Center Report, Special Supplement,* 25, ser. 1, S19–S22.

Stevens, E. 1973. Marianismo: The other face of machismo. In *Female and male in Latin America.* Pittsburgh: University of Pittsburgh Press.

Stroup-Benham, C. A., and F. M. Trevino. 1991. Reproductive characteristics of Mexican-American, mainland Puerto Rican, and Cuban-American women: Data from the Hispanic health and nutrition examination survey. *Journal of the American Medical Association* 265 (2): 222–226.

Stycos, J. M. 1954 Female sterilization in Puerto Rico. *Eugenics Quarterly* 1 (June): 3–9.

————. 1955. *Family and fertility in Puerto Rico: A study of the lower income group.* New York: Columbia University Press.

Stycos, J. M., R. Hill, and K. Back. 1959. *The family and population control: A Puerto Rican experiment in social change.* Chapel Hill: University of North Carolina Press.

Toro-Morn, M. 2005. Boricuas en Chicago: Gender and class in the migration and settlement of Puerto Ricans. In *Puerto Rican diaspora: Historical Perspectives,* ed. C. T. Whalen and V. Vasquez-Hernandez, 125–150. Philadelphia: Temple University Press.

U.S. Bureau of Labor Statistics. 2007. Local area unemployment statistics: Puerto Rico. http://data.bls.gov.

U.S. Census Bureau. 2006. Percent of people below poverty level in the past 12 months for whom poverty status is determined: 2006. http://factfinder.census.gov.

U.S. Department of Health and Human Services. 2006. Fibroid tumor fact sheet. http://womenshealth.gov.

Valentine, C. A. 1968. *Culture and poverty: Critique and counterproposals.* Chicago: University of Chicago Press.

Vazquez-Calzada, J. L. 1973. La esterilización femenina en Puerto Rico. *Revista de ciencias sociales* 173 (September): 281–308.

————. 1982. Female sterilization in Puerto Rico and its demographic effectiveness. *Puerto Rico Health Sciences Journal* 1 (2): 68–79.

————. 1988. *La población de Puerto Rico y su trayectoria historica.* San Juan: Universidad de Puerto Rico, Escuela Graduada de Salud Pública.

Vazquez-Calzada, J. L., and J. Carnivali. 1982. *El uso de métodos anticonceptivos en Puerto Rico: Tendencias recientes.* Centro de Investigaciones Demográficas, Escuela de Salud Publica, Recinto de Ciencias Médicas, Monografí a número III. San Juan: Universidad de Puerto Rico.

Vazquez-Calzada, J. L., and Z. Morales del Valle. 1981. *La esterilización feminina y su efectividad demografica: El caso de Puerto Rico.* Escuela de Salud Publica, Recinto de Ciencias Medicas. San Juan: Universidad de Puerto Rico.

Velez, C. G. 1978. Se me acabó la canción: An ethnography of non-consenting sterilizations among Mexican women in Los Angeles. In *Mexican women in the United States: Struggles past and present,* ed. L. Castillo. Berkeley: University of California Press.

Wajcman, J. 1994. Delivered into men's hands? The social construction of reproductive technology. In *Power and decision: The social control of reproduction,* ed. Gita Sen and Rachel C. Snow, 153–175. Cambridge, MA: Harvard University Press.

Waldinger, R. 1996. *Still the promised city? African Americans and the new immigrants in postindustrial New York.* Cambridge, MA: Harvard University Press.

Wallach, E., and N. Vlahos. 2004. Uterine myomas: An overview of development, clinical features and management. *Obstetric Gynecology* 104:393.

Warren, C. W. 1986. Contaceptive sterilization in Puerto Rico. *Demography* 23 (3): 351–365.

———. 1988. Tubal sterilization: Questioning the decision. *Population Studies* 42 (3): 407–418.

Westhoff, C., and A. Davis. 2000. Tubal sterilization: Focus on the U.S. experience. *Fertility and Sterility* 735 (May): 913–22.

White E. C., ed. 1993. *The black women's health book: Speaking for ourselves*. Seattle: Seal Press.

Wilber, K. 2000. *Integral psychology: Consciousness, spirit, psychology, therapy*. Boston: Shambhala.

Wilson, W. J. 1987. *The truly disadvantaged: The inner city, the underclass, and public policy*. Chicago: University of Chicago Press.

Zambrana, R. E. 1982. *Work, family and health: Latina women in transition*. Monograph No. 7. New York: Fordham University Hispanic Research Center.

Zavella, P. 1996. Feminist insider dilemmas: Constructing identity with "Chicana" informants. In *Feminist Dilemmas in Fieldwork*, ed. D. L. Wolfe, 138–169. Boulder, CO: Westview.

———. 1997. "Playing with Fire": The gendered construction of Chicana/Mexicana sexuality. In *The gendered/sexuality reader: Culture, history, political economy*, ed. R. N. Lancaster and M. di Leonardo, 402–418. New York: Routledge.

———. 2003. Talking sex: Chicanas and Mexicanas theorize about silences and sexual pleasures. In *Chicana feminisms: A critical reader*, ed. G. Arredondo, A. Hurtado, N. Klahn, O. Najera Ramirez, and P. Zavella, 228–253. Durham: Duke University Press.

Zavella, P., and X. Castañeda. 2003. Changing constructions of sexuality and risk: Migrant Mexican women farmworkers in California. *Journal of Latin American Anthropology* 8 (2): 126–150.

Zuberi T. 2003. *Thicker than blood: How statistics lie*. Minneapolis: University of Minnesota Press.

Zurawin, R. K. 2006. Tubal sterilization. http://www.emedicine.com/med/topic3313.htm.

Index

abortion, 41, 58, 144; to avoid difficult pregnancy, 103; Catholic Church and, 19; legalization of, 17–18; moral reasons for having, 48–49; as necessary evil, 80; and *Roe v. Wade*, 18; self-, 24
Academies Institute of Medicine, 129
adoption, 108, 109, 110, 111
African Americans, stereotype of, 129–130
agency/victim binary framework, xvii–xviii, xxi, 125, 143–144, 151, 154
Aid for Dependent Children (AFDC), 29, 66
AIDS, 39, 40–41, 104, 105

baby maker stereotype, 70
Belaval, J., 13
bipolar tubal coagulation, 127–128
birth control: availability of information on, 41, 54–56, 57, 97; lack of access to, 7–8, 11, 14, 19, 38, 119; *vs.* population control, xiii–xiv; as woman's responsibility, 38, 53–54, 67, 75, 149. *See also* birth control methods; birth control movement, in Puerto Rico
Birth Control League of Puerto Rico, 11
birth control methods: condoms, 14, 53–54, 59, 60, 75, 95, 97, 149; diaphragm, ix, xviii, 14, 15, 18, 53, 75, 147; intrauterine device (IUD), ix, 38, 48, 53, 67, 75, 115, 116, 120, 153; loop, 53, 67, 95, 120; pill (*see* birth control pill); rhythm, 14, 53. *See also* sterilization
birth control movement, in Puerto Rico:

birth control pill testing, 16–18; Catholic Church opposition to, 10, 13, 14, 18, 19; colonialism and, 18, 19; eugenics influence on, 9–11, 15, 18, 19; feminists and, 10, 18; government sterilization policy, 7–8, 14; government view on temporary birth control, 18; legislation, 12, 16, 18; medical profession's acceptance of sterilization, 8–9, 16, 19; origins of, 9–10; privatization of market, 15–16, 18; Puerto Rico as test laboratory, 15–17, 153; roots of, 3–4; sexist population policy, 18; sterilization for health reasons, 12; sterilization of poor and mentally diseased, 11–12; trajectory of, 10–15; U.S. involvement, 11–18
birth control pill, ix, xiii, xviii; failure of, 67, 147; side effects, 17, 38, 57, 67, 87, 95, 105, 115, 132; testing on Puerto Rican women, 17, 153
bodegas, 62, 78
Bourne, J., 12–13, 14
breast cancer scare, 50–51
Briggs, L., 9, 10, 11, 15, 16, 17, 18, 30, 164n6 (chap. 1)

caesarean section (C-section), 55, 60, 89, 91–92, 135, 137–138, 141
cancer fear, as reason for hysterectomy, 49–50, 59, 60, 83, 84, 135–137, 145, 151
Catholic Church: on birth control, 10, 11, 13, 15, 23, 164n2 (chap. 2); on sterilization, 19, 48–49, 103

About the Author

IRIS LOPEZ is an engaged urban anthropologist who has worked extensively with Latino communities in New York City. Her work focuses on gender, immigration, and reproductive rights. She is the director of Latin American and Latino Studies and the former director of Women's Studies at City College of New York.